Allan Cunningham

Traditional Tales

Of the English and Scottish Peasantry

Allan Cunningham

Traditional Tales
Of the English and Scottish Peasantry

ISBN/EAN: 9783337072643

Printed in Europe, USA, Canada, Australia, Japan

Cover: Foto ©ninafisch / pixelio.de

More available books at **www.hansebooks.com**

OF THE

ENGLISH AND SCOTTISH PEASANTRY

BY

ALLAN CUNNINGHAM

WITH AN INTRODUCTION BY HENRY MORLEY
LL.D., PROFESSOR OF ENGLISH LITERATURE AT
UNIVERSITY COLLEGE, LONDON

LONDON
GEORGE ROUTLEDGE AND SONS
BROADWAY, LUDGATE HILL
GLASGOW AND NEW YORK
1887

MORLEY'S UNIVERSAL LIBRARY.

1. Sheridan's Plays.
2. Plays from Molière. By English Dramatists.
3. Marlowe's Faustus and Goethe's Faust.
4. Chronicle of the Cid.
5. Rabelais' Gargantua and the Heroic Deeds of Pantagruel.
6. Machiavelli's Prince.
7. Bacon's Essays.
8. Defoe's Journal of the Plague Year.
9. Locke on Civil Government and Filmer's "Patriarcha."
10. Butler's Analogy of Religion.
11. Dryden's Virgil.
12. Scott's Demonology and Witchcraft.
13. Herrick's Hesperides.
14. Coleridge's Table-Talk.
15. Boccaccio's Decameron.
16. Sterne's Tristram Shandy.
17. Chapman's Homer's Iliad.
18. Mediæval Tales.
19. Voltaire's Candide, and Johnson's Rasselas.
20. Jonson's Plays and Poems.
21. Hobbes's Leviathan.
22. Samuel Butler's Hudibras.
23. Ideal Commonwealths.
24. Cavendish's Life of Wolsey.
25 & 26. Don Quixote.
27. Burlesque Plays and Poems.
28. Dante's Divine Comedy. LONGFELLOW's Translation.
29. Goldsmith's Vicar of Wakefield, Plays, and Poems.
30. Fables and Proverbs from the Sanskrit. (Hitopadesa.)
31. Lamb's Essays of Elia.
32. The History of Thomas Ellwood.
33. Emerson's Essays, &c.
34. Southey's Life of Nelson.
35. De Quincey's Confessions of an Opium-Eater, &c.
36. Stories of Ireland. By Miss EDGEWORTH.
37. Frere's Aristophanes: Acharnians, Knights, Birds.
38. Burke's Speeches and Letters.
39. Thomas à Kempis.
40. Popular Songs of Ireland.
41. Potter's Æschylus.
42. Goethe's Faust: Part II. ANSTER's Translation.
43. Famous Pamphlets.
44. Francklin's Sophocles.
45. M. G. Lewis's Tales of Terror and Wonder.
46. Vestiges of the Natural History of Creation.
47. Drayton's Barons' Wars, Nymphidia, &c.
48. Cobbett's Advice to Young Men.
49. The Banquet of Dante.
50. Walker's Original.
51. Schiller's Poems and Ballads.
52. Peele's Plays and Poems.
53. Harrington's Oceana.
54. Euripides: Alcestis and other Plays.
55. Praed's Essays.
56. Traditional Tales. ALLAN CUNNINGHAM.

"Marvels of clear type and general neatness."—*Daily Telegraph.*

INTRODUCTION.

ALLAN CUNNINGHAM was born in 1785, and died at the age of fifty-seven, in October 1842. He was born into a poor household at Blackwood, in Dumfriesshire, and had little schooling. When a child of eleven he was apprenticed to a stonemason. But he was born with a quick fancy and a love of song. In 1810 R. H. Cromek published "Remains of Nithsdale and Galloway Song, with Historical and Traditional Notices relative to the Manners and Customs of the Peasantry." Allan Cunningham, then twenty-five years old, had taken special delight in the fireside tales and songs of the little world of peasantry to which he himself belonged, and he supplied to Cromek's Nithsdale and Galloway volume Ballads of his own making as if they were traditions of the past. They were good enough to draw towards Allan Cunningham the sympathies of James Hogg, the Ettrick Shepherd, who had also come into the world with a small gift, that if small was true.

Walter Scott, who had warmly recognized the genius of the Ettrick Shepherd, was as prompt in generous appreciation of young Allan Cunningham, made his acquaintance, and the more he knew of him liked "honest Allan" the better. Encouraged by this recognition of his native power the stonecutter went, in the same year, 1810, to seek his fortune in London as a poet.

In London, Allan Cunningham endeavoured to live by his pen. He found admission among the writers in *The London Magazine,* and plied his pen with great industry until his death. From the worst anxieties of the struggle on which he had ventured, he was saved by the friendship of Chantrey the sculptor. Francis Chantrey was only four years older than Allan Cunningham. Chantrey had shown his bent for sculpture when apprenticed to a carver and gilder at Sheffield. He had afterwards got some instruction in London at the Royal Academy, and returned to Sheffield, where he received in 1809 from an architect an order for four colossal busts. This started Chantrey upon his career of rising power and prosperity, only a year before young Allan Cunningham appeared in London. Chantrey's fame was rising; his work was growing on his hands; Walter Scott was among those who sat to him; and when he recognized the touch of finer thought and fancy in Allan Cunningham and found that he had left the trade of stone-cutting, he restored him to it in a form that harmonized with his best aspirations; Chantrey appointed Allan Cunningham to be the principal assistant in his studio.

The work in the studio made daily bread secure, and Allan Cunningham had leisure for such reading as would in some degree train and advance his powers. He found time also for free use of his pen. He wrote a play, "Sir Marmaduke Maxwell." He wrote novels, "Paul Jones" and "Sir Michael Scott." He wrote a "Life of Burns." He wrote songs. The best of his story-books is that which is here reprinted. It was first published in 1822.

In 1826 Allan Cunningham published, in four volumes, "Songs of Scotland, ancient and modern; with an Essay and Notes, historical and critical, and Characters of the most eminent Lyrical Poets of Scotland." In 1830 he completed for John Murray's Family Library, in six volumes, his "Lives of the most eminent British Painters, Sculptors and Architects." That was his most successful work in prose. His keen interest in Art as well as Literature was shown again by his editing, in 1834, a "Cabinet Gallery of Pictures by the first masters of the Foreign and English Schools;" and in 1843, the year after his death, appeared his "Life of Sir David Wilkie, with his Journals and Tours." In 1847 Allan Cunningham's "Poems and Songs" were collected and published with an Introduction, Glossary and Notes, by Peter Cunningham, his son.

Why reprint among the works of the great masters this book that bears witness only to a little gift though true? Allan Cunningham as a storyteller caught the now obsolete fashion of his time, and there are passages of phrase and sentiment, and even of incident—as in the first part of the Selbys—that although healthy in nature are conventional in tone, with conventions that were established in a day of broken health. The true love of Literature does not walk only on the mountain tops, it leads us also to the copse and meadow on the lower slopes, and gives us rest upon the moss beside the small rills of the valley. Wherever the voice is true, if there be but a little touch of the divine gift that makes man look below the outward shows with sympathetic insight, and give poetic form to the life common to us all, the right reader has a ready ear, and passes easily through accidental fault to the essential life with which he communes.

In another way also this book has interest for the student of literature. Allan Cunningham took pleasure from early childhood in the stories of the country-side, and he here puts upon record the latest memories of the itinerant storyteller in whom the earliest form of our national literature, once dependent wholly on the recitations of the Scóp and gleeman, after many changes finally became extinct. At this day, probably, there is not one man left in the three kingdoms who earns his bread by carrying from house to house, for oral recitation, the tales and traditions of his country-side. At the end of the last century such a custom, as Allan Cunningham here tells us, was not wholly extinct. Though his Traditional Tales may be mainly of his own invention, they are the outcome of a mind that had been in much real contact with North Country peasantry, had taken eager delight in their "stories told of many a feat," and felt the music in them. The free sprinkling of song over the tales, gives us the pleasant sense also that our entertainer is a poet, while, however out of fashion some points in his style may be, we feel the artist in his prose.

Next flight is upward to the heights again.

H. M.

November 1887.

TRADITIONAL TALES

OF THE

ENGLISH AND SCOTCH PEASANTRY.

EZRA PEDEN.

I SAT and watched while a'l men slept, and lo !
Between the green earth and the deep green sea
I saw bright spirits pass, pure as the touch
Of May's first finger on the eastern hill.
Behind them followed fast a little cloud ;
And from the cloud an evil spirit came—
A damnéd shape—one who in the dark pit
Held sovereign sway ; and power to him was given
To chase the blessed spirits from the earth,
And rule it for a season.
                    Soon he shed
His hellish slough, and many a subtle wile
Was his to seem a heavenly spirit to man.
First he a hermit, sore subdued in flesh,
O'er a cold cruse of water and a crust,
Poured out meek prayers abundant. Then he changed
Into a maid when she first dreams of man,
And from beneath two silken eyelids sent
The sidelong light of two such wondrous eyes,
That all the saints grew sinners. He subdued
Those wanton smiles, and grew a reverend dame,
With wintry ringlets, and grave lips, which dropt
Proverbial honey in her grandson's ear.
Then a professor of God's word he seemed,
And o'er a multitude of upturned eyes
Showered blessed dews, and made the pitchy path,
Down which howl damnéd spirits, seem the bright
Thrice hallowed way to Heaven. Yet grimly through
The glorious veil of those seducing shapes
Frowned out the fearful Spirit.

THE religious legend which supplies my story with the motto affords me no farther assistance in arranging and interpreting the varying traditional remembrances of the colloquies between one of the chiefs of the ancient Presbyterian Kirk and one of the inferior spirits of darkness. It is seldom that tradition requires any illustration; its voice is clear, and its language simple—it seeks to conceal nothing: what it can explain it explains, and scorns, in the homely accuracy of its protracted details, all mystery and reservation. But in the present story there is much which the popular spirit of research would dread to have revealed; a something too mystical and hallowed to be sought into by a devout people. Often as I have listened to it, I never heard it repeated without mutual awe in the teller and the auditor. The most intrepid peasant becomes graver and graver as he proceeds, stops before the natural termination of the story, and hesitates to pry into the supernatural darkness of the tradition. It would be unwise therefore to seek to expound or embellish the legend—it shall be told as it was told to me: I am but as an humble priest responding from the traditionary oracles, and the words of other years pass without change from between my lips.

Ezra Peden was one of the shepherds of the early Presbyterian flock, and distinguished himself as an austere and enthusiastic pastor; fearless in his ministration, delighting in wholesome discipline, and guiding in the way of grace the peer as well as the peasant. He grappled boldly with the infirmities and sins of the times; he spared not the rod in the way of his ministry; and if in the time of peril he laid his hand on the sword, in the time of peace his delight was to place it on the horns of the altar. He spared no vice, he compounded with no sin, and he discussed men's claims to immortal happiness with a freedom which made them tremble. Amid the fervour of his eloquence, he aspired, like some of his fellow-professors of that period, to the prophetic mantle. Plain and simple in his own apparel, he counted the mitred glory and exterior magnificence of the hierarchy a sin and an abomination, and preferred preaching on a wild hill or in a lonesome glen to the most splendid edifice.

Wherever he sojourned, dance and song fled: the former he accounted a devoting of limbs, which God made, to the worship of Satan; the latter he believed to be a sinful meting out of wanton words to a heathen measure. Satan, he said, leaped and danced, and warbled and sung, when he came to woo to perdition the giddy sons and daughters of men. He dictated the colour and the cut of men's clothes—it was seemly for those who sought salvation to seek it in a sober suit—and the ladies of his parish were obliged to humble their finery, and sober down their pride, before his sarcastic sermons on female paintings, and plumings, and perfumings, and the unloveliness of lovelocks. He sought to make a modest and sedate grace abound among women; courtship was schooled and sermoned into church controversy, and love into mystical professions; the common civilities between the sexes were doled out with a suspicious hand and a jealous charity, and the primrose path through the groves of dalliance to the sober vale of marriage was planted with thorns and sown with briars.

He had other endowments not uncommon among the primitive teachers of the Word. In his day, the empire of the Prince of Darkness was more manifest among men than now, and his ministry was distinguished, like the reign of King Saul, by the persecution of witches, and elves, and evil spirits. He made himself the terror of all those who dealt in divinations, or consulted the stars, or sought to avert witchcraft by sinful spell and charm, instead of overcoming it by sorrowings and spiritual watchings. The midnight times of planetary power he held as the prime moments of Satan's glory on earth, and he punished Hallowmass revellers as chief priests in the infernal rites. He consigned to church censure and the chastening of rods a wrinkled dame who sold a full sea and a fair wind to mariners, and who insulted the Apostles, and made a mystical appeal to the twelve signs of Heaven in setting a brood goose with a dozen eggs. His wrath, too, was observed to burn against all those who compounded with witches, and people who carried evil influence in their eyes—this was giving tribute to the Fiend, and bribing the bottomless pit.

He rebuked a venerable dame, during three successive Sundays, for placing a cream bowl and new-baked cake in the paths of the nocturnal elves, who, she imagined, had plotted to steal her grandson from the mother's bosom. He turned loose many Scripture threatenings against those diminutive and capricious beings, the fairies, and sought to preach them from the land. He prayed on every green hill, and held communings in every green valley. He wandered forth at night, as a spiritual champion, to give battle to the enemies of the light. The fairies resigned the contest with a foe equipped from such an armoury, and came no more among the sons and daughters of men. The sound of their minstrelsy ceased on the hill; their equestrian processions were seen no more sweeping past at midnight beneath the beam of the half-veiled moon; and only a solitary and sullen elf or two remained to lament the loss of their immemorial haunts. With the spirits of evil men and the lesser angels of darkness he waged a fierce and a dubious war; he evoked an ancient ghost from a ruined tower, which it had shared for generations with the owl; and he laid or tranquillized a fierce and troubled spirit which haunted the abode of a miser in a neighbouring churchyard, and seemed to gibber and mumble over his bones. All these places were purified by prayer, and hallowed by the blessing of the gifted pastor, Ezra Peden.

The place of his ministry seemed fitted by nature, and largely endowed by history, for the reception and entertainment of all singular and personified beliefs. Part was maritime and part mountainous, uniting the aërial creeds of the shepherds with the stern and more imposing beliefs of the husbandman, and the wild and characteristic superstitions of the sailors. It often happened, when he had marched against and vanquished a sin or a superstition of native growth, he was summoned to wage war with a new foe; to contend with a legion of errors and a strange race of spirits from the haunted coasts of Norway and Sweden. All around him on every side were records of the mouldering influence of the enemies of faith and charity. On the hill, where the heathen Odin had appeared to his worshippers in the circle of granite, the pillars of his Runic temple promised to be immortal; but the god was gone, and his worship was extinct. The sword, the spear, and the banner had found sanctuary from fields of blood on several lofty promontories; but shattered towers and dismantled castles told that for a time hatred, oppression, and revenge had ceased to triumph over religion. Persecution, now passed and gone, a demon exorcised by the sword, had hallowed three wild hills and sanctified two little green valleys with the blood of martyrs. Their gravestones, bedded among heather or long grass, cried up to Heaven against their oppressors in verses which could not surely fail to elude the punishment awarded by the Kirk against poesy. Storms, and quicksands, and unskilful mariners, or, as common belief said, the evil spirits of the deep, had given to the dangerous coast the wrecks of three stately vessels; and there they made their mansions, and raised whirlwinds, and spread quicksands, and made sandbanks, with a wicked diligence which neither prayer nor preaching could abate. The forms under which these restless spirits performed their pranks have unfortunately been left undefined by a curious and a poetical peasantry.

It happened one winter, during the fifteenth year of the ministry of Ezra Peden, and in the year of grace 1705, that he sat by his fire pondering deep among the treasures of the ancient Presbyterian worthies, and listening occasionally to the chafing of the coming tide against cliff and bank, and the fitful sweep of heavy gusts of wind over the roof of his manse. During the day he had seemed more thoughtful than usual; he had consulted Scripture with an anxious care, and fortified his own interpretation of the sacred text by the wisdom of some of the chiefs and masters of the calling. A Bible, too, bound in black oak, and clasped with silver, from the page of which sin had received many a rebuke, and the abominations of witchcraft and sorcery had been cleansed from the land, was brought from its velvet sanctuary, and placed beside him. Thus armed and prepared, he sat like a watcher of old on the towers of Judah; like one who girds up his loins and makes bare his right arm for some fierce and dubious contest.

All this stir and preparation passed not unnoticed of an old man—his predecessor's coeval, and prime minister of the household; a person thin, religious, and faithful, whose gifts in prayer were reckoned by some old people nearly equal to those of the anointed pastor. To such a distinction Josiah never thought of aspiring; he contented himself with swelling the psalm into something like melody on Sunday, visiting the sick as a forerunner of his master's approach, and pouring forth prayers and graces at burials and banquetings as long and dreary as a hill sermon. He looked on the minister as something superior to man, a being possessed by a divine spirit; and he shook his head with all its silver hairs, and uttered a gentle groan or two, during some of the more rapt and glowing passages of Ezra's sermons.

This faithful personage stood at the door of his master's chamber, unwilling to go in, and yet loth to depart. "Josiah, thou art called, Josiah," said Ezra in a grave tone; "so come hither. The soul of an evil man, a worker of iniquity, is about to depart; one who drank the blood of saints, and made himself fat with the inheritance of the righteous. It hath been revealed to me that his body is sorely troubled; but I say unto you he will not go from the body without the strong compulsion of prayer, and therefore am I summoned to war with the enemy; so I shall arm me to the task."

Josiah was tardy in speech, and before he could reply, the clatter of a horse's hoofs was heard at the gate: the rider leaped down, and, splashed with mire and sprinkled with sleet, he stood in an instant before the minister. "Ah! sir," said the unceremonious messenger, "haste—snatch up the looms of redemption, and bide not the muttering of prayer, else auld Mahoun will haurl his friend Bonshaw to his cauldrons, body and saul, if he has nae him half-way hame already. God-sake, sir, start and fly, for he cannot shoot owre another hour!—he talks of perdition, and speaks about a broad road and a great fire, and friends who have travelled the way before him. He's no his lane, however, that's one comfort; for I left him conversing with an old cronie, whom no one saw but himself—ane whose bones are ripe and rotten; and mickle they talked of a place called Tophet, a hot enough region, if one can credit them; but I aye doubt the accounts of such travellers—they are like the spies of the land of promise——"

"Silence thy unreverent tongue, and think of thy latter end with fear and trembling," said Ezra, in a stern voice. "Mount thy horse, and follow me to the evil man, thy master; brief's the time, and black's the account, and stern and inexorable will the summoning angel be." And, leaping on their horses, they passed from the manse, and sought out the bank of a little busy stream, which, augmented by a fall of sleet, lifted up a voice amid its rocky and desolate glen equal to the clamour of a mightier brook. The glen or dell was rough with sharp and projecting crags, which, hanging forward at times from opposite sides, seemed to shut out all farther way; while from between their dark grey masses the rivulet leaped out in many divided streams. The brook again gathered together its waters, and subsided into several clear deep pools, on which the moon, escaping for a moment from the edge of a cloud of snow, threw a cold and wavering gleam. Along the sweeps of the stream a rough way, shaped more by nature than by the hands of man, winded among the rocks, and along this path proceeded Ezra, pondering on the vicissitudes of human life.

At length he came where the glen expanded, and the sides became steep and woody: amid a grove of decaying trees the mansion of Bonshaw rose, square and grey. Its walls of rough granite were high and massive; the roof, ascending steep and sharp, carried a covering of red sandstone flags; around the whole the rivulet poured its scanty waters in a deep moat, while a low-browed door, guarded by loopholes, gave it the character of a place of refuge and defence. Though decayed and war-worn now, it had in former times been a fair and a courtly spot. A sylvan nook or arbour, scooped out of the everlasting rock, was wreathed about with honeysuckles; a little pool, with a margin studded with the earliest primroses, lay at its entrance; and a garden, redeemed by the labour of man from the sterile upland, had its summer roses and its beds of lilies, all bearing token of some gentle and departed inhabitant.

As he approached the house a candle glimmered in a small square window, and threw a line or two of straggling light along the path. At the foot of the decayed porch he observed the figure of a man kneeling, and presently he heard a voice chanting what sounded like a psalm or a lykewake hymn. Ezra alighted, and approached: the form seemed insensible of his presence, but stretched his hands towards the tower; and while the feathery snow descended on his grey hair, he poured his song forth in a slow and melancholy manner. "I protest," said the messenger, "here kneels old William Cameron, the Covenanter. Hearken, he pours out some odd old-world malison against Bonshaw. I have heard that the laird hunted him long and sore in his youth, slew his sons, burned his house, threw his two bonnie daughters desolate—that was nae gentle deed, however—and brake the old mother's heart with downright sorrow. Sae I canna much blame the dour old carle for remembering it even now, though the candles of Bonshaw are burning in the socket, and his light will be extinguished for ever. Let us hearken his psalm or his song; it is no every winter night we have minstrelsy at Bonshaw gate, I can tell ye that." The following are the verses, which have been preserved under the title of "Ane godly exultation of William Cameron, a chosen vessel, over Bonshaw, the persecutor." I have adopted a plainer but a less descriptive title.

THE DOWNFALL OF DALZELL.

The wind is cold, the snow falls fast,
　The night is dark and late,
As I lift aloud my voice and cry
　By the oppressor's gate.
There is a voice in every hill,
　A tongue in every stone;
The greenwood sings a song of joy,
　Since thou art dead and gone;
A poet's voice is in each mouth,
　And songs of triumph swell,
Glad songs that tell the gladsome earth
　The downfall of Dalzell.

As I raised up my voice to sing
　I heard the green earth say,
Sweet am I now to beast and bird,
　Since thou art passed away:
I hear no more the battle-shout,
　The martyrs' dying moans;
My cottages and cities sing
　From their foundation-stones;
The carbine and the culverin's mute—
　The deathshot and the yell
Are turned into a hymn of joy,
　For thy downfall, Dalzell.

I've trod thy banner in the dust,
　And caused the raven call
From thy bride-chamber to the owl
　Hatched on thy castle wall;
I've made thy minstrels' music dumb,
　And silent now to fame
Art thou, save when the orphan casts
　His curses on thy name.
Now thou mayst say to good men's prayers
　A long and last farewell:
There's hope for every sin save thine—
　Adieu, adieu, Dalzell!

The grim pit opes for thee her gates,
　Where punished spirits wail,
And ghastly death throws wide her door,
　And hails thee with a Hail!
Deep from the grave there comes a voice,
　A voice with hollow tones,
Such as a spirit's tongue would have
　That spoke through hollow bones:
"Arise, ye martyred men, and shout
　From earth to howling hell;
He comes, the persecutor comes!
　All hail to thee, Dalzell!"

O'er an old battlefield there rushed
  A wind, and with a moan
The severed limbs all rustling rose,
  Even fellow-bone to bone.
"Lo! there he goes," I heard them cry,
  "Like babe in swathing-band,
Who shook the temples of the Lord,
  And passed them 'neath his brand.
Cursed be the spot where he was born,
  There let the adders dwell,
And from his father's hearthstone hiss:
  All hail to thee, Dalzell!"

I saw thee growing like a tree—
  Thy green head touched the sky—
But birds far from thy branches built,
  The wild deer passed thee by;
No golden dew dropt on thy bough,
  Glad summer scorned to grace
Thee with her flowers, nor shepherds wooed
  Beside thy dwelling-place:
The axe has come and hewn thee down,
  Nor left one shoot to tell
Where all thy stately glory grew:
  Adieu, adieu, Dalzell!

An ancient man stands by thy gate,
  His head like thine is grey;
Grey with the woes of many years,
  Years fourscore and a day.
Five brave and stately sons were his;
  Two daughters, sweet and rare;
An old dame, dearer than them all,
  And lands both broad and fair:
Two broke their hearts when two were slain,
  And three in battle fell—
An old man's curse shall cling to thee:
  Adieu, adieu, Dalzell!

And yet I sigh to think of thee,
  A warrior tried and true
As ever spurred a steed, when thick
  The splintering lances flew.
I saw thee in thy stirrups stand,
  And hew thy foes down fast,
When Grierson fled, and Maxwell failed,
  And Gordon stood aghast,
And Graeme, saved by thy sword, raged fierce
  As one redeemed from hell.
I came to curse thee—and I weep:
  So go in peace, Dalzell!

When this wild and unusual rhyme concluded, the Cameronian arose and departed, and Ezra and his conductor entered the chamber of the dying man.

He found him stretched on a couch of state, more like a warrior cut in marble than a breathing being. He had still a stern and a martial look, and his tall and stalwart frame retained something of that ancient exterior beauty for which his youth was renowned. His helmet, spoiled by time of its plumage, was placed on his head; a rusty corslet was on his bosom; in his arms, like a bride, lay his broad and famous sword; and as he looked at it, the battles of his youth passed in array before him. Armour and arms hung grouped along the walls, and banners, covered with many a quaint and devotional device, waved in their places as the domestic closed the door on Ezra and the dying warrior in the chamber of presence.

The devout man stood and regarded his ancient parishioner with a meek and sorrowful look; but nothing visible or present employed Bonshaw's reflections or moved his spirit—his thoughts had wandered back to earlier years, and to scenes of peril and blood. He imagined himself at the head of his horsemen in the hottest period of the persecution, chasing the people from rock to rock, and from glen to cavern. His imagination had presented to his eye the destruction of the children of William Cameron: he addressed their mother in a tone of ironical supplication: "Woman, where is thy devout husband, and thy five holy sons? Are they busied in interminable prayers or everlasting sermons? Whisper it in mine ear, woman—thou hast made that reservation doubtless in thy promise of concealment. Come, else I will wrench the truth out of thee with these gentle catechists, the thumscrew and the bootikin. Serving the Lord, sayest thou, woman? Why, that is rebelling against the king. Come, come, a better answer, else I'll make thee a bride for a saint on a bloody bed of heather." Here he paused and waved his hand like a warrior at the head of armed men, and thus he continued: "Come, uncock thy carbine, and harm not the woman till she hear the good tidings. Sister, saint, how many bairns have ye? I bless God, saith she, five—Reuben, Simon, Levi, Praisegod, and Patrick. A bonny generation, woman. Here, soldier, remove the bandages from the faces of those two young men before ye shoot them. There stands Patrick, and that other is Simon: dost thou see the youngest of thy affections? The other three are in Sarah's bosom—thyself shall go to Abraham's. The woman looks as if she doubted me: here, toss to her those three heads—often have they lain in her lap, and mickle have they prayed in their time. Out, thou simpleton! Canst thou not endure the sight of the heads of thine own fair-haired sons, the smell of powder, and the flash of a couple of carbines?"

The re-acting of that ancient tragedy seemed to exhaust for a little while the old persecuter: he next imagined himself receiving the secret instructions of the Council. "What, what! my lord, must all this pleasant work fall to me? A reeking house and a crowing cock shall be scarce things in Nithsdale. Weepings and wailings shall be rife—the grief of mothers, and the moaning of fatherless babes. There shall be smoking ruins, and roofless kirks, and prayers uttered in secret, and sermons preached at a venture and a hazard on the high and solitary places. Where is General Turner?—gone where the wine is good? And where is Grierson?—has he begun to talk of repentance? Gordon thinks of the unquenchable fire which the martyred Cameronian raved about; and gentle Graeme vows he will cut no more throats unless they wear laced cravats. Awell, my lords, I am the king's servant and not Christ's, and shall boune me to the task."

His fancy flew over a large extent of time, and what he uttered now may be supposed to be addressed to some invisible monitor; he seemed not aware of the presence of the minister. "Auld, say you, and grey-headed, and the one foot in the grave; it is time to repent, and spice and perfume over my rottenness, and prepare for Heaven? I'll tell ye, but ye must not speak on't—I tried to pray late yestreen—I knelt down and I held up my hands to Heaven—and what think ye I beheld? A widow woman and her five fair sons standing between me and the Most High, and calling out 'Woe, woe on Bonshaw!' I threw myself with my face to the earth, and what got I between my hands? A gravestone which covered five martyrs, and cried out against me for blood which I had wantonly shed. I heard voices from the dust whispering around me; and the angel which watched of old over the glory of my house hid his face with his hands, and I beheld the evil spirits arise with power to punish me for a season. I'll tell ye what I will do—among the children of those I have slain shall my inheritance be divided; so sit down, holy sir, and sit down, most learned man, and hearken to my bequest. To the children of three men slain on Irongrey Moor; to the children of two slain on Closeburn Hill; to—no, no, all that crowd, that multitude, cannot be the descendants of those whom I doomed to perish by the rope, and the pistol, and the sword. Away, I say, ye congregation of zealots and psalm-singers! Disperse, I say, else I shall trample ye down beneath my horse's hoofs! Peace, thou white-headed stirrer of sedition, else I shall cleave thee to the collar! Wilt thou preach still?"

Here the departing persecutor uttered a wild imprecation, clenched his teeth, leaped to his feet, waved his sword, and stood for several moments, his eyes flashing from them a fierce light, and his whole strength gathered into a blow which he aimed at his imaginary adversary. But he stiffened as he stood—a brief shudder passed over his frame, and he was dead before he fell on the floor, and made the hall re-echo. The minister raised him in his arms: a smile of military joy still dilated his stern face, and his hand grasped the sword-hilt so firmly that it required some strength to wrench it from his hold. Sore, sore the good pastor lamented that he had no death-bed communings with the departing chief, and he expressed this so frequently that the peasantry said, on the day of his burial, that it would bring back his spirit to earth and vex mankind, and that Ezra would find him particularly intractable and bold. Of these whisperings he took little heed, but he became somewhat more grave and austere than usual.

It happened on an evening about the close of the following spring, when the cat beard was flourishing, and the barley shot its sharp green spikes above the clod, carrying the dew on the third morning, that Ezra Peden was returning from a wedding at Buckletiller. When he left the bridal chamber it was about ten o'clock. His presence had suppressed for a time the natural ardour for dancing and mirth which characterizes the Scotch; but no sooner was he mounted, and the dilatory and departing clatter of his horse's hoofs heard, than musicians and musical instruments appeared from their hiding-places. The floor was disencumbered of the bridal dinner-tables, the maids bound up their long hair, and the hinds threw aside their mantles, and taking their places and their partners, the restrained mirth broke out like a whirlwind. Old men looked on with a sigh, and uttered a feeble and faint remonstrance, which they were not unwilling should be drowned in the abounding and augmenting merriment.

The pastor had reached the entrance of a little wild and seldom-frequented glen, along which a grassy and scarce visible road winded to an ancient burial-ground. Here the graceless and ungodly merriment first reached his ears, and made the woody hollow ring and resound. Horse and rider seemed possessed of the same spirit : the former made a full halt when he heard the fiddle note; while the latter, uttering a very audible groan, and laying his bridle on his horse's neck, pondered on the wisest and most effectual way of repressing this unseemly merriment—of cleansing the parish of this ancient abomination. It was a beautiful night : the unrisen moon had yet a full hour of travel before she could reach the tops of the eastern hills; the wind was mute, and no sound was abroad save the chafing of a small runnel, and the bridal mirth.

While Ezra sat casting in his own mind a long and a dubious contest with this growing and unseemly sin, something like the shadowy outline of a horse and rider appeared in the path. The night was neither light nor dark, and the way, grassy and soft, lay broad and uninterrupted between two hazel and holly groves. As the pastor lifted up his eyes, he beheld a dark rider reining up a dark horse side by side with his own, nor did he seem to want any accoutrement necessary for ruling a fine and intractable steed. As he gazed, the figure became more distinct—it seemed a tall martial form, with a slouched hat and feather, and a dark and ample mantle, which was muffled up to his eyes. From the waist downward all was indistinct, and horse and rider seemed to melt into one dark mass visible in the outline alone. Ezra was too troubled in spirit to court the intrusion of a stranger upon his meditations ; he bent on him a look particularly forbidding and stern, and having made up his mind to permit the demon of mirth and minstrelsy to triumph for the present, rode slowly down the glen.

But side by side with Ezra, and step by step, even as shadow follows substance, moved the mute and intrusive stranger. The minister looked at his companion, and stirred his steed onward ; with corresponding speed moved the other, till they came where the road branched off to a ruined castle. Up this way, with the wish to avoid his new friend, Ezra turned his horse—the other did the same: the former seemed suddenly to change his mind, and returned to the path that led to the old burial-ground; the latter was instantly at his side, his face still hidden in the folds of his mantle.

Now Ezra was stern and unaccommodating in kirk controversy, and the meek and gentle spirit of religion, and a sense of spiritual interest, had enough to do to appease and sober down a temper naturally bold and even warlike. Exasperated at this intruding stranger, his natural triumphed over his acquired spirit, and lifting his riding-stick, and starting up in his stirrups, he aimed a blow equal to the unhorsing of any ordinary mortal. But the weapon met with no obstruction—it seemed to descend through air alone. The minister gazed with dread on this invulnerable being; the stranger gazed on him; and both made a halt like men preparing for a mortal affray. Ezra, who felt his horse shuddering beneath him, began to suspect that his companion pertained to a more dubious state of existence than his own, and his grim look and sable exterior induced him to rank him at once among those infamous and evil spirits which are sometimes permitted to trouble the earth, and to be a torment to the worthy and the devout.

He muttered a brief and pithy prayer, and then said: "Evil shape, who art thou, and wherefore comest thou unto me? If thou comest for good, speak; if for my confusion and my harm, even do thine errand; I shall not fly from thee." "I come more for mine own good than for thy harm," responded the figure. "Far have I ridden and much have I endured, that I might visit thee and this land again." "Do you suffer in the flesh, or are you tortured in the spirit?" said the pastor, desirous to know something certain of his unwelcome companion. "In both," replied the form: "I have dwelt in the vale of fire, in the den of punishment, hollow, and vast, and dreadful; I have ridden through the region of snow and the land of hail; I have swam through the liquid wilderness of burning lava; passed an illimitable sea; and all for the love of one hour on this fair green earth, with its fresh airs and its new-sprung corn."

Ezra looked on the figure with a steady and a penetrating eye; the stranger endured the scrutiny. "I must know of a truth to whom and what I speak; I must see you face to face. Thou mayest be the grand artificer of deceit come to practise upon my immortal soul. Unmantle thee, I pray, that I may behold if thou art a poor and an afflicted spirit, punished for a time, or that fierce and restless fiend who bears the visible stamp of eternal reprobation." "I may not withstand thy wish," uttered the form in a tone of melancholy; and dropping his mantle, and turning round on the pastor, said, "Hast thou forgotten me?" "How can I forget thee?" said Ezra, receding as he spoke; "the stern and the haughty look of Bonshaw has been humbled indeed. Unhappy one, thou art sore'y changed since I beheld thee on earth with the helmet plume fanning thy hot and bloody brow as thy right hand smote down the blessed ones of the earth. The Almighty doom, the evil and the tormenting place, the vile companions, have each in their turn done the work of retribution upon thee: thou art indeed more stern and more terrible, but thou art not changed beyond the knowledge of one whom thou hast hunted and hounded, and sought to slay utterly."

The shape or spirit of Bonshaw dilated with anger, and in a quicker and a fiercer tone said: "Be charitable; flesh and blood, be charitable—doom not to hell-fire and grim companions one whose sins thou canst not weigh but in the balance of thine own prejudices. I tell thee, man of God, the uncharitableness of the sect to which thou pertainest has thronged the land of punishment as much as those who headed, and hanged, and stabbed, and shot, and tortured. I may be punished for a time, and not wholly reprobate." "Punished in part, or doomed in whole, thou needs must be," answered the pastor, who seemed now as much at his ease as if this singular colloquy had happened with a neighbouring divine. "A holy and a blessed spirit would have appeared in a brighter shape. I like not thy dubious words, thou half-punished and half-pardoned spirit. Away, vanish! Shall I speak the sacred words which make the fiends howl, or wilt thou depart in peace?" "In peace I come to thee," said the spirit, "and in peace let me be gone: hadst thou come sooner when I summoned thee, and not loitered away the precious death-bed moments, hearkening the wild and fanciful song of one whom I have deeply wronged, this journey might have been spared—a journey of pain to me and peril to thyself." "Peril to me!" said the pastor: "be it even as thou sayest. Shall I fly for one cast down, over whose prostrate form the purging fire has passed? Wicked was thy course on earth—many and full of evil were thy days; and now thou art loose again, thou fierce and persecuting spirit—a woe, and a woe to poor Scotland." "They are loose who were never bound," answered the spirit of Bonshaw, darkening in anger and expanding in form, "and that I could soon show thee. But, behold, I am not permitted; there is a watcher—a holy one, come nigh, prepared to resist and to smite; I shall do thee no harm, holy man, I vow by the pains of punishment and the conscience pang, now the watcher has departed."

"Of whom speakest thou?" inquired Ezra; "have we ministering spirits who guard the good from the plots of the wicked ones? Have we evil spirits, who tempt and torment men, and teach the maidens ensnaring songs, and lighten their feet and their heads for the wanton dance?" "Stay, I pray thee," said the spirit; "there are spirits of evil men and of good men made perfect who are permitted to visit the earth, and power is given them for a time to work their will with men. I behold one of the latter even now, a bold one and a noble; but he sees I mean not to harm thee, so we shall not war together."

At this asssurance of protection, the pastor inclined his shuddering steed closer to his companion, and thus he proceeded: "You have said that my sect—my meek, and lowly, and broken, and long-persecuted remnant—have helped to people the profound hell: am I to credit thy words?" "Credit them or no as thou wilt," said the spirit: "whoso spilleth blood by the sword, by the word, and by the pen, is there—the false witness—the misinterpreter of the gospel— the profane poet—the profane and presumptuous preacher— the slayer and the slain—the persecutor and the persecuted —he who died at the stake, and he who piled the faggot— all are there, enduring hard weird and penal fire for a time reckoned and days numbered. They are there whom thou wottest not of," said the confiding spirit, drawing near as he spoke, and whispering the names of some of the worthies of the Kirk, and the noble, and the far-descended.

"I well believe thee," said the pastor; "but I beseech thee to be more particular in thy information: give me the names which some of the chief ministers of woe in the nether world were known by in this—I shall hear of those who built cathedrals and strongholds, and filled thrones spiritual and temporal." "Ay, that thou wilt," said the spirit, "and the names of some of the mantled professors of God's humble Presbyterian Kirk also; those who preached a burning fire and a devouring hell to their dissenting brethren, and who called out, with a loud voice, perdition to the sons and daughters of men; 'draw the sword; slay and smite utterly.'" "Thou art a false spirit assuredly," said the pastor; "yet tell me one thing. Thy steed and thou seem to be as one, to move as one, and I observed thee even now conversing with thy brute part; dost thou ride on a punished spirit, and is there injustice in hell as well as on earth?" The spirit laughed. "Knowest thou not this patient and obedient spirit on whom I ride—what wouldest thou say if I named a name renowned at the holy altar?— the name of one who loosed the sword on the bodies of men, because they believed in a humble Saviour, and he believed in a lofty. I have bestrode that mitred personage before now—he is the hack to all the Presbyterians in the pit, but he cannot be spared on a journey so distant as this." "So thou wilt not tell me the name of thy steed?" said Ezra; "well, even as thou wilt." "Nay," said the spirit, "I shall not deny so good a man so small a matter. Knowest thou not George Johnstone, the captain of my troop, as bold a hand as ever bore a sword and used it among fanatics?—we lived together in life, and in death we are not divided." "In persecution and in punishment, thou mightest have said, thou scoffing spirit," said the pastor; "but tell me, do men lord it in perdition as they did on earth; is there no retributive justice among the condemned spirits?" "I have condescended on that already," said the spirit, "and I will tell thee further: there is thy old acquaintance and mine, George Gordon, punished and condemned though he be, he is the scourge, and the whip, and the rod of fire to all those brave and valiant men who served those equitable and charitable princes, Charles Stuart, and James his brother." "I suspect why those honourable cavaliers are tasting the cup of punishment," said the pastor; "but what crime has sedate and holy George done that his lot is cast with the wicked?" "Canst thou not guess it, holy Ezra?" said the spirit; "his crime was so contemptible and mean that I scorn to name it. Hast thou any further questions?"

"You spoke of Charles Stuart, and James his brother,"

said the pastor: "when sawest thou the princes for whom thou delugedst thy country with blood, and periledst thine own soul?" "Ah! thou cunning querist," said the spirit with a laugh, "canst thou not ask a plain question? Thou askest questions plain and pointed enough of the backsliding damsels of thy congregation; why shouldst thou put thy sanctified tricks on me, a plain and a straightforward spirit as ever uttered response to the godly? Nevertheless, I will tell thee. I saw them not an hour ago: Charles saddled me my steed; wot ye who held my stirrup?—even James his brother. I asked them if they had any message to the devout people of their ancient kingdom of Scotland. The former laughed, and bade me bring him the Kirk repentance-stool for a throne. The latter looked grave, and muttered over his fingers like a priest counting his beads; and hell echoed far and wide with laughter at the two princes." "Ay, ay!" said the pastor, "so I find you have mirth among you: have you dance and song also?" "Ay, truly," answered the spirit, "we have hymns and hallelujahs from the lips of that holy and patriotic band who banished their native princes, and sold their country to an alien, and the alien himself rules and reigns among them; and when they are weary with the work of praise, certain inferior and officious spirits moisten their lips with cupfuls of a curious and a cooling liquid, and then hymn and thanksgiving recommence again." "Ah, thou dissembler," said the pastor; "and yet I see little cause why they should be redeemed, when so many lofty minds must wallow with the sinful for a season. But, tell me, it is long since I heard of Claud Hamilton; have you seen him among you? He was the friend and follower of the alien—a mocker of the mighty minds of his native land—a scoffer of that gifted and immortal spirit which pours the glory of Scotland to the uttermost ends of the earth: tell me of him, I pray." Loud laughed the spirit, and replied in scorn: "We take no note of things so mean and unworthy as he; he may be in some hole in perdition, for aught I know or care; but stay, I will answer thee truly. He has not passed to our kingdom yet; he is condemned to the punishment of a long and useless life on earth; and even now you will find him gnawing his flesh in agony to hear the name he has sought to cast down renowned over all the earth!"

The spirit now seemed impatient to be gone: they had

emerged from the glen, and vale and lea, brightened by the moon and sown thick with evening dew, sparkled far and wide. " If thou wouldest question me farther," said the frank and communicative spirit of Bonshaw, "and learn more of the dead, meet me in the old burial-ground an hour before moonrise on Sunday night: tarry at home if thou wilt; but I have more to tell thee than thou knowest to ask about, and hair of thy head shall not be harmed." Even as he spoke the shape of horse and rider underwent a sudden transformation—the spirit sank into the shape of a steed, the steed rose into the form of the rider, and wrapping his visionary mantle about him, and speaking to his unearthly horse, away he started, casting as he flew a sudden and fiery glance on the astonished pastor, who muttered as he concluded a brief prayer: "There goes Captain George Johnstone, riding on his fierce old master."

The old burial-ground, the spirit's trysting-place, was a fair but a lonely spot. All around lay scenes renowned in tradition for blood, and broil, and secret violence. The parish was formerly a land of warriors' towers and of houses for penance, and vigil, and mortification. But the Reformation came, and sacked and crushed down the houses of devotion; while the peace between the two kingdoms curbed the courage and extinguished for ever the military and predatory glory of those old Galwegian chieftains. It was in a burial-ground pertaining to one of those ancient churches, and where the peasants still loved to have their dust laid, that Ezra trusted to meet again the shadowy representative of the fierce old laird of Bonshaw.

The moon, he computed, had a full hour to travel before her beams would be shed on the place of conference, and to that eerie and deserted spot Ezra was observed to walk, like one consecrating an evening hour to solitary musing on the rivulet side. No house stood within half a mile; and when he reached the little knoll on which the chapel formerly stood, he sat down on the summit to ponder over the way to manage this singular conference. A firm spirit and a pure heart, he hoped, would confound and keep at bay the enemy of man's salvation; and he summed up, in a short historical way, the names of those who had met and triumphed over the machinations of fiends. Thus strengthened and reassured, he rose and looked around, but he saw no approaching shape. The road along which he expected the steed and rider to come was empty, and he walked towards the broken gate, to cast himself in the way, and show with what confidence he abode his coming.

Over the wall of the churchyard, repaired with broken and carved stones from the tombs and altar of the chapel, he now looked, and it was with surprise that he saw a new-made widow, kneeling over her husband's grave, and about to pour out her spirit in lamentation and sorrow. He knew her form and face, and the deepest sorrow came upon him. She was the daughter of an old and a faithful elder: she had married a seafaring youth, and borne him one fair child. Her husband was returning from a distant voyage, had entered the sea of Solway—his native hills, his own home rose to his view, and he saw the light streaming from the little chamber window where his wife and his sweet child, sat awaiting his return. But it was not written that they were to meet again in life. She heard the sweep of a whirlwind, and she heard a shriek, and, going to her chamber door, she saw the ship sinking, and her husband struggling in the agitated water. It is needless to lengthen a sorrowful story: she now threw herself weeping over his grave, and poured out the following wail:

"He was the fairest among men, yet the sea swept him away: he was the kindest-hearted, yet he was not to remain. What were all other men compared to him—his long curling hair, and his sweet hazel eyes, and his kind and gladsome tongue? He loved me long, and he won me from many rivals; for who could see his face and not love him?—who could listen to his speech, and refuse him aught? When he danced, maids stood round, and thought his feet made richer music than the instruments. When he sang, the maids and matrons blessed him; and high-born dames loved the song of my frank and gentle sailor. But there is no mercy in the ocean for the sons of men, and there is nought but sorrow for their daughters. Men go grey-headed to the grave, who, had they trusted the unstable deeps, would have perished in their prime, and left fatherless babes and sorrowing widows. Alas, alas! in lonely night on this eerie spot, on thy low and early grave, I pour forth my heart! Who now shall speak peace to my mind, and open the latch of my little lonely home with thy kind and anxious hand? Who now shall dandle my sweet babe on his knee, or love to go with me to kirk and to preaching—

to talk over our old tales of love and courtship—of the secret tryst and the bridal joy?" And, concluding her melancholy chant, she looked sorrowfully and steadfastly at the grave, and recommenced anew her wailing and her tears.

The widow's grief endured so long that the moon began to make her approach manifest by shooting up a long and a broad stream of thin, lucid, and trembling light over the eastern ridge of the Cumberland hills. She rose from her knees, shed back her moist and disordered locks, showing a face pale but lovely, while the watery light of two large dark eyes of liquid and roving blue was cast mournfully on the way homewards, down which she now turned her steps to be gone. Of what passed in the pastor's mind at this moment, tradition, which sometimes mocks and at other times deifies the feelings of men, gives a very unsatisfactory account. He saw the hour of appointment with his shadowy messenger from the other world arrive and pass without his appearance; and he was perhaps persuaded that the pure, and pious, and overflowing grief of the fair young widow had prevented the intrusion of a form so ungracious and unholy. As she advanced from the burial-ground the pastor of her parish stood mute and sorrowful before her. She passed him as one not wishing to be noticed, and glided along the path with a slow step and a downcast eye.

She had reached the side of a little lonely stream, which glided, half-seen, half-hid, underneath its banks of broom and honeysuckle, sprinkled at that hour with wild daisies and spotted with primroses, when the voice of Ezra reached her ears. She made a full stop, like one who hears something astounding, and turned round on the servant of the altar a face radiant with tears, to which her tale of woe and the wild and lonely place added an interest and a beauty. "Young woman," he began, "it is unseemly in thee to bewail thy loss at this lonely hour and in this dreary spot: the youth was given to thee, and ye became vain. I remarked the pride of thy looks, and the gaudiness of thine apparel, even in the house of holiness: he is taken from thee, perhaps, to punish thy pride. There is less meekness in thy sorrow than there was reason in thy joy; but be ye not discomforted." Here the weeping lady turned the sidelong glance of her swimming eyes on Ezra, shed back the locks which usurped a white brow and snowy temples, and folding her hands over a bosom the throbbings of which made the cambric that concealed it undulate like water, stood still, and drank in his words of comfort and condolence.

Tradition always conducts Ezra and the mariner's widow to this seldom-frequented place: a hundred and a hundred times have I mused over the scene in sunlight and moonlight; a hundred and a hundred times have I hearkened to the wild and variable accounts of the peasantry, and sought to make bank, and bush, and stream, and tree assist in unravelling the mystery which must still hang over the singular and tragic catastrophe. Standing in this romantic place, a pious man, not overstricken in years, conversing with a rosy young widow, a vain and a fair creature, a bank of blossomed flowers beside them, and the new-risen moon scattering her slant and ineffectual beams on the thick budded branches above them—such is the picture which tradition ever and invariably draws, while imagination endeavours to take up the tender thread of the story, and imagination must have this licence still. Truth contents herself with the summary of a few and unsatisfactory particulars. The dawn of morning came, says Truth, and Ezra had not returned to his manse. Something evil hath happened, said Imagination, scattering as she spoke a thousand tales of a thousand hues, many of which still find credence among the pious people of Galloway.

Josiah, the old and faithful servant of Ezra, arrived in search of his master at the lonely burial-ground about the dawn of the morning. He had become alarmed at his long absence, and his alarm was not abated by the unholy voices which at midnight sailed round the manse and kirk, singing, as he imagined, a wild and infernal hymn of joy and thanksgiving. He traced his steps down the footpath by the rivulet side till he came to the little primrose bank, and found it trodden upon and pressed as if two persons had been seated among the flowers. Here all further traces ceased, and Josiah stood pondering on the power of evil spirits, and the danger of holding tryst with Beelzebub or any of the lesser spirits of darkness.

He was soon joined by an old shepherd, who told a tale which pious men refuse to believe, though they always listen to it. The bright moonlight had made him imagine it was morning, and he arose and walked forth to look at his lambs on the distant hill: the moon had been up for nearly an hour. His way lay near the little lonely primrose bank, and as he walked along he heard the whispering of tongues: he deemed it some idle piece of love-making, and he approached to see who they might be. He saw what ought not to be seen, even the reverend Ezra seated on the bank and conversing with a buxom young dame and a strange cne. They were talking wondrous kindly. He observed them for a little space: the young dame was in widow's weeds; the mariner's widow wore the only weeds, praise be blest, in the parish; but she was a raven to a swan compared to the quean who conversed with the minister. She was indeed passing fair, and the longer he looked on her she became the lovelier—owre lovely for mere flesh and blood. His dog shrunk back and whimpered, and an owl that chased a bird in the grove uttered a scream of terror as it beheld her, and forsook its prey. At length she turned the light of her eyes on himself; Will wi' the Wisp was but a proverb to them: they had a glance he should never get the better of, and he hardly thought his legs carried him home, he flew with such supernatural speed.

"But, indeed," added the cautious peasant, "I have some doubts that the whole was a fiction of the Auld Enemy, to make me think ill of the douce man and the godly; and if he be spared to come home, so shall I tell him. But if Ezra, pious man, is heard of nae mair, I shall be free to believe that what I heard I heard, and what I saw I saw. And Josiah, man, I may as weel give ye the benefit of my own opinion. I'll amaist aver on my Bible, that the minister, a daring man and a courageous—owre courageous, I doubt—has been dared out to the lonely place by some he- or maybe she-fiend—the latter maist likely; and there he has been overcome by might or temptation, and now Satan may come atween the stilts of the Gospel plough, for the right hand of Ezra will hold it no longer; or I should nae wonder," said the peasant, "but that the old dour persecutor Bonshaw has carried him away on his fiend steed Geordie Johnstone—conscience, nought more likely—and I'll warrant even now they are ducking him in the dub of perdition, or picking his banes ahint the hallan o' hell."

The whole of this rustic prediction was not fulfilled. In a little deep wild dell, at the distance of a gunshot, they found Ezra Peden lying on the ground, uttering words which will be pardoned, since they were the words of a delirious tongue. He was carried home amid the sympathy and sorrow of his parishioners: he answered no question nor seemed to observe a single face, though the face of many a friend stood round him. He only raved out words of tenderness and affection, addressed to some imaginary person at his side; and concluded by starting up, and raising such an outcry of horror and amazement, as if the object of his regard had become a demon: seven strong men could hardly hold him. He died on the third day, after making a brief disclosure, which may be readily divined from this hasty and imperfect narrative.

THE SELBYS OF CUMBERLAND.

Part I.

THUS would she sit a summer eve, and shed
The withered tresses from her faded brow;
Stretch forth her long and feeble arm, which nursed
Three generations—moving thus her knee,
And smiling as a mother smiles who dandles
Her first-born darling mid the sunny air.
And then she chanted an old chivalrous ballad,
And muttered snatches of our old sad stories—
Such tales as stay the peasant at his plough,
The shepherd's sharp shears as they reap the fleece,
The household damsel while she twines the thread,
And make the maid, even as the ewe-milk reeks
Between her whiter fingers, pause and sigh
To think of old how gentle love was crossed
In green and gladsome Cumberland.

AMONG the pastoral mountains of Cumberland dwells an unmingled and patriarchal race of people, who live in a primitive manner, and retain many peculiar usages different from their neighbours of the valley and the town. They are imagined by antiquarians to be descended from a colony of Saxon herdsmen and warriors, who, establishing themselves among the mountainous wastes, quitted conquest and spoliation for the peaceful vocation of tending their flocks, and managing the barter of their rustic wealth for the luxuries fabricated by their more ingenious neighbours. In the cultivation of corn they are unskilful or uninstructed; but in all that regards sheep and cattle they display a knowledge and a tact which is the envy of all who live by the fleece and shears. Their patriarchal wealth enables them to be hospitable, and dispense an unstinted boon among all such people as chance, curiosity, or barter scatter over their inheritance.

It happened on a fine summer afternoon that I found myself engaged in the pursuit of an old fox which annually preyed on our lambs, and eluded the vigilance of the most skilful huntsmen. Leaving Keswick far behind, I pursued my cunning adversary from glen to cavern, till at last he fairly struck across an extensive tract of upland, and sought refuge from the hotness of pursuit in one of the distant mountains. I had not proceeded far on this wide and desolate tract ere I became fatigued and thirsty, and—what true sportsmen reckon a much more serious misfortune—found myself left alone and far behind—while the shout and the cheer of my late companions began to grow faint and fainter, and I at last heard only the bleat of the flocks or the calling of the curlew. The upland on which I had entered appeared boundless on all sides, while amid the brown wilderness arose innumerable green grassy knolls, with herds of small black cattle and sheep grazing or reposing on their sides and summits. They seemed so many green islands floating amid the ocean of brown blossom with which the heath was covered.

I stood on one of the knolls, and, looking around, observed a considerable stream gushing from a small copse of hazel and lady-fern, which, seeking its way into a green and narrow glen, pursued its course with a thousand freakish windings and turnings. While following with my eye the course of the pure stream out of which I had slaked my thirst, I thought I heard something like the sound of a human voice coming up the glen; and, with the hope of finding some of my baffled companions of the chase, I proceeded along the margin of the brook. At first, a solitary and stunted alder or hazel bush, or mountain ash, in which the hooded crow had sought shelter for her young, was all the protection the stream obtained from the rigour of the mid-day sun. The glen became broader and the stream deeper—gliding over a bed of pebbles, shining, large, and round, half-seen, half-hid beneath the projection of the grassy sward it had undermined; and raising all the while that soft and simmering din which contributes so much music to pastoral verse. A narrow footpath, seldom frequented, winded with the loops and turns of the brook. I had wandered along the margin nearly a quarter of a mile when I approached a large and doddered tree of green holly, on the top of which sat a raven, grey-backed and bald-headed from extreme age, looking down intently on something which it thought worthy of watching beneath.

I reached the tree unheard or unheeded, for the soft soil returned no sound to my foot; and on the sunward side I found a woman seated on the grass. She seemed bordering on seventy years of age, with an unbent and unbroken frame, a look of lady-like stateliness, and an eye of that sweet and shining hazel colour of which neither age nor sorrow had been able to dim the glance. Her mantle, once green, and garnished with flowers of gold thread at the extremities, lay folded at her feet, together with a broad flat straw hat—an article of dress common seventy or eighty years ago—and a long staff worn smooth as horn by daily employment. Her hair, nut-brown and remarkably long in her youth, was now become as white as December's snow, and its profusion had also yielded, like its colour, to time; for it hung, or rather flowed, over her shoulders in solitary ringlets, and scarcely afforded a minute's employment to her fingers, which seemed to have been once well acquainted with arranging in all its beauty one of Nature's finest ornaments. As she disposed of each tress, she accompanied the motion of her hands with the verse of a legendary ballad, which she chanted, unconscious of my presence, and which probably related to an adventure of her ancestors:

LADY SELBY.

On the holly tree sat a raven black,
    And at its foot a lady fair
Sat singing of sorrow, and shedding down
    The tresses of her nut-brown hair:
And aye as that fair dame's voice awoke,
The raven broke in with a chorusing croak:

"The steeds they are saddled on Derwent banks;
    The banners are streaming so broad and free;
The sharp sword sits at each Selby's side,
    And all to be dyed for the love of me:
And I maun give this lily-white hand
To him who wields the wightest brand:

"She coost her mantle of satin so fine,
    She kilted her gown of the deep sea-green,
She wound her locks round her brow, and flew
    Where the swords were glimmering sharp and sheen:
As she flew, the trumpet awoke with a clang,
And the sharp blades smote, and the bowstrings sang.

'The streamlet that ran down the lonely vale,
    Aneath its banks, half-seen, half-hid,
Seemed melted silver—at once it came down,
    From the shocking of horsemen, reeking and red;
And that lady flew, and she uttered a cry,
As the riderless steeds came rushing by.

"And many have fallen, and more have fled:
    All in a nook of bloody ground
That lady sat by a bleeding knight,
    And strove with her fingers to stanch the wound:
Her locks, like sunbeams when summer's in pride,
She plucked and placed on his wounded side.

"And aye the sorer that lady sighed,
    The more her golden locks she drew;
The more she prayed, the ruddy life's blood
    The faster and faster came trickling through:
On a sadder sight ne'er looked the moon
That o'er the green mountain came gleaming down.

"He lay with his sword in the pale moonlight;
    All mute and pale she lay at his side:
He, sheathed in mail from brow to heel;
    She, in her maiden bloom and pride:
And their beds were made, and the lovers were laid,
All under the gentle holly's shade.

"May that Selby's right hand wither and rot,
    That fails with flowers their bed to strew!
May a foreign grave be his who doth rend
    Away the shade of the holly bough!
But let them sleep by the gentle river,
And waken in love that shall last for ever."

As the old dame ceased her song, she opened her lap, from which she showered a profusion of flowers—such as are gathered rather in the wood or the wild than the garden—on two green ridges which lay side by side beneath the shade of the green holly. At each handful she strewed she muttered, in an under-tone, what sounded like the remains of an ancient form of prayer; when, turning toward the path, she observed me, and said: "Youth, comest thou here to smile at beholding a frail woman strew the dust of the beautiful and the brave with mountain thyme, wild mint, and scented hawthorn?" I soothed her by a tone of submission and reverence: "Eleanor Selby, may the curse of the ballad, which thou sangest even now, be mine, if I come to scorn those who honour the fair and the brave. Had I known that the ancient lovers, about whom we so often sing, slept by this lonely stream, I would have sought Cumberland for the fairest and rarest flowers to shower on their grassy beds." "I well believe thee, youth," said the old dame, mollified at once by my respect for the surname of Selby; "how could I forget the altar of Lanercost and thee? There are few at thy wilful and froward time of life who would not mock the poor wandering woman, and turn her wayward affections into ridicule; but I see thy respect for her sitting shining in those sweet and moist eyes of hazel."

While she indulged in this language she replaced her long white locks under her bonnet, resumed her mantle and her staff, and, having adjusted all to her liking, and taken a look at the two graves, and at the raven, who still maintained his seat on the summit of the bush, she addressed me again : " But, come, youth, come—the sun is fast walking down the side of the western mountains : Fremmet-ha' is a good mile distant, and we shall be wise to seek the friendship of its porch with an unset sun above our heads." She took my hand, and, exerting an energy I little expected, we descended the glen together, keeping company with the brook, which received and acknowledged, by an augmented murmur, the accession of several lesser streams. At length we came where the glen, suddenly expanding into a beautiful vale, and the brook into a small, deep, and clear lake, disclosed to my sight the whole domestic establishment of one of the patriarchal portioners of the mountainous regions of Cumberland.

On the northern side of the valley, and fronting the midday sun, stood a large old-fashioned house, constructed of rough and undressed stones, such as are found in abundance on the northern uplands, and roofed with a heavy coating of heath, near by an ell in thickness; the whole secured with bands of wood and ropes of flax, in a manner that resembled the checks of a Highland plaid. Something which imitated a shepherd's crook and a sheathed sword was carved on a piece of hewn stone in the front, and underneath was cut in rude square raised letters, "Randal Rode, 1545." The remains of old defences were still visible to a person of an antiquarian turn ; but sheep-folds, cattle-folds, and swine-pens usurped the trench and the rampart, and filled the whole southern side of the valley. In the middle of the lake shattered walls of squared stone were visible, and deep in the clear water a broken and narrow causeway might be traced, which once secured to the proprietor of the mansion a safe retreat against any hasty incursion from the restless borderers, who in former times were alternately the plunderers or defenders of their country. The descendants of Randal Rode seemed to be sensible that their lot was cast in securer times, and instead of practising with the bow, or that still more fatal weapon the gun, or with the sword or with the spear, they were collected on a small green plat of ground on the margin of the lake, to the number of twelve or fourteen, indulging in the rustic exercises of wrestling, leaping, throwing the bar, and casting the stone. Several old white-headed men were seated at a small distance on the ground, maidens continually passed backwards and forwards, with pails of milk, or with new-moulded cheese, casting a casual glance at the pastime of the young men—the valley all the while re-murmuring with the din of the various contests.

As we approached a young man, who had thrown the stone—a pebble massy and round—beyond all the marks of his companions, perceived us coming, and came running to welcome the old woman with all the unrestrained joyousness of eighteen. "Welcome, Dame Eleanor Selby, welcome to Fremmet-ha'! For thy repose I have ordered a soft warm couch, and from no fairer hands than those of my own sister, Maude Rode; and for thy gratification, as well as mine own, have I sought far and wide for a famous ballad of the Selbys; but we are fallen on evil days—the memory of our oldest men only yielded me fragments: these I have pieced together, and shall gladly sing it with all the grace I may." "Fair fall thee, youth," said the old woman, pleased at the revival of a traditional rhyme recording the fame of her house; "thy companions are all clods of the valley, no better than the stones they cast, the bars they heave, and the dull earth they leap upon, compared to thee. But the Selbys' blood within thee overcomes that of the Rodes." The young man came close to her ear, and in an interceding whisper said: "It is true, Dame Eleanor Selby, that my father is but a tender of flocks, and nowise comparable to the renowned house of Selby, with whom he had the fortune to intermarry; but, by the height of Skiddaw and the depth of Solway, he is as proud of his churl's blood as the loftiest of the land; and the welcome of that person would be cold, and his repulse certain, who should tell him the unwelcome tale that he wedded above his degree." "Youth, youth," said the old woman, with hasty and marked impatience, " I shall for thy sake refrain from comparing the churlish name of Rode with the gentle name of Selby ; but I would rather sit a winter night on Skiddaw than have the best who bear the name of Rode to imagine that the hem of a Selby's robe had not more of gentleness than seven acres of Rode's. But thou hast promised me a song : even let me hearken to it now in the free open air, sitting by an ancient summer-seat of the Selbys; it will put me in a mood to enter thy mother's abode." She seated herself on the margin of the lake, while the young man, surrounded by his companions, sung in a rough free voice this legendary ballad, of which I had the good fortune to obtain a copy :

SIR ROLAND GRAEME.

The trumpet has rung on Helvellyn side,
   The bugle in Derwent vale;
And an hundred steeds came hurrying fleet,
   With an hundred men in mail :
And the gathering cry and the warning word
Was " Fill the quiver and sharpen the sword."

And away they bound—the mountain deer
   Starts at their helmets' flash :
And away they go—the brooks call out
   With a hoarse and a murmuring dash ;
The foam flung from their steeds as they go
Strews all their track like the drifting snow.

What foe do they chase, for I see no foe ;
   And yet, all spurred and gored,
Their good steeds fly—say, seek they work
   For the fleet hound or the sword ?
I see no foe—yet a foe they pursue,
With bow and brand, and horn and halloo.

Sir Richard spurs on his bonnie brown steed,
   Sir Walter on his black ;
There are a hundred steeds, and each
   Has a Selby on its back :
And the meanest man there draws a brand
Has silver spurs and a baron's land.

The Eden is deep in flood—lo! look
 How it dashes from bank to bank!
To them it seems but the bonnie green lea,
 Or the vale with brackens rank.
They brave the water and breast the banks,
And shake the flood and foam from their flanks.

The winding and haunted Esk is nigh,
 With its woodlands wild and green;
"Our steeds are white with foam; shall we wash
 Their flanks in the river sheen?"
But their steeds may be doomed to a sterner task
Before they pass the woodland Esk.

All at once they stoop on their horses' necks,
 And utter a long shrill shout;
And bury their spurs in their coursers' flanks,
 And pluck their bright blades out:
The spurned-up turf is scattered behind,
For they go as the hawk when he sails with the wind.

Before them not far on the lilied lea
 There is a fair youth flying,
And at his side rides a lovely maid,
 Oft looking back and sighing:
On his basnet dances the heron's plume,
And fans the maid's cheek, all of ripe rose bloom.

"Now do thy best, my bonnie grey steed,
 And carry my true love over,
And thy corn shall be served in a silver dish,
 And heaped and running over:
Oh! bear her safe through dark Esk's fords,
And leave me to cope with her kinsmen's swords!"

Proud looked the steed, and had braved the flood
 Had it foamed a full mile wider;
Turned his head in joy, and his eye seemed to say,
 "I'm proud of my lovely rider;
And though Selbys stood thick as the leaves on the tree,
All scatheless I'd bear thee o'er mountain and lea."

A rushing was heard on the river banks,
 Wide rang wood, rock, and linn;
And that instant an hundred horsemen at speed
 Came foaming and fearless in:
"Turn back, turn back, thou Scottish loon;
Let us measure our swords 'neath the light of the moon!"

An hundred horsemen leaped lightly down,
 With their silver spurs all ringing;
And drew back, as Sir Richard his good blade bared,
 While the signal trump kept singing:
Sir Roland Graeme down his mantle threw
With a martial smile, and his bright sword drew.

With a measuring eye and a measured pace,
   Nigher they came and nigher;
Then made a bound and made a blow,
   And the smote helms yielded fire:
December's hail, or the thunder blast,
Ne'er flashed so bright, or fell so fast.

"Now yield thee, Graeme, and give me back
   Lord Selby's beauteous daughter;
Else I shall sever thy head and heave't
   To thy light love o'er the water."
"My sword is steel, Sir Richard, like thine,
And thy head's as loose on thy neck as mine."

And again their dark eyes flashed, and again
   They closed—on sweet Eskside,
The ring-doves sprang from their roosts, for the blows
   Were echoing far and wide:
Sir Richard was stark, and Sir Roland was strong;
And the combat was fierce, but it lasted not long.

There's blood upon young Roland's blade,
   There's blood on Sir Richard's brand;
There's blood showered o'er their weeds of steel
   And rained on the grassy land;
But blood to a warrior's like dew to the flower;
The combat but waxed still more deadly and dour.

A dash was heard in the moonlit Esk,
   And up its banks of green
Fair Edith Selby came with a shriek,
   And knelt the knights between:
"Oh spare him, Sir Richard!" She held her white hands,
All spotted with blood 'neath the merciless brands.

Young Roland looked down on his true love and smiled,
   Sir Richard looked also, and said—
"Curse on them that true love would sunder!" He sheathed
   With his broad palm his berry-brown blade;
And long may the Selbys abroad and at hame,
Find a friend and a foe like the good gallant Graeme!

While the ballad proceeded, the old representative of the house of Selby sat with a look of demure dignity and importance, and regarded this minstrel remembrance of the forcible engrafting of the predatory name of Graeme on the stately tree of the Selbys with a look of the darkest displeasure. When the youth finished, she arose hastily, and, elevating herself to her utmost stature, said: "May that ignorant minstrel be mute for ever, or confine his strains to the beasts of the field and the churls who tend them, who has presumed to fashion the ballad of Roland Graeme's wooing of Edith Howard of Naworth into a rhyme reproaching with this ungentle marriage the spotless house of Selby ! A gentle Selby wed a border Graeme! May the heavens forfend! Who will lay a dog in a deer's den? No," said she, muttering in continuance, as she walked into the house of her ancestors; "we have had sad mishaps among us, but nothing like that. One branch of the stately Selby tree carried the kite's nest of a Forster, another the rook's nest of a Rode; but neither scion nor bough have sheltered the hooded-crow brood of the men of the debateable land— men neither of predatory Scotland nor haughty England, but begotten in the haste of a mutual inroad—and the herald's office cannot divine by whom." The mutterings of the wayward woman fell unregarded in the ear of fair Maude Rode, one of the sweetest maidens that ever pressed curd or milked ewes among the pastoral mountains of Cumberland. She welcomed old Eleanor with one of those silent glances which says so much, and spread her a seat, and ministered to her with the demeanour of the humblest handmaid of the house of Selby when its splendour was fullest. This modest kindness soon had its effect on the mutable descendant of this ancient house; she regained her serenity, and her wild legends and traditional tales were related to no ungrateful ears.

Part II.

AND when she came to yon kirkyard,
   Where graves are green and low,
She saw full thirty coal-black steeds
   All standing in a row.

And out she stretched her trembling hand,
   Their mighty sides to stroke:
And aye she reached, and aye she stretched—
   'Twas nothing all but smoke.

They were but mere delusive forms
   Of films and sulph'ry wind;
And every wave she gave her hand
   A gap was left behind.
                         JAMES HOGG.

"A BRIGHT fire, a clean floor, and a pleasant company," is one of the proverbial wishes of domestic comfort among the wilds of Cumberland. The moorland residence of Randal

Rode exhibited the first and second portions of the primitive wish, and it required no very deep discernment to see that around the ample hearth we had materials for completing the proverb. In each face was reflected that singular mixture of gravity and humour peculiar, I apprehend, to the people of the North. Before a large fire, which it is reckoned ominous ever to extinguish, lay half a dozen sheepdogs, spreading out their white bosoms to the heat, and each placed opposite to the seat of its owner. The lord—or rather portioner—of Fremmet-ha' himself lay apart on a large couch of oak antiquely carved, and ornamented, like some of the massive furniture of the days of the olden church, with beads, and crosses, and pastoral crooks. This settee was bedded deep with sheepskins, each retaining a fleece of long white wool. At each end lay a shepherd's dog, past its prime, like its master, and, like him, enjoying a kind of half-ruminating and drowsy leisure peculiar to old age. Three or four busy wheels, guided by as many maidens, manufactured wool into yarn for rugs, and mauds, and mantles. Three other maidens, with bared arms, prepared curds for cheese, and their hands rivalled in whiteness the curdled milk itself. Under the light of a large candlestick several youths pursued the amusement of the popular game of draughts. This piece of rude furniture ought not to escape particular description. It resembled an Etruscan candelabrum, and was composed of a shaft, capable of being depressed or elevated by means of a notched groove, and sunk secure in a block of wood at the floor, terminated above in a shallow cruse or plate, like a three-cocked hat, in each corner of which stood a large candle, rendering the spacious hall where we sat as light as day. On this scene of patriarchal happiness looked my old companion, Eleanor Selby, contrasting, as she glanced her eye in succession over the tokens of shepherds' wealth in which the house abounded, the present day with the past; the times of the fleece, the shears, and the distaff, with those of broils, and blood, and mutual inroad and invasion, when the name of Selby stood high in the chivalry of the North. One might observe in her changing looks the themes of rustic degradation and chivalrous glory on which she brooded; and the present peaceful time suffered by the comparison, as the present always does in the contemplation of old age. The constant attention of young Maude Rode, who ministered to the comfort of her ancient and wayward relative, seemed gradually to soothe and charm down the demon of proud ancestry who maintained rule in her breast; and, after interchanging softer and softer looks of acknowledgment and kindness with her fair young kinswoman, she thus proceeded to relate some of the adventures she had witnessed in the time of her youth. These she poured out in a very singular manner, unconscious, apparently, at times, of the presence of others, and often addressing herself to the individuals whom her narrative recalled to life, as if they stood lifelike and breathing before her.

"When I was young like thee, Maude Rode, a marvel happened which amazed many: it is, and will be, a lasting tale and a wonder; for it came even as a vision, and I beheld it with these eyes. In those days the crown of this land, which now stands so sure and so shining on the brows of him who rules us, was held as one of ambition's baubles, that might be transferred by the sword to some adventurous head; and men of birth and descent were ready with trumpet and with brand to do battle for the exiled branch of the house of Stuart. Rumours of rebellions and invasions were as frequent as the winds on our heaths; and each day brought a darker and more varied tale of risings in the east, and risings in the west; for the king abroad, and for the king at home; and each relater gave a colour and a substance to his tidings, even as his wishes were. The shepherd went armed to the pasturage of his flocks, the lover went armed to the meeting with his mistress; those who loved silver and gold sought the solitary and silent place, and buried their treasure; the father and mother gazed at their sons and their daughters, and thought on the wrongs of war; and the children, armed with hazel rods for spears and swords of lath, carried on a mimic and venturous war with one another, under the hostile banners of the Lion and the bonnie White Rose. Those who still loved the ancient Church were dreaded by those who loved the new; and the sectarians hated both, and hoped for the day when the jewelled mitre would be plucked off the prelate's head, and when austerity, that denies itself, yet giveth not to others, and zeal, which openeth the gates of mercy but for a tithe of mankind, should hold rule and dominion in the land. Those who had broad lands and rich heritages wished for peace; those who had little to lose hoped acquisitions by a convulsion; and there were many of the fiery and intractable spirits of the land who wished for strife and commotion for the sake of variety of pursuit, and because they wished to see coronets and crowns staked on the issue of a battle. Thus, hot discussion and sore dispute divided the people of this land.

"It happened on a fine summer evening that I stopped at the dwelling of David Forester, of Wilton Hall, along with young Walter Selby of Glamora, to refresh myself after the chase on the banks of Derwentwater. The mountain air was mild and balmy, and the lofty and rugged outline of Soutrafell appeared on a canopied background of sky so pure, so blue, and so still, that the earth and heaven seemed blended together. Eagles were visible, perched among the starlight, on the peaks of the rocks; ravens roosted at a vast distance below; and, where the greensward joined the acclivity of rock and stone, the flocks lay in undisturbed repose, with their fleeces shining in dew, and reflected in a broad deep lake at the bottom, so pure and so motionless, that it seemed a sea of glass. The living, or rather human portion of the picture, partook of the same silent and austere character, for inanimate nature often lends a softness or a sternness to man; the meditative melancholy of the mountain and the companionable garrulity of the vale have not escaped proverbial observation. I had alighted from my horse, and, seated on a little green hillock before the house, which the imagination of our mountaineers had not failed to people at times with fairies and elves, tasted some of the shepherds' curds and cream, the readiest and the sweetest beverage which rustic hospitality supplies. Walter Selby had seated himself at my feet, and behind me stood the proprietor of Wilton Hall and his wife, awaiting my wishes with that ready and respectful frankness which those of birth and ancestry always obtain among our mountain peasantry. A number of domestics, shepherds and maidens, stood at a distance, as much for the purpose of listening to our conversation, as from the desire to encumber us with their assistance in recommencing our journey.

"'Young lady,' said David Forester, 'have you heard tidings of note from the North or from the South? The Selbys are an ancient and renowned race, and in days of old held rule from sunny Carlisle to the vale of Keswick—a day's flight for a hawk. They are now lordless and landless;

but the day may soon come when to thee I shall go hat in hand to beg a boon, and find thee lady of thy lands again, and the noble house of Lanercost risen anew from its briars and desolation.' I understood better than I wished to appear this mysterious address of my entertainer, and was saved from the confusion of a reply, either direct or oblique, by the forward tongue of his wife. 'Marry, and God forbid,' said she, 'that ever old Lady Popery should hold rule in men's homes again! Not that I wholly hate the old dame either; she has really some good points in her character; and if she would put fat flesh in her pot o' Fridays, and no demand o' one a frank confession of failings and frailties, she might hold rule i' the land again for aught I care; though I cannot say I think well of the doctrine that denies nourishment to the body in the belief of bettering the soul. That's a sad mistake in the nature of us moorland people; if a shepherd lacks a meal a minute beyond the sounding of the horn, all the house hears on't: it's a religion, my lady, that will never take root again in this wild place, where men scorn the wheat and haver food, and make, for lack o' kitchen, the fat mutton eat the lean.'

"The good woman of the house was interrupted in her curious speech by the arrival of one of those personages, who, with a horse and pack, distribute the luxuries and the comforts of the city over the mountainous regions of the provinces. His horse, loaded with heavy panniers, came foremost, anxious for a resting-place; and behind came the owner, a middle-aged man, tall and robust, with hair as black as the raven, curled close beneath a very broad bonnet, and in his hand one of those measuring rods of root-grown oak, piked with iron at the under end, and mounted with brass at the upper, which seemed alike adapted for defending or measuring his property. He advanced to the spot where we were seated, like an old acquaintance, asked for and obtained lodgings for the evening, and having disposed of his horse, he took out a small box resembling a casket, which he placed on the grass, and, seating himself beside it, assumed one of those looks of mingled gravity and good humour, prepared alike for seriousness or mirth.

"He was not permitted to remain long in silence. 'Ye come from the North, Simon Packpin,' said one of the menials; 'one can know that by yere tongue; and as ye are a cannie lad at a hard bargain, ye can tell us, in yere own sly and cannie way, if it be true that the Highland gentlemen are coming to try if they can set with targe and claymore the crown of both lands on the brow it was made for.' I looked at the person of the querist, a young man of the middle size, with a firm limb and a frank martial mien, and something in his bearing which bespoke a higher ambition than that of tending flocks; his face, too, I thought I had seen before, and under very different circumstances. 'Goodsooth, Wattie Graeme,' said another of the menials, 'ye might as well try to get back butter out o' the black dog's throat, as extract a plain answer from Sleekie Simon. I asked him no further than a month ago, if he thought we would have a change in the land soon. "The moon," quoth he, "will change in its season, and so maun all things human." "But do you think," said I, "that the people will continue to prefer the cold blood of the man who keeps the chair to the warm kindly, English blood o' him that's far away?" "Ay, ay," quoth he; "nae doubt, nae doubt, when we would drink ditch-water rather than red wine." "But," said I, "would it not be better for the land that we had the throne made steadfast under our own native king, than have it shaken by every blast that blows, as I hear it will soon be?" "Say ye sae?" said he, "say ye sae? Better have a finger off than a ye wagging." And so he continued for an hour to reply to every plain question with such dubious responses of northern proverb, that I left him as wise as I found him.'

"This historical sketch of the pedlar obtained the notice of the farmer's wife, who, with the natural impatience of womankind, thus abruptly questioned him: 'We honest moorland people hate all mystery: if you are a man loyal in your heart, and upright in your dealings, you may remain and share our supper; but if ye be a spy from these northern marauders, who are coming with houghs as bare as their swords to make a raid and a foray upon us—arise, I say, and depart! But stay, tell us truly when this hawk of the old uncannie nest of the Stuarts will come to wreck and herrie us?' To all this Simon the pedlar opposed a look of the most impenetrable serenity, and turning over his little oaken box, undid a broad strap and buckle, applied a key to the lock, took out combs, and knives, and spectacles, and some of his cheap ornaments for the bosom and the hair, and all the while he continued chanting over the following curious song, addressed obliquely to the good dame's queries, and perfectly intelligible to all who knew, the poetic language and allegorical meaning which the adherents of the house of Stuart employed to convey tidings of importance to each other :

THE CUCKOO IS A GENTLE BIRD.

The Cuckoo is a gentle bird,
  And gentle is his note,
And April it is pleasant,
  While the sun is waxing hot ;
For amid the green woods growing,
  And the fresh flowers' blooming throng,
Forth comes the gentle Cuckoo
  With his meek and modest song.

The eagle slays the little lambs
  On Skiddaw high and hoar ;
The hawk he covets carnage, and
  The grey glede griens for gore :
The raven croaks aloud for blood,
  Through spring and summer long ;
While the bonnie Cuckoo gladdens us
  With many a merry song.

The woodcock comes, and with the swan
  Brings winter on his wing ;
The groves cast off their garments green,
  The small birds cease to sing :
The wild birds cease their singing, till
  The lilies scent the earth ;
But the Cuckoo scatters roses round
  Whenever he goes forth.

The Cuckoo is a princely bird,
  And we will wait awhile,
And welcome him with shout and song,
  In the morn of green April ;
We'll lay our thighs o'er our good steeds,
  And gird our claymores on,
And chase away the hooded crows
  That croak around the throne.

"I could not help glancing my eye on this curious and demure traveller; but the perfect simplicity of his looks baffled all the scrutiny which the mysterious import of his song induced me to make. Walter Graeme, one of the shepherds, sat down at his side, desirous of purchasing some of his commodities, but the frank mountaineer was repulsed in an attempt to dip his hands among the motley contents of the pack ; and had it come to the arbitration of personal strength, there could be little doubt of the issue, for the merchant had a willing hand and a frame of iron.

"Silence ensued for a little while; the pedlar, who for some time had stolen a look at me, seemed all at once to come to some conclusion how to proceed, and, fastening up his little box, approached me with a look of submission and awe. 'Fair lady, the pedlar is but a poor man, who earns an honest penny among the peasantry; but he has a reverence and a love for the noble names which grace our verse and our chivalry; and who has an English heart that knows not and beats not high at the sound of Selby's name? and who bears a Scottish heart that sorrows not for the wreck and the desolation of our most ancient and most noble foe? I tell thee, lady, that I honour thee more—lady, as thou seemest to be, but of a kirtle and a steed—than if thou satest with a footstool of gold, and hadst nobles' daughters bearing up thy train. This cross and rosary'—and he held in his hand these devotional symbols, carved of dark wood, and slightly ornamented with gold—'are of no common wood: a princess has sat under the shadow of its bough, and seen her kingdom won and lost; and may the fair one who will now wear it warm it in her bosom till she sees a kingdom, long lost, won as boldly and as bravely as ever the swords of the Selbys won their land!' And throwing the rosary around my neck as he concluded, away he went, opened his pack anew, resuming again his demure look and the arrangement of his trinkets.

"Walter Selby, who all this while—though then a hot and forward youth—had remained mute, addressed me in a whisper: 'Fair Eleanor, mine own giddy cousin, this pedlar—this dispenser of rosaries, made of Queen Mary's yew tree—he, whom the churls call Simon Packpin, is no seeker of profit from vulgar merchandise. I'll wager a kiss of thine own ruddy lips against one of mine, that he carries swords made of good Ripon steel, and pistols of good Swedish iron, in yon horse-pack of his: wilt thou pledge a kiss on this wager, my gentle cousin? And instead of a brain stored with plans for passing an English yard for a Scottish ell, and making pieces of homespun plaiding seem costly works from the looms of Arras or even of Leeds, it is furnished with more perilous stuff, pretty Eleanor; and no man can tell us better how many of the Scottish cavaliers have their feet ready for the stirrup, and on what day they will call on the Selbys to mount and strike for their ancient lord and their lost inheritance.' Something of this matter had been passing in my own mind, but the temper of the Selbys ever required more to be repressed than encouraged, and so I endeavoured to manage thee, poor Walter Selby!" She sighed while she named the name of him who had guided and gladdened her youth, and, in a tone low and almost inaudible, she addressed herself to the image which her affections had thus charmed into life : "I saw thee, thou last and thou bravest of all the Selbys, with thy banner spread, thy sword bright, and thy long golden locks waving on thy shoulders, when the barriers of Preston were lost and won, and the gallant laird of Ashiestiel fought like a brother by thy side. Oh, that this last bright picture were all I remembered of thee ! But can the heart of woman, though her head be grey, forget that she saw those long locks which made the dames sigh, waving, soiled and bloody, on the gates of Carlisle. There is much done in this world must be answered for in the next, and this cruel and remorseless deed is one." She looked while she spoke as if her wild and agitated fancy had given motion to the picture which she drew of her lover; her face changed, and her eyes, from beneath their moist and depressed lids, became fixed and frozen, like stars in a winter night. This passed away with a smothered groan and a moving of her hand over her bosom: she again resumed her narrative. "'Truly,' said I, 'my froward cousin, thou art the best soldier our poor prince could peril his cause with—thou canst make a pedlar churl into a deep-plodding politician, capable of overturning a throne ; and his pack, filled with shreds of lace and remnants of ribbon, into a magazine of weapons fit for furnishing an army. What will thy most wise head make of these dubious sibyl verses which this mysterious politician of thine has been doling out for thy especial instruction ?' 'By the rood, my witty Eleanor,' said Walter Selby, 'I shall win a battle, and wed thee in revenge for this. But thinkest thou not that the box, which has endowed that round white neck of thine with a cross and rosary of gold, and wood still more precious, may not contain things equally curious and strange ? Some golden information this pedlar—since pedlar thou wilt have him—carries in his looks; I wish I could find the way to extract it.' The stranger, as if guessing by our looks and our whispers what was passing between us, proceeded to instruct us in his own singular way: he described the excellent temper of his Sheffield whittles; praised the curious qualities of his spectacles, which might enable the wearer to see distant events; and after soothing over some lines of a psalm or hymn common to the Presbyterians, he proceeded to chant the following ballad, of which I regret the loss of several verses:—

THE PEDLAR'S BALLAD.

It is pleasant to sit on green Saddleback top,
    And hearken the eagle's cry;
It is pleasant to roam in the bonnie greenwood,
    When the stags go bounding by;
And it's merry to sit, when the red wine goes round,
'Mid the poet's sweet song and the minstrel's sweet sound.

It is merry in moonshine to lead down the dance,
    To go starting away when the string
Shakes out its deep sound, and the fair maidens fly
    Like the sunlight—or birds on the wing;
And it's merry at gloaming, aneath the boughs green,
To woo a young maiden and roam all unseen.

But it's blither by far when the pennon is spread,
    And the lordly loud trumpet is pealing,
When the bright swords are out, and the war-courser neighs,
    As high as the top of Helvellyn;
And away spurs the warrior, and makes the rocks ring
With the blows that he strikes for his country and king.

Our gallants have sprung to their saddles, and bright
    Are the swords in a thousand hands;
I came through Carlisle, and I heard their steeds neigh
    O'er gentle Eden's sands.
And seats shall be emptied, and brands shall be wet,
Ere all these gay gallants in London are met.

Lord Maxwell is mounted by winding Nith,
    Lord Kenmore by silver Dee;
The blithe lads spur on from the links of the Orr
    And Durisdeer's greenwood tree;
And the banners which waved when Judea was won
Are all given again to the glance of the sun.

The Johnstone is stirring in old Annandale,
    The Jardine, the Halliday's coming
From merry Milkwater and haunted Dryfe bank,
    And Esk, that shall list at the gloaming
The war shout, the yell, and of squadrons the dash,
And gleam to the claymore and carabine's flash.

Then come with the war-horse, the basnet, and sword,
    And bid the big trumpet awaken;
The bright locks that stooped at a fair lady's feet
    Mid the tempest of war must be shaken.
It is pleasant to spur to the battle the steed,
And cleave the proud helmet that holds a foe's head.

Thy sword's rusty, Howard; hot Dacre, art thou
    So cool when the war-horse is bounding?
Come Percy, come thou, like a Percy of yore,
    When the trumpet of England is sounding:
And come, gallant Selby—thy name is a name,
While a soldier has soul and a minstrel has flame.

And come, too, ye names that are nameless—come mount,
    And win ye a name in proud story:
A thousand long years at the sock and the share
    Are not worth one moment of glory.
Come arm ye, and mount ye, and make the helms ring
Of the Whigs, as ye strike for your country and king!

"The whole household of Wilton Hall, including Walter Selby and myself, had gradually gathered around this merchant-minstrel, whose voice, from an ordinary chant, had arisen, as we became interested, into a tone of deep and martial melody. Nor was it the voice alone of the stranger that became changed: his face, which at the commencement of the ballad had a grave and a dubious expression, brightened up with enthusiasm; his frame grew erect, and his eyes gleamed with that fierce light which has been observed in the eyes of the English soldiers on the eve of battle. 'What thinkest thou, pretty Eleanor, of our merchant now?' said Walter Selby. 'I should like to have such a form on my right hand when I try to empty the saddles of the southern horse of some of the boldest Whigs.' 'And I'll pledge thee, young gentleman,' said the pedlar, raising his voice at once from the provincial drawl and obscurity of lowland Scotch into the purest English, 'any vow thou askest of me, to ride on which hand thou wilt, and be to thee as a friend and a brother when the battle is at the hottest; and so I give thee my hand on't.' 'I touch no hand,' said Walter Selby, 'and I vow no vow, either in truce or battle, till I know thy name, if thou art of the lineage of the gentle or the churl. I am a Selby, and the Selbys——' 'The Selbys,' said the stranger, in a tone slow and deliberate, 'are an ancient and a noble race; but this is no time, young gentleman, to scruple precedence of blood. In the fields where I have ridden noble deeds have been achieved by common hands, while the gentle and the far-descended have sat apart, nor soiled their swords. I neither say I am of a race churlish nor noble, but my sword is as sharp as other men's, and might do thee a friendly deed were it nigh thee in danger.' 'Now, God help us,' said the dame of Wilton Hall, 'what will old England become? Here's young Wat Selby debating lineage and blood with a packman churl. In good truth, if I had but one drop of gentle blood in my veins, I would wrap him up in his own plaid, and beat him to death with his ellwand, which I'll warrant is a full thumb-breadth short of measure.' I stood looking on Walter Selby and on the stranger; the former standing aloof with a look of haughty determination; and the latter, with an aspect of calm and intrepid resolution, enduring the scoff of the hot-headed youth and the scorn of the vulgar matron.

"It might be now about nine o'clock: the air was balmy and mute, the sky blue and unclouded, and the moon, yet unrisen, had sent as much of her light before her as served, with the innumerable stars, to lighten the earth from the summit of the mountains to the deepest vales. I never looked upon a more lovely night, and gladly turned my face from the idle disputants to the green mountain-side, upon which that forerunner gleam which precedes the moon had begun to scatter its light. While I continued gazing, there appeared a sight on Soutra Fellside, strange, ominous, and obscure to many, at that time, but which was soon after explained in desolation and in blood. I saw all at once a body of horsemen coming swiftly down the steep and impassable side of the mountain, where no earthly horse ever rode. They amounted to many hundreds, and trooped onwards in succession, their helmets gleaming and their drawn swords shining amid the starlight. On beholding this vision I uttered a faint scream, and Walter Selby, who was always less or more than other men, shouted till the mountain echoed: 'Saw ever man so gallant a sight? A thousand steeds and riders on the perpendicular side of old Soutra—see, where they gallop along a linn, where I could hardly fly a hawk! Oh! for a horse with so sure and so swift a foot as these, that I might match me with this elfin chivalry! My wanton brown, which can bound across the Derwent like a bird with me on its back, is but a packhorse to one of these.' Alarm was visible in every face around, for we all knew what the apparition foreboded—a lost battle and a ruined cause. I heard my father say that the like sight appeared on Helvellyn-side before the battle of Marston Moor, with this remarkable difference: the leader wore on his head the semblance of a royal crown, whereas the leaders of the troop whom I beheld wore only earls' coronets.

"'Now, his right hand protect us!' said the dame of Wilton Hall. 'What are we doomed to endure?—what will follow this?' 'Misery to many,' answered the pedlar, 'and sudden and early death to some who are present.' 'Cease thy croak, thou northern raven!' said Walter Selby; 'if they are phantoms, let them pass—what care we for men of mist? And if they are flesh and bone, as I guess by their bearing they must surely be, they are good gallant soldiers of our good king, and thus do I bid them welcome with my bugle.' He winded his horn till the mountain echoed far and wide; the spectre horsemen, distant nearly a quarter of a mile, seemed to halt; and the youth had his horn again at his lips to renew the note, when he was interrupted by the pedlar, who, laying his hand on the instrument, said: 'Young gentleman, be wise, and be ruled; yon vision is sent for man's instruction, not for his scoff and his scorn.' The shadowy troop now advanced, and passed toward the south at the distance of a hundred yards. I looked on them as they went, and I imagined I knew the forms of many living men—doomed speedily to perish in the battle-field or on the scaffold. I saw the flower of the Jacobite chivalry—the Maxwells, the Gordons, the Boyds, the Drummonds, the Ogilvys, the Camerons, the Scotts, the Foresters, and the Selbys. The havoc which happened among these noble names it is needless to relate: it is written in tale, related in ballad, sung in song; and, deeper still it is written in family feeling and national sympathy. A supernatural light accompanied this pageant, and rendered perfectly visible horse and man: in the rear I saw a form that made me shudder; a form still present to my eye and impressed upon my heart, old and sorrow-worn as it is, as vividly as in early youth. I saw the shape of Walter Selby—his short cloak, his scarlet dress, his hat and feather, his sword by his side; and that smiling glance in his deep dark eye which was never there but for me, and which I could know among the looks of a thousand thousand.

As he came, he laid his bridle on his horse's neck, and leaned aside, and took at me a long, long look. The youth himself, full of life and gladness beside me, seemed to discover the resemblance between the spectre rider and himself, and it was only by throwing myself in his bosom that I hindered him from addressing the apparition. How long I remained insensible in his arms I know not, but when I recovered I found myself pressed to the youth's bosom, and a gentleman, with several armed attendants, standing beside me—all showing by their looks the deep interest they took in my fate."

Part III.

DEATH OF WALTER SELBY.

I REDE ye, my lady—I rede ye, my lord,
To put not your trust in trumpet and sword :
Else the proud name of Selby, which gladdened us long,
Shall pass from the land like the sough of a song.
OLD BALLAD.

BEFORE Dame Eleanor Selby had concluded her account of the Spectre Horsemen of Soutra Fell, the sun had set ; and the twilight, warm, silent, and dewy, had succeeded: that pleasant time, between light and dark, in which domestic labour finds a brief remission. The shepherd, returned from hill or moor, spread out his hose, moistened in morass or rivulet, before the hearth fire, which glimmered far and wide, and, taking his accustomed seat, sat mute and motionless as a figure of stone. The cows came lowing homewards from the pasture-hills; others, feeding out of cribs filled with rich moist clover, yielded their milk into a score of pails ; while the ewes, folded on the sheltered side of the remote glen, submitted their udders, not without the frequent butt and bleat, to the pressure of maidens' hands. Pastoral verse has not many finer pictures than what it borrows from the shepherd returning from the hill and the shepherdess from the fold, the former with his pipe and dogs, and the latter with her pail of reeking milk, each singing with a hearty country freedom of voice, and in their own peculiar way, the loves and the joys of a pastoral life. The home of Randal Rode presented a scene of rough plenty, and abounded in pastoral wealth; the head of the house associated with his domestics, and maintained that authority over their words and conduct which belonged to simpler times; and something of the rustic dignity of the master was observable in his men. His daughter Maude busied herself among the maidens with a meekness and a diligence which had more of the matron than is commonly found in so young a dame. All this escaped not the notice of her old and capricious kinswoman Eleanor Selby; but scenes of homely and domestic joy seemed alien to her heart. The intrusion, too, of the churlish name of Rode among the martial Selbys, never failed to darken the picture which she would have enjoyed had this rustic alloy mixed with the precious metal of any other house. It was her chief delight, since all the males of her name had perished, to chant ballads in their praise, and relate their deeds from the time of the Norman invasion down to their ruin in the last rebellion. Many snatches of these chivalrous ballads are still current on the Border—the debateable land of song as well as of the sword, where minstrels sought their themes, and entered, harp in hand, into rivalry—a kind of contest which the sword, the critic's weapon of those days, was often drawn to decide. Much of this stirring and heroic Border-life mingles with the traditionary tales of Eleanor Selby. Her narratives contain occasionally a vivid presentment of character and action. I shall endeavour to preserve something of this, and retain at the same time their dramatic cast, while I prune and condense the whole, to render them more acceptable to the impatience of modern readers. She thus pursued her story:

"I am now to tell a tale I have related a thousand times to the noble and the low; it is presented to me in my dreams, for the memory of spilt blood clings to a young mind—and the life's-blood of Walter Selby was no common blood to me. The vision of the spectre horsemen, in which human fate was darkly shadowed forth, passed away, and departed too, I am afraid, from the thoughts of those to whom it came as a signal and a warning—as a cloud passes from the face of the summer-moon. Seated on horseback, with Walter Selby at my bridle-rein, and before and behind me upwards of a score of armed cavaliers, I had proceeded along the mountain-side about a mile, when a horn was winded at a small distance in our front. We quickened our pace; but the way was rough and difficult, and we were obliged to go a sinuous course, like the meanderings of a brook, round rock and cairn and heathy hill, while the horn, continuing to sound, still seemed as far ahead as when we first heard it. It was about twelve o'clock; and the moon, large and bright and round, gleamed down from the summit of a green pasture mountain, and lighted us on our way through a narrow wooded valley, where a small stream glimmered and sparkled in the light, and ran so crooked a course as compelled us to cross it every hundred yards. Walter Selby now addressed me in his own singular way: 'Fair Eleanor, mine own grave and staid cousin, knowest thou whither thou goest? Comest thou to counsel how fifty men may do the deeds of thousands, and how the crown of this land may be shifted like a prentice's cap?' 'Truly,' said I, 'most sage and considerate cousin, I go with thee like an afflicted damsel of yore, in the belief that thy wisdom and valour may reinstate me in my ancient domains, or else win for me some new and princely inheritance.' 'Thou speakest,' said the youth, 'like one humble in hope, and puttest thy trust in one who would willingly work miracles to oblige thee. But ponder, fair damsel: my sword, though the best blade in Cumberland, cannot cut up into relics five or six regiments of dragoons, nor is this body, though devoted to thee, made of that knight-errant stuff that can resist sword and bullet. So I counsel thee, most discreet coz, to content thyself with hearing the sound of battle afar off, for we go on a journey of no small peril.' To these sensible and considerate words I answered nothing, but rode on, looking, all the while, Walter Selby in the face, and endeavouring to say something witty or wise. He resumed his converse: 'Nay, nay, mine own sweet and gentle cousin—my sweet Eleanor—I am too proud of that troubled glance of thine to say one word more about separation'; and our horses' heads and our cheeks came closer as he spoke. 'That ballad of the pedlar—for pedlar shall the knight be still to oblige thee—his ballad told more truth than I reckoned a minstrel might infuse into verse. All the Border cavaliers of England and Scotland are near us or with us; and now for the game of coronets and crowns

—a coffin, coz, or an earl's bauble—for we march upon Preston.'

"Prepared as I was for these tidings, I could not hear them without emotion, and I looked on Walter Selby with an eye that was not calculated to inspire acts of heroism. I could not help connecting our present march on Preston with the shadowy procession I had so recently witnessed, and the resemblance which one of the phantoms bore to the youth beside me, pressed on my heart. 'Now do not be afraid of our success, my fair coz,' said he, 'when to all the proud names of the Border—names thou hast long since learned by heart, and rendered musical by repeating them— we add the names of two most wise and prudent persons, who shall hereafter be called the setters-up and pluckers-down of kings; even thy cool and chivalrous cousin, and a certain staid and sedate errant damosel.' This conversation obtained for us the attention of several stranger cavaliers who happened to join us, as, emerging from the woody glen, we entered upon a green and wide moor or common. One of them, with a short cloak and slouched hat and heron's feather, rode up to my right hand, and, glancing his eye on our faces, thus addressed himself to me in a kind-hearted old Scottish style: 'Fair lady, there be sights less to a warrior's liking than so sweet a face beside a wild mountain about the full of the moon. The cause that soils one of these bright tresses in dew must be a cause dear to man's heart; and, fair one, if thou wilt permit me to ride by thy bridle-rein, my presence may restrain sundry flouts and jests which young cavaliers, somewhat scant of grace and courtesy—and there be such in our company—may use, on seeing a lady so fair and so young bowne on such a dangerous and unwonted journey.' I thanked this northern cavalier for his charitable civility, and observed, with a smile: 'I had the protection of a young person who would feel pleased in sharing the responsibility of such a task.' 'And, fair lady,' continued he,' since Walter Selby is thy protector, my labour will be the less.' My cousin, who during this conversation had ridden silent at my side, seemed to awaken from a reverie, and glancing his eye on the cavalier, and extending his hand, said: 'Sir, in a strange dress, uttering strange words, and busied in a pursuit sordid and vulgar, I knew you not, and repelled your frank courtesy with rude words. I hear you now in no disguised voice, and see you with the sword of honour at your side, instead of the pedlar's staff: accept, therefore, my hand, and be assured that a Selby—as hot and as proud as the lordliest of his ancestors—feels honoured in thus touching in friendship the hand of a gallant gentleman.'

"I felt much pleased with this adventure, and looked on the person of the stalwart Borderer as he received and returned the friendly grasp of Walter Selby: he had a brow serene and high, an eye of sedate resolution, and something of an ironic wit lurking amid the wrinkles which age and thought had engraven on his face. I never saw so complete a transformation; and could hardly credit that the bold, martial-looking, and courteous cavalier at my side had but an hour or two before sung rustic songs and chaffered with the peasants of Cumberland about the price of ends of ribbon and twopenny toys and trinkets. He seemed to understand my thoughts, and thus resolved the riddle in a whisper: 'Fair lady, these are not days when a knight of loyal mind may ride with sound of horn and banner displayed, summoning soldiers to fight for the good cause; of a surety, his journey would be brief. In the disguise of a calling—low, it is true, but honourable in its kind—I have obtained more useful intelligence, and enlisted more good soldiers, than some who ride aneath an earl's pennon.'

"Our party, during this nocturnal march, had been insensibly augmented; and when the grey day came I could count about three hundred horsemen—young, well mounted, and well armed—some giving vent to their spirit or their feelings in martial songs, others examining and proving the merits of their swords and pistols, and many marching on in grave silence, forecasting the hazards of war and the glory of success. Leaving the brown pastures of the moorlands, we descended into an open and cultivated country, and soon found ourselves upon the great military road which connects all the north country with the capital. It was still the cold and misty twilight of the morning, when I happened to observe an old man close beside me, mounted on a horse seemingly coeval with himself—wrapped, or rather shrouded, in a grey mantle or plaid, and all the while looking steadfastly at me from under the remains of a broad slouched hat. I had something like a dreamer's recollection of his looks; but he soon added his voice to assist my recollection, and I shall never forget the verses the old man chanted with a broken and melancholy, and I think I may add prophetic, voice:

OH! PRESTON, PROUD PRESTON.

Oh! Preston, proud Preston! come hearken the cry
Of spilt blood against thee—it sounds to the sky;
Thy richness a prey to the spoiler is doomed,
Thy homes to the flame, to be smote and consumed:
Thy sage with grey locks, and thy dame with the brown,
Descending long tresses and grass-sweeping gown,
Shall shriek when there's none for to help them: the hour
Of thy fall is not nigh, but it's certain and sure.
Proud Preston, come humble thy haughtiness—weep—
Cry aloud; for the sword it shall come in thy sleep.

What deed have I done, that thou liftst thus thy cry,
Thou bard of ill-omen, and doomst me to die?
What deed have I done thus to forfeit the trust
In high Heaven, and go to destruction and dust?
My matrons are chaste and my daughters are fair;
Where the battle is hottest my sword's shining there;
And my sons bow their heads, and are on their knees kneeling,
When the prayer is poured forth and the organ is pealing:
What harm have I wrought, and to whom offered wrong,
That thou comest against me with shout and with song?

What harm hast thou wrought! List and hearken: the hour
Of revenge may be late, but it's certain and sure:
As the flower to the field and the leaf to the tree,
So sure is the time of destruction to thee.
What harm hast thou wrought! Haughty Preston, now hear:
Thou hast whetted against us the brand and the spear;
And thy steeds through our ranks rush, all foaming and hot,
And I hear thy horns sound and the knell of thy shot:
The seal of stern judgment is fixed on thy fate
When the life-blood of Selby is spilt at thy gate.

Oh! Selby, brave Selby, no more thy sword's braving
The foes of thy prince, when thy pennon is waving;
The Gordon shall guide and shall rule in the land;
The Boyd yet shall battle with buckler and brand;
The Maxwells shall live, though diminished their shine,
And the Scotts in bard's song shall be all but divine;
Even Forster of Derwent shall breathe for a time,
Ere his name it has sunk to a sound and a rhyme;
But the horn of the Selbys has blown its last blast,
And the star of their names from the firmament cast.

"I dropped the bridle from my hand, and all the green expanse of dale and hill grew dim before me. The voice of the old man had for some time ceased before I had courage to look about; and I immediately recognized in the person of the minstrel an old and faithful soldier of my father's,

whose gift at song, rude and untutored as it was, had
obtained him some estimation on the Border, where the
strong, lively imagery and familiar diction of the old
ballads still maintain their ground against the classic
elegance and melody of modern verse. I drew back a little,
and, shaking the old man by the hand, said: 'Many years
have passed, Harpur Harberson, since I listened to thy
minstrel skill at Lanercost; and I thought thou hadst gone,
and I should never see thee again. Thy song has lost some
of its ancient grace and military glee since thou leftest my
father's hall.' ''Deed, my bonnie lady,' said the Borderer
with a voice suppressed and melancholy, while something of
his ancient smile brightened his face for a moment, 'sangs
of sorrow and dule have been rifer with me than ballads of
merriment and mirth. It's long now since I rode and
fought by my gallant master's side, when the battle waxed
fierce and desperate; and my foot is not so firm in the
stirrup now, nor my hand sae steeve at the steel, as it was
in those blessed and heroic days. It's altered days with
Harpur Harberson since he harped afore the nobles of the
North in the home of the gallant Selbys, and won the cup
of gold. I heard that my bonnie lady and her gallant
cousin were on horseback; so I e'en put my old frail
body on a frail horse, to follow where I cannot lead. It's
pleasant to mount at the sound of the trumpet again; and
it's better for an auld man to fall with a sound of battle in
his ear, and be buried in the trench with the brave, and the
young, and the noble, than beg his bread from door to
door, enduring the scoff and scorn of the vulgar and sordid,
and be found, some winter morning, streeked stiff and dead
on a hassock of straw in some churl's barn. So I shall e'en
ride on, and see the last of a noble and a hopeless cause.' He
drew his hat over his brow, while I endeavoured to cheer
him by describing the numbers, resources, and strength of
the party. And I expressed rather my hope than firm
belief when I assured him 'there was little doubt that the
house of Selby would lift its head again and flourish, and
that the grey hairs of its ancient and faithful minstrel would
go down in gladness and glory to the grave.' He shook his
head, yet seemed almost willing to believe for a moment,
against his own presentiment, in the picture of future glory I
had drawn. It was but for a moment. ' 'Deed no—'deed
no, my bonnie, bonnie lady, it canna—canna be. Glad

would I be could I credit the tale that our house would hold up its head again, high and lordly. But I have too strong faith in minstrel prediction, and in the dreams and visions of the night, to give credence to such a pleasant thought. It was not for nought that horsemen rode in ranks on Soutraside last night, where living horseman could never urge a steed, and that the forms and semblances of living men were visible to me in this fearful procession. Nor was it for nought that my grandfather, old minstrel Harberson, caused himself to be carried in his last hour to the summit of Lanercost Hill, that he might die looking on the broad domains of his master. His harp—for his harp and he were never parted—his harp yielded involuntary sounds, and his tongue uttered unwilling words—words of sad import, the fulfilment of which is at hand. I shall repeat you the words: they are known but to few, and have been scorned too much by the noble race of Selby:

I rede ye, my lady—I rede ye, my lord,
To put not your trust in the trumpet and sword;
To follow no banner that comes from the flood,
To march no more southward to battle and blood.
League not with Dalzell—no, nor seek to be fording
The clear stream of Derwent with Maxwell and Gordon;
To a Forester's word draw nor bridle nor glaive;
Shun the gates of proud Preston like death and the grave;
And the Selbys shall flourish in life and in story,
While eagles love Skiddaw and soldiers love glory.

"'These are the words of my ancestor—what must be must. I shall meet thee again at the gates of Preston. As he uttered these words he mingled with the ranks of horsemen under the banner of a Border knight, and I rode up to the side of my cousin and his companion.

"It is not my wish to relate all I heard and describe all I saw on our way southward; but our array was a sight worth seeing, and a sight we shall never see again; for war is now become a trade, and men are trained to battle like hounds to the hunting. In those days the noble and the gentle, each with his own banner, with kinsmen and retainers, came forth to battle; and war seemed more a chivalrous effort than it seems now, when the land commits its fame and its existence to men hired by sound of trumpet and by beat of drum. It was soon broad daylight; all the adherents of the house of Stuart had moved towards Lancashire, from the south of

Scotland and the north of England, and, forming a junction where the Westmoreland mountains slope down to the vales, now covered the road as far as my eye could reach—not in regular companies, but in clusters and crowds, with colours displayed. There might be, in all, one thousand horsemen and fifteen hundred foot—the former armed with sword and pistol and carbine, the latter with musket and spear. It was a fair sight to see so many gentlemen dressed in the cavalier garb of other days, some with head and bosom pieces of burnished mail, others with slouched hats and feathers and scarlet vests, and all with short cloaks or mantles of velvet or woollen, clasped at the bosom with gold, and embroidered each according to their own or their mistress's fancy. A body of three hundred chosen horsemen, pertaining to my Lord Kenmore, marched in front, singing, according to the fashion of the Scotch, rude and homely ballads in honour of their leader:

> Kenmore's on and awa, Willie,
>   Kenmore's on and awa;
> And Kenmore's lord is the gallantest lord
>   That ever Galloway saw.
>
> Success to Kenmore's band, Willie,
>   Success to Kenmore's band;
> There was never a heart that feared a Whig
>   E'er rode by Kenmore's hand.
>
> There's a rose in Kenmore's cap, Willie,
>   There's a rose in Kenmore's cap;
> He'll steep it red in ruddy life's blood
>   Afore the battle drap.

"Such were some of the verses by which the rustic minstrels of those days sought to stimulate the valour of their countrymen. One hundred horse, conducted by Lord Nithsdale, succeeded; those of Lord Derwentwater followed: a band numerous, but divided in opinion—unsteady in resolution, and timid in the time of need and peril, like their unfortunate lord. The foot followed: a band of warriors, strange and even savage in their appearance; brave and skilful, and unblenching in battle, with plaid and bonnet and broadsword, bare-kneed, and marching to a kind of wild music, which, by recalling the airs of their ancestors, and the battles in which they fought and bled, kindles a military fury and resolution which destroys all against which it is directed. These were men from the mountains of Scotland, and they were led by chieftain Mackintosh, who was to them as a divinity—compared to whom the prince in whose cause they fought was a common being, a mere mortal. I admired the rude, natural courtesy of these people, and lamented the coward counsels which delivered them up to the axe and the cord without striking a single blow. The rear—accounted in this march, with an enemy behind as well as before, a post of some peril—was brought up by about two hundred Border cavaliers and their adherents; and with them rode Walter Selby and his new companion. The command seemed divided among many, and without obeying any one chief in particular, all seemed zealous in the cause, and marched on with a rapidity regulated by the motions of the foot.

"No serious attempt was made to impede us: some random shots were fired from the hedgerows and groves; till at length, after a fatiguing journey, we came within sight of Preston; and there the enemy made his appearance in large masses of cavalry and foot, occupying the distant rising grounds, leaving our entry into the town free and uninterrupted. Something in my face showed the alarm I felt on seeing the numbers and array of our enemies: this passed not unobserved of the cavalier at my side, who said with a smile: 'Fair lady, you are looking on the mercenary bands which sordid wealth has marched against us; these are men bought and sold, and who hire their best blood for a scarlet garb and a groat. I wish I had wealth enough to tempt the avarice of men who measure all that is good on earth by the money it brings. And yet, fair one, I must needs own that our own little band of warriors is brought strangely together and bound by ties of a singular kind. It would make a curious little book were I to write down all the motives and feelings which have put our feet in the stirrup. There's my Lord Kenmore, a hot, a brave, and a self-willed, and the Scotch maidens say a bonnie Gordon: his sword had stuck half-drawn from the scabbard, but for the white hand of his wife; but he that lives under the influence of bright eyes, Lady Eleanor, lives under a spell as powerful as loyalty. And what would the little book say of my Lord Nithsdale, with whom ride so many of the noble name of Maxwell? Can scorn for the continual cant and sordid hearts of some acres of psalm-singing Covenanters, who haunt the hill-tops of Terreagles and Dalswinton, cause the good lord to put the fairest domains on the Border in jeopardy? or does he hope to regain all the sway held by his ancestors of yore over the beautiful vale of Nith, humbling into dust, as he arises, the gifted weaver who preaches, the inspired cordwainer who expounds, and the upstart grocer who holds rule—the two former over men's minds, and the latter over men's bodies? There's my Lord Carnwath——'

"At this moment I heard the sounding of trumpets, and the rushing of horses behind us; and ere I could turn round, my cavalier said, in the same equal and pleasant tone in which he was making his curious communication of human character: 'Fair lady, here be strange auditors, some of my friend General Willis's troopers come to try the edges of their new swords. Halbert, lead this fair lady to a place where she may see what passes; and now for the onset, Walter Selby.' The latter, exchanging a glance with me, turned his horse's head; swords were bared in a moment; and I heard the dash of their horses, as they spurred them to the contest, while a Scottish soldier hurried me towards the town. I had not the courage to look back; the clashing of swords, the knelling of carbines, the groans of the wounded, and the battle-shout of the living, came all blended in one terrible sound: my heart died within me.

"I soon came up to the Scottish mountaineers, who, with their swords drawn and their targets shouldered, stood looking back on the contest, uttering shouts of gladness or shrieks of sorrow, as their friends fell or prevailed. I looked about, and saw the skirmish, which at first had only extended to a few blows and shots, becoming bloody and dubious; for the enemy, reinforced with fresh men, now fairly charged down the open road, and the place where they contended was soon covered with dead and dying. I shrieked aloud at this fearful sight; and quitting my horse's bridle, held up my hands, and cried out to the mountaineers: 'Oh! haste and rescue, else they'll slay him! they'll slay him!' An old Highlander, at almost the same instant, exclaimed, in very corrupt English: 'God! she'll no stand and see the Border lads a' cut to pieces!' And, uttering a kind of military yell, flew off with about two hundred men to the assistance of his friends.

"I was not allowed to remain and witness the charge of

these northern warriors, but was led into Preston, and carried into a house, half-dead, where several of the ladies who followed the fortune of their lords in this unhappy expedition endeavoured to soothe and comfort me. But I soon was the gayest of them all; for in came Walter Selby and his companion, soiled with blood and dust from helmet to spur. I leaped into my cousin's bosom, and sobbed with joy: he kissed my forehead, and said: 'Thank him, my Eleanor—the gallant knight, Sir Thomas Scott; but for him I should have been where many brave fellows are.' I recovered presence of mind in a moment, and turning to him, said: 'Accept, sir, a poor maiden's thanks for the safety of her kinsman, and allow her to kiss the right hand that wrought this deliverance.' 'Bless thee, fair lady,' said the knight, 'I would fight a dozen such fields for the honour thou profferest; but my hand is not in trim for such lady courtesy; so let me kiss thine as a warrior ought.' I held out my hand, which he pressed to his lips; and washing the blood from his hands, removing the soils of battle from his dress, and resuming his mantle, he became the gayest and most cheerful of the company.

"It was evident, from the frequent and earnest consultations of the leaders of this rash enterprise, that information had reached them of no pleasing kind. Couriers continually came and went, and some of the chiefs began to resume their weapons. As the danger pressed, advice and contradiction, which at first were given and urged with courtesy and respect, now became warm and loud; and the Earl of Derwentwater, a virtuous and amiable man, but neither warrior nor leader, instead of overawing and ruling the tumultuary elements of his army, strode to and fro, a perfect picture of indecision and dismay, and uttered not a word.

"All this while Sir Thomas Scott sat beside Walter Selby and me, calm and unconcerned; conversing about our ancient house, relating anecdotes of the lords of Selby in the court and in the camp, quoting, and in his own impressive way of reciting verse lending all the melody of music to, the old minstrel ballads which recorded our name and deeds. In a moment of less alarm I could have worshipped him for this; and my poor Walter seemed the child of his companion's will, and forgot all but me in the admiration with which he contemplated him.

"The conference of the chiefs had waxed warm and

tumultuous, when Lord Nithsdale, a little high-spirited and intrepid man, shook Sir Thomas by the shoulder, and said: 'This is no time, Sir Knight, for minstrel lore and lady's love; betake thee to thy weapon, and bring all thy wisdom with thee, for truly we are about to need both.' Sir Thomas rose, and having consulted a moment with Lord Kenmore, returned to us and said: 'Come, my young friend, we have played the warrior; now let us play the scout, and go forth and examine the numbers and array of our enemies. Such a list of their generals and major-generals has been laid before our leaders as turns them pale; a mere muster-roll of a regiment would make some of them lay down their arms and stretch out their necks to the axe. Lord Kenmore, fair Eleanor, who takes a lady's counsel now and then, will have the honour of sitting by your side till our return.' So saying, Walter Selby and Sir Thomas left us, and I listened to every step in the porch, till their return, which happened within an hour.

"They came splashed with soil, their dress rent with hedge and brake; and they seemed to have owed their safety to their swords, which were hacked and dyed to the hilts. The leaders questioned them: 'Have you marked the enemy's array and learned aught of their numbers?' 'We have done more,' said Sir Thomas; 'we have learned from the tongues of two dying men that Willis, with nine regiments of horse, and Colonel Preston, with a battalion of foot, will scarcely await for dawn to attack you.' This announcement seemed to strike a damp to the hearts of several of the chiefs, and instead of giving that consistency to their councils which mutual fear often inspires, it only served to bewilder and perplex them. 'I would counsel you,' said Sir Thomas, 'to make an instant attack upon their position before their cannon arrive; I will lead the way. We are inferior in number, but superior in courage. Let some of our Border troopers dismount, and with the clansmen open a passage through Colonel Preston's troops which line the hedgerows and enclosures; the horse will follow, and there can be no doubt of a complete victory.' Some opposed this advice, others applauded it; and the precious hours of night were consumed in unavailing debate and passionate contradiction.

"This was only interrupted by the sound of the trumpet and the rushing of horse; for Willis, forcing the barriers at two places, at once made good his entry into the principal street of Preston. I had the courage to go into the street, and had not proceeded far till I saw the enemy's dragoons charging at the gallop; but their saddles were emptied fast with shot and with sword; for the clansmen, bearing their bucklers over their heads, made great havoc among the horsemen with their claymores, and at length succeeded in repulsing them to the fields. As soon as the enemy's trumpets sounded a retreat, our leaders again assembled— assembled not to conquer or fall like cavaliers, with their swords in their hands, but to yield themselves up, to beg the grace of a few days, till they prepared their necks for the rope and the axe. The Highland soldiers wept with anger and shame, and offered to cut their way or perish; but the leaders of the army, unfit to follow or fight, resolved on nothing but submission, and sent Colonel Oxburgh with a message to General Willis to propose a capitulation.

"Sir Thomas Scott came to Walter Selby and me, and said, with a smile of bitter scorn: 'Let these valiant persons deliver themselves up to strain the cord and prove the axe; we will seek, Lady Eleanor, a gentler dispensation. Retreat now is not without peril; yet let us try what the good greenwood will do for poor outlaws. I have seen ladies, and men too, escape from greater peril than this.'

"We were in the saddle in a moment; and, accompanied by about twenty of the Border cavaliers, made our way through several orchard enclosures, and finally entered upon an extensive common or chase, abounding in clumps of dwarf holly and birch, and presenting green and winding avenues, into one of which we gladly entered, leaving Preston half a mile behind. That pale and trembling light which precedes day began to glimmer; it felt intensely cold, for the air was filled with dew, and the boughs and bushes sprinkled us with moisture. We hastened on at a sharp trot, and the soft sward returning no sound, allowed us to hear the trumpet summons and military din which extended far and wide around Preston.

"As we rode along I observed Sir Thomas motion with his hand to his companions, feel his sword and his pistols, glance to the girths of his horse, and finally drop his mantle from his right arm, apparently baring it for a contest. In all these preparations he was followed by his friends, who at the same time closed their ranks, and proceeded with caution and silence. We had reached a kind of road, half the work of Nature and half of man's hand, which divided the chase or waste in two; it was bordered by a natural hedge of holly and thorn. All at once, from a thicket of bushes, a captain, with about thirty of Colonel Preston's dragoons, made a rush upon us, calling out, 'Yield! Down with the traitors!' Swords were bare in a moment, pistols and carbines were flashing, and both parties spurred, alike eager for blood.

"Of this unexpected and fatal contest I have but an indistinct remembrance: the glittering of the helmets, the shining of drawn swords, the flashing of pistols and carbines, the knell of shot, the rushing of horses, and the outcry of wounded men, come all in confusion before me; but I cannot give a regular account of such a scene of terror and blood. It was of brief duration. I laid my bridle on my horse's neck, and wrung my hands, and followed with my looks every motion of Walter Selby. He was in the pride of strength and youth, and spurred against the boldest; and, putting soul and might into every blow, made several saddles empty. I held up my hands, and prayed audibly for success. A dragoon, who had that moment killed a cavalier, rode to my side, and exclaimed: 'Down with thy hands, thou cursed nun—down with thy hands; woot pray yet, woot thou; curse tha, then!' And he made a stroke at me with his sword. The eyes of Walter Selby seemed to lighten as a cloud does on a day of thunder, and at one blow he severed the dragoon's head, bone and helmet, down to his steel collar. As the trooper fell, a pistol and carbine flashed together, and Walter Selby reeled in the saddle, dropped his head and his sword, and saying faintly, 'Oh, Eleanor!' fell to the ground, stretching both hands towards me. I sprang to the ground, clasped him to my bosom, which he covered with his blood, and entreated Heaven to save him; and oh, I doubt I upbraided the Eternal with his death! But Heaven will pity the ravings of despair. He pressed my hand faintly, and lay looking on my face alone, though swords were clashing and pistols were discharged over us.

"Ere the contest had ceased, Sir Thomas sprang from his horse, took Walter Selby in his arms, and tears sparkled in his eyes as he saw the blood flowing from his bosom. 'Alas! alas!' said he, 'that such a spirit, so lofty and heroic, should be quenched so soon, and in a skirmish such as this! Haste, Frank—Elliot; haste, and frame us a litter of green boughs; cover it thick with our mantles; place this noble youth upon it, and we will bear him northward on our horses' necks. Ere I leave his body here, I will leave mine own aside it; and you, minstrel Harberson, bring some water from the brook for this fair and fainting lady.'

"All these orders, so promptly given, were as quickly executed; and we recommenced our journey to the north, with sorrowful hearts and diminished numbers. I rode by the side of the litter, which, alas! became a bier, ere we reached the green hills of Cumberland. We halted in a lonely glen; a grave was prepared; and there, without priest, prayer, or requiem, was all that I loved of man consigned to a sylvan grave. 'The dust of our young hero,' said Sir Thomas, 'must lie here till the sun shines again on our cause, and it shall be placed in consecrated earth.' The minstrel of the ancient name of Selby stood gazing on the grave, and burst out into the following wail or burial song, which is still to be heard from the lips of the maids and matrons of Cumberland:

LAMENT FOR WALTER SELBY.

Mourn, all ye noble warriors—
  Lo! here is lying low
As brave a youth as ever
  Spurred a courser on the foe.
Hope is a sweet thing to the heart,
  And light unto the e'e,
But no sweeter and no dearer
  Than my warrior was to me:
He rode a good steed gallantly,
  And on his foes came down,
With a war-cry like the eagle's,
  From Helvellyn's haughty crown:
His hand was wight, and his dark eye
  Seemed born for wide command;
Young Selby has nae left his like
  In all the northern land.

Weep for him, all ye maidens,
  And weep for him, all ye dames;
He was the sweetest gentleman
  From silver Tweed to Thames.

Wail all for Walter Selby,
  Let your tears come dropping down ;
Wail all for my young warrior,
  In cottage, tower, and town.
Cursed be the hand that fired the shot,
  And may it never know
What beauty it has blighted,
  And what glory it laid low !
Shall some rude peasant sit and sing
  How his rude hand could tame
Thy pride, my Walter Selby,
  And the last of all thy name?

And mourn too, all ye minstrels good,
  And make your harp-strings wail,
And pour his worth through every song,
  His deeds through every tale.
His life was brief, but wondrous bright :
  Awake your minstrel story !
Lo ! there the noble warrior lies,
  So give him all his glory.
When Skiddaw lays its head as low
  As now 'tis green and high,
And the Solway sea grows to a brook,
  Now sweeping proudly by ;
When the soldier scorns the trumpet sound,
  Nor loves the tempered brand ;
Then thy name, my Walter Selby,
  Shall be mute in Cumberland.

"But, alas ! the form of the lovely and the brave was not permitted to sink silently into dust—it was plucked out of its lonely and obscure grave, displayed on a gibbet, and the head, separated from the body, was placed on the gate of Carlisle. All day I sat looking, in sadness and tears, on this sorrowful sight, and all night I wandered about, wild and distracted, conjuring all men who passed by to win me but one tress of the long bright hair of Walter Selby. Even the rude sentinels were moved by my grief, but no one dared to do a deed so daring and so perilous.

I remember it well—it was on a wild and stormy night, the rain fell fast, the thunder rocked the walls, and the lightnings, flashing far and wide, showed the castle's shattered towers and the river Eden rolling deep in flood. I wrapped my robe about me, and approached the gate. The sentinels, obeying the storm, had sought shelter in the turrets, and no living soul seemed abroad but my own unhappy self. I gazed up to the gate—where, alas ! I had often gazed—and I thought I beheld a human form ; a flash of lightning passed, and I saw it was a living being. It descended and approached me, motioning me back with its hand. I retired in awe, and still the figure followed. I turned suddenly round and said, 'Whether thou comest for evil or for good, farther shall I not go till I know thy errand.'

"' Fair and unhappy lady,' said a voice which I had often heard before, 'I have come, not without peril, from a distant place; for I heard the story of your daily and nightly sorrowings, and I vowed I would not leave a relic of the noble and the brave to gladden the eyes of vulgar men and feast the fowls of heaven. Here, take this tress of thy lover's hair, and mourn over it as thou wilt—men shall look on the morrow for the golden locks of Walter Selby waving on Carlisle gate, and when they see nothing there they shall know that the faithful and the valiant are never without friends. His body has been won and his head removed, and his dust shall mingle with the knightly and the far-descended, even as I vowed when we laid him in his early grave.' With these words Sir Thomas Scott departed, and I placed the ringlet in my bosom, from which it shall never be separated."

Such was the story of Eleanor Selby. In a later day some unknown Scottish minstrel heard the uncertain and varying tradition, and, with a minstrel's licence, wove it into verse, suppressing the name of Selby and giving the whole a colour and character most vehemently Scottish. A northern lady is made to sing the following rude and simple lament

CARLISLE YETTS.

White was the rose in my love's hat
  While he rowed me in his Lowland plaidie,
His heart was true as death in love,
  His hand was aye in battle ready;
His lang, lang hair in yellow hanks
  Waved o'er his cheeks sae sweet and ruddy,
But now it waves o'er Carlisle yetts
  In dripping ringlets soiled and bloody.

When I came first through fair Carlisle
  Ne'er was a town sae gladsome seeming,
The white rose flaunted o'er the wall,
  The thistled pennons far were streaming.
When I came next through fair Carlisle,
  Oh! sad, sad seemed the town, and eerie,
The old men sobbed, and grey dames wept,
  "O lady! come ye to seek your dearie?"

THE SELBYS OF CUMBERLAND.

I tarried on a heathery hill,
   My tresses to my cheeks were frozen,
And far adown the midnight wind
   I heard the din of battle closing.
The grey day dawned, where 'mang the snow
   Lay many a young and gallant fellow,
But the sun came visiting in vain
   Two lovely een 'tween locks of yellow.

There's a tress of soiled and yellow hair
   Close in my bosom I am keeping:
Oh! I have done with delight and love,
   So welcome want, and woe, and weeping.
Woe, woe upon that cruel heart,
   Woe, woe upon that hand so bloody,
That lordless leaves my true love's hall,
   And makes me wail a virgin widow.

PLACING A SCOTTISH MINISTER.

> LANG patronage, wi' rod o' airn,
>   Has shored the Kirk's undoin',
> As lately Fenwick, sair forfairn,
>   Has proven to its ruin ;
> Our patron, honest man ! Glencairn,
>   He saw mischief was brewin' ;
> And, like a godly elect bairn,
>   He's waled us oot a true ane,
>   And soun', this day.
>   BURNS.

THE pleasantest hour, perhaps, of human life, is when a man, becoming master of his own actions, and with his first-earned money in his hand, gazes along the opening vista of existence, and sees, in silent speculation, the objects of his ambition appearing before him in their shadowy succession of peace, and enjoyment, and glory. Out of a few hard-won shillings the peasant frames visions of rustic wealth, whitens the mountains with his flocks, and covers the plain with clover and corn. The seaman casts his future anchor on a coast of silver, and gold, and precious stones; and sees his going and returning sails wafting luxury and riches. The poet, in his first verse, feels a thrill of unbounded joy he is never to experience again ; he hears Fame sounding her trumpet at his approach, and imagines his songs descending through the most delightful of all modes of publication—the sweet lips of millions of fair maidens—now and for evermore. It was with feelings of this kind that I arranged the purchases my first wealth made, in a handsome pack secured with bolt and lock, and proceeded to follow the gainful and healthful calling of a packman among the dales of Dumfriesshire and the green hills of Galloway. On the first morning of my trade I halted in every green lane, spread out the motley contents of my box in orderly array before me, surveyed them with silent and growing joy, then placed them again in the box, and recommenced my march, amid busy calculation of the probable proceeds of my industry.

A little before noon, on a sweet morning of summer, I had seated myself on the summit of a little green fairy hill which overlooks the ancient Abbey of Bleeding Heart; and spreading out before me all the articles I had to offer for sale, I indulged, unconsciously, in the following audible speculation: "A pleasant story and a merry look will do much among the young; and a sedate face and a grave tale will win me a lodging from the staid and devout. For the bonnie lass and the merry lad have I not the choicest ballads and songs? For the wise and the grave do I lack works of solemn import, from the ' Prophecies of Peden,' and the 'Crumb of Comfort,' up to 'Salvation's Vantage-Ground,' or a ' Louping-on-Stone for Heavy Believers'? Then, for those who are neither lax on the one hand nor devout on the other, but stand as a stone in the wall, neither in the kirk nor out of it, have I not books of as motley a nature as they? And look at these golden laces, these silken snoods, and these ivory bosom-busks, though I will not deny that a well-faured lass has a chance to wheedle me out of a lace or a ribbon with no other money than a current kiss, and reduce my profit, yet I must even lay it the heavier on new-married wives, rosy young widows, and lasses with fee and bounty in their laps. It would be a sad thing if love for a sonsie lass should make me a loser."

An old dame in a grey linsey-woolsey gown, a black silk riding-hood pinned beneath her chin, with a large calf skin-covered Bible under her arm, had approached me unseen. She fell upon me like a whirlwind: "Oh! thou beardless trickster, thou seventeen-year-old scant-o'-grace, wilt thou sit planning among God's daylight how to over-reach thy neighbour? My sooth, lad, but thou art a gleg one. I question if William Mackfen himself, who has cheated my goodman and me these twenty-seven summers, is half such a wily loon as thyself. A night's lodging ye need never ask at Airnaumrie. And yet it would be a sore matter to my conscience to turn out a face so young and so well faured to the bensel of the midnight blast." And away the old lady walked, and left me to arrange the treasures of my pack at my leisure.

Her words were still ringing in my ears when an old man, dressed in the antique Scottish fashion—a grey plaid wound about his bosom, a broad westland bonnet on his head, which shaded, but did not conceal, a few shining white hairs, and with a long white staff in his hand, came up and addressed me: "Gather up thy books and thy baubles, young man; this is not the time to spread out these worldly toys to the eyes of human infirmity. Gather them together, and cast them into that brook, and follow me. Alas!" said he, touching my treasures with the end of his staff, "here are gauds for our young and our rosy madams—bosom-busks, brow-snoods, and shining brooches for ensnaring the eyes of youth. I tell thee, young man, woman will fall soon enough from her bright station by her own infirmities without thy helping hand to pluck her down. Much do I fear thou hast been disposing of sundry of thy snares to the vain old dame of Airnaumrie. She is half-saint and half-sinner; and the thoughts of her giddy youth are still too strong for her grey hairs: seest thou not that she carries the book of redemption in her hand, when she should bear it in her head? But she gleaned her scanty knowledge on an Erastian field among the Egyptian stubble. Ah! had she been tightly targed by a sound professor on the Proof Catechism, she had not needed that printed auxiliary under her arm. But I waste precious time on an unprofiting youth. I hasten whither I am called—for patronage, with its armed hand, will give the kirk of Galloway a sad stroke to-day, if there be no blessed interposition." And my male followed my female monitor, leaving me to wonder what all this religious bustle and preparation might mean.

I was about to follow, when loud talk and louder laughter came towards me through the green avenue of a neighbouring wood. A bevy of lads and lasses in holiday clothes, with books of devotion in their hands, soon appeared; and they were not slack in indulging themselves in week-day merriment. "A pretty Whig, indeed!" said a handsome girl with brown locks, and coats kilted half-way up a pair of very white legs; "a pretty Whig, indeed! I'll tell thee, lad, thou'lt never be the shining star in the firmament thy aunt speaks of when she prays. I have seen a lad with as much grace in his eye as thyself endure a sore sermon by himself when the kirk should have scaled." "And I have seen," retorted the swain, "as great a marvel as a pair of white legs, rosy lips, and mischievous eyes, making as wise a man as myself pay dear for an hour's daffin'." "Daffin'," said the maiden, laughing till the woods rang again; "daffin' will be scant when a lass seeks for't with such a world's wonder as thee. It sets thy mother's oldest son well to speak of daffin'." "I have climbed a higher tree and harried a richer nest," murmured the ploughman; "but what, in the name of patronage, have we here? Here's an abstract personification, as somebody called John Goudie the Cameronian, of old Willie Mackfen the pedlar—in the days of his youth." So saying, a crowd of lads and lasses surrounded my pack and me, and proceeded to examine and comment on my commodities with an absence of ceremony which would have vexed even a veteran traveller.

"As I shall answer for it," said one youth, "here's the very snood Jenny Birkwhistle lost amang Andrew Lorrance's broom." "And I protest," retorted the maiden, justly offended at this allusion to the emblem of maidenhood, "I protest, here's the wisest of all printed things—even 'A Groat's Worth of Wit for a Penny,' which thy mother longed to read ere she was lightened of thee. Thy father has much to answer for." A loud laugh told that truth was mingled with the wit of the maiden. Utter ruin seemed to wait on my affairs, when a woman, with a sour, sharp visage and a tongue that rang like a steel hammer on a smith's anvil, came up, and interposed. "Ye utterly castaway and graceless creatures, are ye making godless mirth on a green hillside?" said she, stretching forth her hands, garnished with long finger-nails, over the crowd—like a hawk over a brood of chickens; "is not this the day when patronage seeks to be mighty, and will prevail? Put yourselves, therefore, in array. The preaching man of Belial, with his red dragons, even now approaches the afflicted kirk of Bleeding Heart. Have ye not heard how they threaten to cast the cope-stone of the kirk into the deep sink, where our forefathers of yore threw the lady of Babylon and her painted and mitred minions? But it is ever this way. Ye would barter the soul's welfare for the body's folly. Ah!" said she to a young peasant, "what would Hezekiah Graneaway, thy devout grandfather, say, were he to see his descendant, on a day of trial like this, standing making mouths at a poor packman-lad, with a bevy of petticoated temptresses around him? Get along, I say, lest I tear those curled love-locks from thy temples. And as for thee, thou young money-changer—thou dealer in maiden trickery and idle gauds—

knowest thou not that this is Ordination Day? So buckle up thy merchandise, and follow. Verily, none can tell from whose hand the blow shall come this day, that will save us from the sinful compliance with that offspring of old Mahoun, even patronage." I was glad of any pretext for withdrawing my goods from the hands of my unwelcome visitors; so I huddled them together, secured them with the lock, and followed the zealous dame, who with a proud look walked down the hill, to unite herself to a multitude of all ranks and sexes which the placing of the parish minister had collected together.

The place where this multitude of motley beliefs and feelings had assembled was one of singular beauty. At the bottom of a woody glen, the margin of a beautiful lake, and the foot of a high green mountain, with the sea of Solway seen rolling and sparkling in the distance, stood a populous and straggling village, through which a clear stream and a paved road winded side by side. Each house had its garden behind, and a bare-headed progeny running wild about the banks of the rivulet; beside which many old men and matrons, seated according to their convenience, enjoyed the light of the sun and the sweetness of the summer air. At the eastern extremity of the village, a noble religious ruin, in the purest style of the Saxons, raised its shattered towers and minarets far above all other buildings; while the wall-flowers, shooting forth in the spring at every joint and crevice, perfumed the air for several roods around. The buttresses and exterior auxiliary walls were covered with a thick tapestry of ivy, which, with its close-clinging and smooth shining leaf, resembled a covering of velvet. One bell, which tradition declares to be of pure silver, remained on the top of one of the highest turrets, beyond the reach of man. It is never rung save by a violent storm, and its ringing is reckoned ominous—deaths at land and drownings at sea follow the sound of the silver bell of Bleeding Heart Abbey. Innumerable swarms of pigeons and daws shared the upper region of the ruin among them, and built and brought forth their young in the deserted niches of saints, and the holes from which corbels of carved wood had supported the painted ceiling. At the very foot of this majestic edifice stood the parish kirk, built in utter contempt of the beautiful proportions of its ancient neighbour, and for the purpose perhaps of proving in how mean a sanctuary the pure and stern devotion of the Presbyterians could humble itself. Men thrash their grain, stall their horses, feed their cattle, and even lodge themselves, in houses dry and comfortable; but for religion they erect edifices which resemble the grave: the moist clay of the floor, the dampness and frequent droppings of water from the walls, are prime matters of satisfaction to the parish grave-digger, and preserve his spade from rust.

Into this ancient abbey, and the beautiful region around it, the whole population of the parish appeared to have poured itself, for the purpose of witnessing, and perhaps resisting, the ordination of a new and obnoxious pastor, whom patronage had provided for their instruction. Youths, more eager for a pleasant sight than religious controversy, had ascended into the abbey towers—the thick-piled gravestones of the kirkyard, each ruined buttress, the broken altar-stone, and the tops of the trees were filled with aged or with youthful spectators. Presbyterians of the Established Kirk, Burghers, Antiburghers, Cameronians, and seceders of all denominations paraded the long crooked street of the village, and whiled away the heavy time, and amused their fancy and soothed their conscience, by splitting anew the straws scattered about by the idle wind of controversy. Something like an attempt to obstruct the entrance to the kirk appeared to have been made. The spirit of opposition had hewn down some stately trees which shaded the kirkyard, and these, with broken ploughs and carts, were cast into the road: the kirk-door itself had been nailed up, and the bell silenced by the removal of the rope. The silver bell on the abbey alone, swept by a sudden wind, gave one gentle toll, and at that moment a loud outcry, from end to end of the village, announced the approach of the future pastor. The peasants thickened round on all sides, and some proceeded to wall up the door of the kirk with a rampart of loose stones. "Let Dagon defend Dagon," said one rustic, misapplying the Scripture he quoted, while he threw the remains of the abbey altar-stone into the path. "And here is the through-stone of the last abbot, Willie Bell: it makes a capital copestone to the defences—I kenned it by the drinking-cup aside the death's head. He liked to do penance with a stoup of wine at his elbow," said another boor, adding the broken stone to the other incumbrances. "A drinking-cup! ye coof," said an old man, pressing through the crowd: "it is a sand-glass—and cut, too, on the headstone of thy own grandfather. Black will be thy end for this." The boor turned away with a shudder; while the dame of Airnaumrie, with the black hood and large Bible, exclaimed: "Take away that foul memorial of old Gomorrha Gunson. The cause can never prosper that borrows defence from that never-do-good's grave. Remove the stone, I say, else I shall brain thee with this precious book." And she shook the religious missile at the descendant of old Gomorrha, who carried off the stone; and no further attempt was made, after this ominous circumstance, to augment the rampart.

Amid all this stir and preparation I had obtained but an indistinct knowledge of the cause which called into action all the grave, impatient, and turbulent spirits of the district. This was partly divulged in a conversation between two persons, to which there were many auditors. One was the male broad-bonneted disciplinarian who rebuked me for displaying the contents of my pack; and the other was the sour-visaged, shrilled-tongued dame who rescued my pack from the peril of pillage on the road, and with the true antique spirit of the Reformed Church lent her voice to swell the clamour of controversy. Their faces were inflamed and their voices exalted by the rancour of mutual contradiction; and it was thus I heard the male stickler for the kirk's freedom of election express himself: "I tell thee once, woman, and I tell thee again, that the kirk of Bleeding Heart there, where it stands so proud and so bonnie, by the side of that auld carcase of the woman of Rome—I tell thee it shall stand empty and deserted, shall send forth on Sunday a dumb silence, and the harmony of her voice be heard no more in the land—rather than she shall take, like a bridegroom, to her bosom that sapless slip of the soul-misleading and Latin-quoting university. Instead of drinking from the pure and fresh well-head, we shall have to drink from the muddy ditch which men have dug for themselves with the spades and shovels of learning. Instead of the downpouring of the frank and heaven-communicated spirit, we shall have the earthly spirit—the gross invention and fancy of man; a long, dull, downcome of a read sermon, which falls as seed on the ocean and chaff on the furrowed land. Besides all this, is not this youth, this Joel Kirkpatrick, a slip or scion from the poisonous tree of patronage, that last legacy from the scarlet lady of Rome?" "I say no to that—the back of my hand to that," interrupted the woman, in red and visible wrath; "I have heard him preach, and I have profited by his prayers; he is a precious youth, and has a happy gift at unravelling the puzzled skein of controversy. He will be a fixed and a splendid star, and that ye will soon see. And here he comes, blessings upon his head; ye shall hear a sermon soon such as has not been heard in the land since that chosen youth, John Rutherford, preached on the text, 'I shall kiss thee with kisses of my mouth.'" "Woman, woman," said her antagonist, "thou art the slipperiest of thy kind; and opposition and controversy turn thee round, even as the bush bends to the blast. To-day hast thou stood for the Kirk in its ancient purity; and lo! now thou wilt take her defiled by patronage, because of that goodly youth Joel Kirkpatrick." "Silence, ye fule-fowk," said a young ploughman at their side; "ye'll no let me hear the sound of the soldiers' bugle; they are coming to plant the gospel with spear and with sword. I have seen many a priest placed, some with pith of the tongue, and some with the pith of malt: Black Ned of the parish of Slokendrouth, was placed in his pulpit by the aid of the brown spirit of malt; and there the same spirit supports him still. But, on my conscience, I never saw a parson guarded to the pulpit with cold steel before. It's a sight worth seeing."

A stir and a movement was now observed at the extremity of the village; and presently the helmets, and plumes, and drawn swords of two hundred horsemen appeared, shining and waving above the crowd. This unusual accompaniment of the ministerial functions was greeted with hissings and hootings; and the scorn and anger of the multitude burst at once into one loud yell. The women and the children, gathering the summer dust in their hands, showered it as thick and as blinding as winter-drift on the persons of the troopers. The anger of the people did not rest here; pebbles were thrown, and symptoms of fiercer hostility began to manifest themselves; for many of the peasants were armed, and seemed to threaten to dispute the entrance to the kirk. In the midst of all this tumult, mounted on a little white horse and dressed in black, rode a young man, around whom the dust ascended and descended as if agitated by a whirlwind. This was the minister. He passed on, nor looked to the right or left, but with singular meekness, and a look of sorrow and resignation, endured the tumultuous scorn of the crowd. Long before he reached the limit of the village he seemed more a pillar of dust than a human being. "Is the Kirk a dog, that thou comest against her with staves?" said one; "Or is she a besieged city, that thou bringest against her thy horsemen and thy chariots?" cried a second; "Or comest thou to slay, whom thou canst not convince?" shouted a third; "Or dost thou come to wash thy garments in the blood of saints?" bawled a fourth; "Or to teach thy flock the exercise of the sword rather than the exercise of devotion?" yelled a fifth; "Or come ye," exclaimed a sixth, at the very limit of the human voice, "to mix the voice of the psalm with that of the trumpet, and to hear how divinity and slaughter will sound together?" Others expressed their anger in hissings and hootings; while an old mendicant ballad-singer paraded, step by step with the minister, through the crowd, and sung to a licentious tune the following rustic lampoon:

PLACING THE PARSON.

Come hasten and see, for the Kirk, like a bride,
Is arrayed for her spouse in sedateness and pride.
Comes he in meek mood, with his hands clasped and sighing
For the godless and doomed, with his hopes set on Zion?
Comes he with the grave, the austere, and the sage—
A warfare with those who scoff Scripture to wage?
He comes—hark! the reins of his war-steeds are ringing;
His trumpet—but 'tis not God's trumpet—is singing.

Clap your hands, all ye graceless; sing loud and rejoice,
Ye young men of Rimmon; and lift up your voice
All ye who love wantonness, wassail, and sinning
With the dame decked in scarlet and fine twined linen.
Scoff louder thou scoffer; scorn on, thou proud scorner;
Satan comes to build kirks, and has laid the first corner.
The Babylon dame, from Perdition's deep pool,
Sings and cradles her babes in the Kirk's cuttie-stool.

He comes! of all parsons the swatch and the pattern,
Shaped out to save souls by the shears of his patron.
He comes steeped in Learning's dark puddle, and chatters
Greek words, and tears all Calvin's creed into tatters,
And vows the hot pit shall shut up its grim portals,
Nor devour to a tithe the sum-total of mortals;
Talks of works, and Morality's Will-o'-wisp glimmer,
And showers Reason's frost on our spiritual simmer.

He comes! Lo! behind on their war-horses ranking,
Ride his bands of the faithful, their steel weapons clanking;
Proud hour for Religion, when God's chosen word
Is proclaimed by the trump, and confirmed by the sword.
Proud hour, when with bayonet, and banner, and brand,
The Kirk spreads her sway o'er old Galloway's land,
Where of yore Sandie Peden looked down on the vales,
Crying, "Clap me hell's flame to their heathenish tails."

Over this minstrel discordance a far louder din now prevailed, though the mendicant raised his voice to its loftiest pitch, and all those who purchased his ballad swelled the noise with their utmost strength. A grove of elm and oak, old and stately, whose broad green branches had shaded the splendid processions of the hierarchy of the Church of Rome when in the height of its glory, presented a short avenue from the end of the village to the door of the parish kirk. Here the peasantry posted themselves in great numbers, and here the horsemen halted to form for the charge which they expected to make before they could obtain access to the church. Nor did this promise to be an easy task. Many of the peasants were well armed; and boat-poles, pitchforks, fish-spears, and hedging-bills—all excellent weapons for resistance and annoyance—began to thicken near the bosoms of the horses; while behind, fowling-pieces, and pistols, and swords, appeared prepared in hands that knew well how to use them. In a remoter line still, the women, their aprons charged with pebbles and staves, stood ready to succour, with hand and with voice, the maintainers of Kirk purity.

The casting of dust, the showering of gravel and stones, and the loud outcry of the multitude, every moment augmented. John Cargill, a gifted Cameronian weaver, from one of the wildest Galloway mountains, brandished an oaken treddle, with which he had armed himself, like a quarter-staff, and cried, "Down with the men of Moab!" Tom Gunson, a smuggler, shouted till he was heard a mile distant, "Down with them, my handy chaps, and we'll drink the auld Kirk's health out of the troopers' helmets;" and, to crown their audacity, Ill-will Tennan, the poacher, hallooed, "I'se shoot the whole troop at a grey groat the pair, and give ye the raven priest to the mends." Open hostility seemed almost unavoidable, when an old farmer, throwing his hat aside, advanced suddenly from the crowd to the side of the minister and said, "Did I ever think I should behold the son of my soothfast friend, Hebron Kirkpatrick, going to glorify God's name at the head of a band of daily brawlers and paid stabbers? His horse's feet shall pass over this frail body first." And he bent himself down at the feet of the minister's horse, with his grey locks nearly touching the dust.

At this unexpected address and remarkable action, Joel Kirkpatrick wakened as from a reverie of despondency, and lighting from his horse, took the old man in his arms with looks of concern and affection. The multitude was hushed while the minister said, "May my head be borne by the scoffer to the grave, and my name serve for a proverb of shame and reproach, if I step another step this day other than thou willest. Thou hast long been an exemplar and a guide to me, John Halberson; and, though God's appointed preacher, and called to the tending of His flock, be assured I will have thy sanction, else my ministry may be barren of fruit." The venerable old man gazed on the young preacher with the light of gladness in his eyes, and taking his hand, said: "Joel Kirkpatrick, heed my words. I question not the authority of the voice permitted by Him whom we serve to call thee to His ministry. The word of the multitude is not always with the wisest, nor the cry of the people with the sound divine and the gifted preacher. I push thee not forward, neither do I pluck thee back; but surely, surely, young man of God, He never ordained the glory of His blessed Kirk to be sustained by the sword, and that he whom He called should come blowing the trumpet against it. Much do I fear for the honour of that ministry which is entered upon with banner and brand." As John Halberson spoke, a sudden light seemed to break upon the preacher: he motioned the soldiers back, and taking off his hat, advanced firmly and meekly down the avenue towards the kirk-door, one time busied in silent prayer, another time endeavouring to address the multitude.

"Hear him not," said one matron; "for he comes schooled from the university of guile and deceit; and his words, sweet as honey in the mouth, may prove bitter in the belly, even as wormwood." "I say, hear him, hear him!" said another matron, shaking her Bible at her neighbour's head, to enforce submission. "Ye think him bitterer than the gourd, but he will be sweeter than the honey-comb." "Absolve thee," said one old man, the garrulity of age making a speech out of what he meant for an exclamation; "absolve thee of the foul guilt, the burning sin, and the black shame of that bane and wormwood of God's Kirk, even patronage; and come unto us—not with the array of horsemen and the affeir of war; but come with the humility of tears and the contrition of sighs, and we will put thee in the pulpit; for we know thou art a gifted youth." Another old man, with a bonnet and plaid, and bearing a staff to reinforce his lack of argument, answered the enemy of patronage: "Who wishes for the choice of the foolish many in preference to the election of the One-wise? The choice of our pastor will be as foolishness for our hearts and a stumbling-block to our feet. When did ignorance lift up its voice as a judge, and the sick heart become its own physician? We are as men who know nothing—each expounding Scripture as seemeth wise in vain eyes; and yet shall we go to say this man, and no other, hath the wisdom to teach and instruct us?" "Well spoken and wisely, Laird of Birkenloan," shouted a ploughman from the summit of the old abbey; "more by token, our nearest neighbours, in their love for the lad who could preach a sappy spiritual sermon, elected to the ministry a sworn and ordained bender of the bicker, whose pulpit, instead of the odour of sanctity, sends forth the odour of smuggled gin." A loud burst of laughter from the multitude acknowledged the truth of the ploughman's sarcasm; while Jock Gillock, one of the most noted smugglers of the coast of Solway, shook his hand in defiance at the rustic advocate of patronage, and said: "If I don't make ye the best thrashed Robson ever stept in black leather shoon, may I be foundered in half a fathom of fresh water." "And if ye fail to know and fear the smell of a ploughman's hand from this day forthwith, compared to that of all meaner men's," cried the undaunted agriculturist, "I will give ye leave to chop me into ballast for your smuggling cutter." And he descended to the ground with the agility of a cat, while the mariner hastened to encounter him; and all the impetuous and intractable spirits on both sides followed to witness the battle.

"So now," said an old peasant, "doth not the wicked slacken their array? Doth not the demon of secession, who hath so long laid waste our Kirk, draw off his forces of his own free will? Let us fight the fight of righteousness, while the workers of wickedness fight their own battles.

Let us open the kirk portals, blocked up and barricaded by the Shimeis of the land." Several times the young preacher attempted to address the crowd, who had conceived a sudden affection for him since the salutary dismissal of the dragoons; but his flock were far too clamorous, impatient, and elated to heed what he had to say. They were unaccustomed to be addressed, save from the pulpit; and the wisest speech from a minister without the imposing accompaniments of pulpits and pews, and ranks of douce unbonneted listeners, is sure to fail in making a forcible impression. It was wise, perhaps, in the minister to follow the counsel of grave John Halberson, and let the multitude work their own way. They lifted him from the ground; and, borne along by a crowd of old and young, he approached the kirk The obstacles which impeded the way vanished before the activity of a thousand willing hands. The kirk-door, fastened with iron spikes by a band of smugglers on the preceding evening, was next assailed, and burst against the wall with a clang that made the old ruin ring again, and in rushed a multitude of heads, filling every seat, as water fills a vessel, from one end of the building to the other. The preacher was borne aloft by this living tide to the door of the pulpit; while the divine to whom was deputed the honour of ordaining and placing him in his ministry was welcomed by a free passage, though he had to listen to many admonitions as he passed. "Oh, admonish him to preach in the ancient spirit of the Reformed Kirk—in a spirit that was wonderful to hear and awful to understand!" said one old man, shaking a head of grey hair as he spoke. "And oh," said another peasant, as the divine turned his head, unwilling thus to be schooled in his calling, "targe him tightly anent chambering and wantonness, the glory of youth and the pride of life; for the follies of the land multiply exceedingly." From him the divine turned away in displeasure; but received in the other ear the cross-fire of an old woman, whose nose and chin could have held a hazel-nut, and almost cracked it between their extremities; and whose upper lip was garnished with a beard matching in length and strength the whiskers of a cat. "And, oh, sir! he's in a state of single innocence and sore temptation even now—warn him, I beseech thee; warn him of the pit into which that singular and pious man fell in the hour of evil—even him whom the scoffers call Sleepy

Samuel. Bid him beware of painted flesh and languishing eyes, of which there be enough in this wicked parish. Tell him to beware of one whose love-locks and whose lures will soon pluck him down from his high calling, even the fair daughter of the old dour trunk of the tree of Papistry, bonnie Bess Glendinning." Here her words were drowned in the more audible counsel of another of the burning and shining lights of the parish, from whose lips escaped, in a tone resembling a voice from a cavern, the alarming words, "Socinians, Arminians, Dioclesians, Erastians, Arians, and Episcopalians—— "Episcopalians!" ejaculated an old woman in dismay and astonishment, who mistook, perhaps, this curtailed catalogue of schismatics for some tremendous anathema or exorcism—"Episcopalians! God protect me! what's that?"

I have no wish to attempt to describe the effects which a very happy, pithy, and fervent inauguration sermon had on the multitude. The topics of election, redemption, predestination, and the duties which he called his brother to perform, with a judicious mind, a Christian feeling, and an ardent but temperate spirit, were handled, perilous as the topics were, with singular tact, and discrimination, and delicacy. The happy mixture of active morality and spiritual belief, of work-day-world practice and elegant theory, which this address contained, deserves a lasting remembrance.

The summary of the preacher's duties, and the description of the impetuous and distempered spirits of the parish, and the contradictory creeds which he had to soothe and to solder, form still a traditionary treasure to the parish. To minds young and giddy as mine, these healthy and solacing things were not so attractive as the follies and outrages of a disappointed crowd; and let not an old man, without reflecting that he too was once eighteen, condemn me for forsaking the presence and precepts of the preacher for the less spiritual and less moral, but no less instructive drama which was acting in the open air.

The dragoons were still in their saddles, but had retired to the extremity of the village, where they emptied bottles of ale and sung English ballads with a gaiety and a life which obtained the notice of sundry of the young maidens, who are observed to feel a regard for scarlet and lace, which I leave to those who love not their pleasant company to explain. As they began to gather round, not unobserved by the sons of Mars, some of the village matrons proceeded to remonstrate. "Wherefore gaze ye on the men with whiskers, pruned and landered, and with coats of scarlet, and with lace laid on the skirts thereof?" said one old woman, pulling at the same time her reluctant niece by the hand, while her eyes, notwithstanding her retrograde motion, were fixed on a brawny trooper. "And, Deborah," said a mother to her daughter, whose white hand and whiter neck, shaded with tresses of glossy auburn, the hands of another trooper had invaded, "what wouldst thou do with him who wears the helmet of brass upon his head? He is an able-bodied man, but a great covenant-breaker, and he putteth trust in the spear and in the sword." The maiden struggled with that earnestness with which a virgin of eighteen strives to escape from the kindness of a handsome man; and kiss succeeding kiss told what penalty she incurred in delaying to follow her mother.

Of the dissenting portion of the multitude, some disposed of themselves in the readiest ale-houses, where the themes of patronage, free-will, and predestination, emptied many barrels, and the clouds of mystery and doubt darkened down with the progress of the tankard. Others, of a more flexible system of morality, went to arrange, far from the tumult of tongues and opinions in which the district gauger figured, a midnight importation of choice Geneva, the rapid consumption of which was hastened by the burning spark of controversy which raged unquenchably in their throats. Many retired sullenly homeward, lamenting that a concourse of men of hostile opinions could collect, controvert, and quarrel, and then coolly separate without blows and bloodshed, cursing the monotony of human existence now, compared with the stirring times of Border forays and Covenant raids. A moiety nearly of the seceding crowd remained in clumps on the village green. They were men chiefly of that glowing zeal to whom mere charity and the silent operations of religious feeling seem cold and unfruitful; those pure and fortunate beings who find nothing praiseworthy, or meriting the hope of salvation, in the actions of mere men; who discover new interpretations of Scripture, and rend anew the party-coloured and patched garments of sect and schism every time they meet, when the liquor is abundant. Their hope of the complete reform in the discipline of the parish kirk, or the creation of a new meeting-house to enjoy the eloquence of a preacher, the choice of their own wisdom, seemed now nearly blasted; and they uttered their discontent at the result, while they praised the dexterity or cunning with which they opposed the ordination of that *protégé* of patronage, Joel Kirkpatrick. "The kirk-session may buy a new bell-rope," said a Cameronian weaver, "for I cut away the tow from their tinkling brass yestreen; more by token, it now tethers my hummel cow on the unmowed side of John Allan's park; he had no business to set himself up against the will of the parish and the word of God." Gilbert Glass, the village glazier, found a topic of worldly consolation amid the spiritual misfortunes of the day: "The kirk windows will cost them a fine penny to repair: some one, whom I'll not name, left not a single pane whole, and each pane will cost the heritors a silver sixpence; that's work my way. It is an evil wind, Saunders Brazely, that blows nobody good; a profitable proverb to you." "All that I know of the proverb," replied Saunders the slater, " is, that it will be the sweet licking of a creamy finger to thee; but alake! what shall I get out of the pain of riding stride-legs over the clouted roof of the old kirk patching a few broken slates? I have heard of many a wind blowing for one's good, but I never heard of a wind that uncovered a kirk yet." To all this answered Micah Meen, a sectarian mason: "Plague on't! I wish there were not a slate on its roof, or one stone of its wall above another. This old kirk, built out of the spare stones of the old abbey, is but a bastard-bairn of the old lady of Rome, and deserves no good to come on't. Look ye to the upshot of my words. Seventeen year have I been kirk-mason, and am still as poor as one of its mice. But bide ye, let us lay our heads together, and build a brent new meeting-house. I will build the walls, and no be too hard about the siller, if I have the letting of the seats. And we will have a preacher to our own liking, one who shall not preach a word save sound doctrine, else let me never bed a stone in mortar more." "Eh, man, but ye speak soundly," said Charlie Goudge, the village carpenter, "in all save the article of kirk-seats, which, being of timber, pertain more to my calling. Howsomever, I would put a roof of red Norway fir over your heads, and erect ye such seats as no man sits in who lends his ears to a read sermon." "And as for us two," said the slater and the glazier, clubbing their callings together, for the sake of making a more serious impression, "we would counsel ye to cover your kirk with blue Lancashire slate, instead of that spongy stone from Locherbrig Hill, which, besides coming from a hill of witch and devil trysting, is fit for nought save laying above a dead man's dwelling, who never complains of a bad roof; and farther, put none of your dull green glass in the windows, but clear pure glass, through which a half-blind body might see to expound the Word." "And I would counsel ye to begin a subscription incontinent," said the keeper of a neighbouring ale-house; "and if ye will come into my home, we can commence the business with moistened throats; and," continued mine host in an under-tone, "I can kittle up your spirits with some rare Geneva from the bosom of my sloop, the Bonnie Nelly Lawson, there, where she lies cosy among Cairnhowrie Birks, and the gauger never the wiser."

A flood of sectarians inundated the parlour of the Thistle and Hand-Hammer, and a noise, rivalling the descent of a Galloway stream down one of its wildest glens, issued, ringing far and wide, from the change-house. "Subscribe!" said Gilpin Johnstone, a farmer of Annandale descent; "I would not give seven placks—and these are but small coins—for the fairest kirk that ever bore a roof above the walls. There's the goodman of Hoshenfoot, a full farmer, who hopes to be saved in his own way—he may subscribe. No but that I am willing to come and listen if the pew-rates be moderate." "Me subscribe!" said he of the Hoshenfoot, buttoning his pockets as he spoke, to fortify his resolution; "where in the wide world, think ye, have I got gold to build into kirk-walls? Besides, I have been a follower of that ancient poetical mode of worship, preaching on the mountain-side; and if ye will give me a day or two's reaping in the throng of harvest, I will lend ye the green hill of Knockhoolie to preach an hour's sound doctrine on any time— save, I should have said, when the peas are in the pod; and then deil have me if I would trust a hungry congregation near them." Similar evasions came from the lips of several more of the wealthy seceders; and, one by one, they dissented and dispersed: not without a severe contest with the landlord whether they were responsible for all the liquor they had consumed, seeing it was for the spiritual welfare of the parish.

If the entry of the minister into his ministry was stormy and troubled, ample reparation was made by the mass of the parishioners, who, after the ordination, escorted him home to the manse, giving frequent testimony of that sedate joy and tranquil satisfaction which the people of Scotland are remarkable for expressing. "Reverend sir, you have had but a cold and a wintry welcome to your ministry," said an old and substantial dame, "and if ye will oblige me by accepting of such a hansel, I will send ye what will make a gallant house-heating." "And ye mauna have all the joy of giving gifts to yourself, goodwife," said an old man with a broad bonnet, and stooping over a staff, "for I shall send our ain Joel Kirkpatrick such a present as no minister o' Bleeding Heart ever received since Mirk Monday, and all too little to atone for the din that my old and graceless tongue raised against God's gifted servant this blessed morning." "And talking of atonements," interrupted an old woman, whose hands were yet unwashed from the dust which she had lately thrown on the minister, "I have an atoning offering to make for having wickedly testified against a minister of God's kirk this morning. I shall send him a stone weight of ewe-milk cheese to-morrow." But no one of the multitude seemed more delighted, or stood higher in general favour, than John Halberson, the wise and venerable man who had given the first check to the fiery spirit that blazed so fiercely in the morning. He walked by the minister's side, his head uncovered, and his remaining white hairs glittering in the descending sun. His words were not many, but they were laid up in the heart and practised in the futurelife of the excellent person to whom they were addressed. "Young man and reverend, thy lot is cast in a stormy season and in a stony land. There be days for sowing, and days for reaping, and days for gathering into the garner. Thou hast a mind gifted with natural wisdom and stored with written knowledge; a tongue fluent and sweet in utterance, and thou hast drunk of the word at the well-head. But trust not thy gifts alone for working deliverance among the people. Thou must know each man and woman by face and by name—pass into their abodes, acquaint thyself with their feelings and their failings, and move them and win them to the paths of holiness, as a young man woos his bride. Thou must dandle their young ones on thy knees, for thy Master loved little children, and it is a seemly thing to be beloved of babes. Should youth go astray in the way in which youth is prone, take it gently and tenderly to task; severity maketh the kirk rancorous enemies, and persecution turneth love into deadly hate; humanity and kindness are the leading-strings of the human heart. One counsel more, and I have done: take unto thee a wife. Ministers are not too good for such a sweet company as woman's, neither are they too steadfast not to fear a fall. Wed, saith the Scripture, and replenish the earth; and I wish not the good, the brave, and ancient name of Kirkpatrick to pass from among us. Peace be with thee, and many days." By following the wise counsel of his venerable parishioner, Joel Kirkpatrick became one of the most popular pastors of the Presbytery, and one of the chief luminaries of the ancient province of Galloway. His eloquence, his kindliness of heart, and the active charity of his nature will be proverbial in parish tradition while eloquence, and kindness, and charity are reverenced on earth.

THE KING OF THE PEAK.

A DERBYSHIRE TALE.

> WHAT time the bird wakes in its bower
> He stood, and looked on Haddon Tower;
> High rose it o'er the woodland height,
> With portals strong and turrets bright,
> And gardens green; with swirl and sweep
> Round rushed the Wye, both broad and deep.
> Leaping and looking for the sun,
> He saw the red deer and the dun;
> The warders with their weapons sheen,
> The watchers with their mantles green;
> The deerhounds at their feet were flung,
> The red blood at their dew-laps hung.
> Adown he leaped, and awhile he stood,
> With a downcast look and pondering mood,
> Then made a step and his bright sword drew,
> And cleft a stone at a stroke in two:
> "So shall the heads of my foemen be,
> Who seek to sunder my love from me.'
> *Derbyshire Rhyme of Dora Vernon.*

REMAINS of the ancient frank and open-hearted hospitality of old England linger yet among her vales and mountains; and travellers are not unfrequently greeted with a patriarchal welcome and a well-spread table, without the chilling formality of a fair-penned and prudently-worded introduction. The open bounty of hill, and wood, and vale, and sea is poured in wholesale profusion on many of the fortunate dwellers in the country; while on those who forsake the wonders of God for the works of man, the green land and the glorious air for the confusion of the city, Nature sprinkles her favours with a sparing and a niggard hand. The city strives in vain to emulate the frank kindness of the country, and opens her doors, but opens them with a sad civility and a constrained and suspicious courtesy. In the country the door stands open, the table is spread, and the bidden guest is the way-wearied man or the fugitive and the wanderer. He enters, he refreshes himself, he reposes, and on the morrow he renews his journey.

It happened once in a northern county that I found myself at a farmer's fireside, and in company which the four winds of heaven seemed to have blown together. The farmer was a joyous old man; and the evening, a wintry one, and wild with wind and snow, flew away with jest, and mirth, and tale, and song. Our entertainer had no wish that our joy should subside, for he heaped the fire till the house shone to its remotest rafter, loaded his table with rustic delicacies, and once, when a pause ensued after the chanting of one of Robin Hood's ballads, he called out: "Why stays the story, and what stops the rhyme? Have I heated my hearth, have I spread my tables, and poured forth my strong drink for the poor in fancy and the lame in speech? Up, up! and give me a grave tale or a gay, to gladden or sadden the present moment, and lend wings to the leaden feet of evening time. Rise, I say; else may the fire that flames so high, the table which groans with food, for which water, and air, and earth, have been sought, and the board that perfumes you with the odour of ale and mead—may the first cease to warm, and the rest to nourish ye."

"Master," said a hail and joyous personage, whose shining and gladsome looks showed sympathy and alliance with the good cheer and fervent blood of merry old England; "since thy table smokes and thy brown ale flows more frankly for the telling of a true old tale, then a true old tale thou shalt have. Shame fall me if I baulk thee, as the pleasant folk say in the dales of bonny Derby.

"Those who have never seen Haddon Hall, the ancient residence of the Vernons of Derbyshire, can have but an imperfect notion of the golden days of old England. Though now deserted and dilapidated—its halls silent, the sacred bell of its chapel mute; though its tables no longer send up the cheering smell of roasted boars and spitted oxen, though the music and the voice of the minstrel are silenced and the light foot of the dancer no longer sounds on the floor, though no gentle knights and gentler dames go trooping hand in hand and whispering among the twilight groves, and the portal no longer sends out its shining helms and its barbed steeds, where is the place that can recall the stately hospitality and glory of former times, like the Hall of Old Haddon?

"It happened on a summer evening, when I was a boy, that several curious old people had seated themselves on a little round knoll near the gate of Haddon Hall; and their talk was of the Vernons, the Cavendishes, the Manners, and many old names once renowned in Derbyshire. I had fastened myself to the apron-string of a venerable dame, at whose girdle hung a mighty iron key, which commanded the entrance of the Hall: her name was Dolly Foljambe, and she boasted her descent from an ancient Red Cross knight of that name, whose alabaster figure in mail may be found in Bakewell Church. This high origin, which, on consulting family history, I find had not the concurrence of clergy, seemed not an idle vanity of the humble portress; she had the straight frame, and rigid, demure, and even warlike cast of face which alabaster still retains of her ancestor; and had she laid herself by his side, she might have passed muster, with an ordinary antiquarian, for a co-eval figure. At our feet the river Wye ran winding and deep; at our side rose the Hall, huge and grey; and the rough heathy hills, renowned in Druidic, and Roman, and Saxon, and Norman story, bounded our wish for distant prospects, and gave us the mansion of the Vernons for our contemplation, clear of all meaner encumbrances of landscape.

"'Ah! Dame Foljambe,' said an old husbandman, whose hair was whitened by acquaintance with seventy winters; 'it's a sore and a sad sight to look at that fair tower, and see no smoke ascending. I remember it in a brighter day, when many a fair face gazed out at the windows, and many a gallant form appeared at the gate. Then were the days when the husbandman could live—could whistle as he sowed, dance and sing as he reaped, and could pay his rent in fatted oxen to my lord and in fatted fowls to my lady. Ah! Dame Foljambe, we remember when men could cast their lines in the Wye; could feast on the red deer and the fallow deer, on the plover and the ptarmigan; had right of the common for their flocks, of the flood for their nets, and of the air for their harquebuss. Ah, Dame! old England is no more the old England it was than that Hall, dark, and silent, and desolate, is the proud Hall that held Sir

George Vernon, the King of the Peak, and his two lovely daughters, Margaret and Dora. Those were days, Dame—those were days!' And as he ceased he looked up to the tower with an eye of sorrow, and shook and smoothed down his white hairs.

"'I tell thee,' replied the ancient portress, sorely moved in mind between present duty and service to the noble owner of Haddon and her lingering affection for the good old times of which memory shapes so many paradises : 'I tell thee the tower looks as high and as lordly as ever; and there is something about its silent porch and its crumbling turrets which gives it a deeper hold of our affections than if an hundred knights even now came prancing forth at its porch, with trumpets blowing and banners displayed.'

"'Ah, Dame Foljambe!' said the husbandman; 'yon deer now bounding so blithely down the old chase, with his horny head held high, and an eye that seems to make nought of mountain and vale, it is a fair creature. Look at him! See how he cools his feet in the Wye, surveys his shadow in the stream, and now he contemplates his native hills again. So! away he goes, and we gaze after him, and admire his speed and his beauty. But were the hounds at his flanks, and the bullets in his side, and the swords of the hunters bared for the brittling—ah, Dame! we should change our cheer; we should think that such shapely limbs and such stately antlers might have reigned in wood and on hill for many summers. Even so we think of that stately old Hall, and lament its destruction.'

"'Dame Foljambe thinks not so deeply on the matter,' said a rustic; 'she thinks, the less the Hall fire, the less is the chance of the Hall being consumed; the less the company, the longer will the old Hall floor last, which she sweeps so clean, telling so many stories of the tree that made it; that the seven Virtues in tapestry would do well in avoiding wild company; and that the lass with the long shanks, Diana, and her nymphs, will hunt more to her fancy on her dusty acre of old arras than in the dubious society of the lords and the heroes of the *Court Gazette*. Moreover, the key at her girdle is the commission by which she is keeper of this cast-off and moth-eaten garment of the noble name of Manners; and think ye that she holds that power lightly which makes her governess of ten thousand bats and owls, and gives her the awful responsibility of an armoury containing almost an entire harquebuss, the remains of a pair of boots, and the relique of a buff jerkin?'

"What answer to this unceremonious attack on ancient things committed to her keeping the portress might have made, I had not an opportunity to learn; her darkening brow indicated little meekness of reply; a voice, however, much sweeter than the dame's, intruded on the debate. In the vicinity of the Hall, at the foot of a limestone rock, the summer visitors of Haddon may and do refresh themselves at a small fount of pure water, which love of the clear element induced one of the old ladies to confine within the limits of a large stone basin. Virtues were imputed to the spring, and the superstition of another proprietor erected beside it a cross of stone, lately mutilated, and now removed, but once covered with sculptures and rude emblems, which conveyed religious instruction to an ignorant people. Towards this fountain a maiden from a neighbouring cottage was observed to proceed, warbling, as she went, a fragment of one of those legendary ballads which the old minstrels, illiterate or learned, scattered so abundantly over the country:

DORA VERNON.

It happened between March and May Day,
  When wood-buds wake which slumbered late,
When hill and valley grow green and gaily,
  And every wight longs for a mate;
When lovers sleep with an open eyelid,
  Like nightingales on the orchard tree,
And sorely wish they had wings for flying,
  So they might with their true love be.

A knight all worthy, in this sweet season
  Went out to Carcliff with bow and gun—
Not to chase the roebuck, nor shoot the pheasant,
  But hunt the fierce fox so wild and dun.
And by his side was a young maid riding,
  With laughing blue eyes and sunny hair;
And who was it but young Dora Vernon,
  Young Rutland's true love and Haddon's heir.

Her gentle hand was a good bow bearing;
  The deer at speed, or the fowl on wing,
Stayed in their flight when the bearded arrow
  Her white hand loosed from the sounding string.
Old men made bare their locks and blessed her
  As blithe she rode down the Durwood side;
Her steed rejoiced in his lovely rider,
  Arched his neck proudly, and pranced in pride.

"This unexpected minstrelsy was soon interrupted by Dame Foljambe, whose total devotion to the family of Rutland rendered her averse to hear the story of Dora Vernon's elopement profaned in the familiar ballad strain of a forgotten minstrel. 'I wonder at the presumption of that rude minion,' said the offended portress, 'in chanting such ungentle strains in my ear. Home to thy milk-pails, idle hussy—home to thy distaff, foolish maiden ; or, if thou wilt sing, come over to my lodge when the sun is down, and I will teach thee a strain of a higher sort, made by a great court lord on the marriage of her late Grace. It is none of your rustic chants, but full of fine words, both long and lordly ; it begins—

> Come, burn your incense, ye godlike graces,
>   Come, Cupid, dip your darts in light ;
> Unloose her starry zone, chaste Venus,
>   And trim the bride for the bridal night.

None of your vulgar chants, minion, I tell thee ; but stuffed with spiced words, and shining with gods, and garters, and stars, and precious stones, and odours thickly dropping; a noble strain indeed.' The maiden smiled, nodded acquiescence, and, tripping homewards, renewed her homely and interrupted song, till the river-bank and the ancient towers acknowledged with their sweetest echoes the native charms of her voice.

"'I marvel much,' said the hoary portress, 'at the idle love for strange and incredible stories which possesses as with a demon the peasants of this district. Not only have they given a saint, with a shirt of haircloth and a scourge, to every cavern, and a Druid, with his golden sickle and his mistletoe, to every circle of shapeless stones ; but they have made the Vernons, the Cavendishes, the Cockaynes, and the Foljambes, erect on every wild place crosses or altars of atonement for crimes which they never committed; unless fighting ankle-deep in heathen blood for the recovery of Jerusalem and the Holy Sepulchre required such outlandish penance. They cast, too, a supernatural light round the commonest story; if you credit them, the ancient chapel bell of Haddon, safely lodged on the floor for a century, is carried to the top of the turret, and, touched by some invisible hand, is made to toll forth midnight notes of dolour and woe when any misfortune is about to befall the noble family of Rutland. They tell you, too, that wailings of no earthly voice are heard around the decayed towers, and along the garden terraces, on the festival night of the saint who presided of old over the fortunes of the name of Vernon. And no longer agone than yesterday, old Edgar Ferrars assured me that he had nearly as good as seen the apparition of the King of the Peak himself, mounted on his visionary steed, and, with imaginary horn, and hound, and halloo, pursuing a spectre stag over the wild chase of Haddon. Nay, so far has vulgar credulity and assurance gone, that the great garden entrance, called the Knight's Porch, through which Dora Vernon descended step by step among her twenty attendant maidens, all rustling in embroidered silks, and shining and sparkling, like a winter sky, in diamonds, and such like costly stones—to welcome her noble bridegroom, Lord John Manners, who came, cap in hand, with his company of gallant gentlemen——'

"'Nay, now, Dame Foljambe,' interrupted the husbandman, 'all this is fine enough, and lordly too, I'll warrant; but thou must not apparel a plain old tale in the embroidered raiment of thy own brain, nor adorn it in the precious stones of thy own fancy. Dora Vernon was a lovely lass, and as proud as she was lovely; she bore her head high, Dame; and well she might, for she was a gallant knight's daughter; and lords and dukes, and what not, have descended from her. But, for all that, I cannot forget that she ran away in the middle of a moonlight night with young Lord John Manners, and no other attendant than her own sweet self. Ay, Dame, and for the diamonds, and what not, which thy story showers on her locks and her garments, she tied up her berry-brown locks in a menial's cap, and ran away in a mantle of Bakewell brown, three yards for a groat. Ay, Dame, and instead of going out regularly by the door, she leapt out of a window; more by token, she left one of her silver-heeled slippers fastened in the grating, and the place has ever since been called the Lady's Leap.'

"Dame Foljambe, like an inexperienced rider whose steed refuses obedience to voice and hand, resigned the contest in despair, and allowed her rustic companion to enter full career into the debateable land where she had so often fought and vanquished in defence of the decorum of the mode of alliance between the houses of Haddon and Rutland.

"'And now, Dame,' said the husbandman, 'I will tell thee the story in my own and my father's way. The last of the name of Vernon was renowned far and wide for the hospitality and magnificence of his house, for the splendour of his retinue, and more for the beauty of his daughters, Margaret and Dorothy. This is speaking in thy own manner, Dame Foljambe; but truth's truth. He was much given to hunting and hawking, and jousting with lances either blunt or sharp; and though a harquebuss generally was found in the hand of the gallant hunters of that time, the year of grace 1560, Sir George Vernon despised that foreign weapon; and well he might, for he bent the strongest bow and shot the surest shaft of any man in England. His chase-dogs, too, were all of the most expert and famous kinds; his falcons had the fairest and most certain flight; and though he had seen foreign lands, he chiefly prided himself in maintaining unimpaired the old baronial grandeur of his house. I have heard my grandsire say how his great-grandsire told him that the like of the Knight of Haddon for a stately form and a noble, free, and natural grace of manner was not to be seen in court or camp. He was hailed in common tale and in minstrel song by the name of the King of the Peak; and it is said his handsome person and witchery of tongue chiefly prevented his mistress, good Queen Bess, from abridging his provincial designation with the headsman's axe.

"'It happened in the fifth year of the reign of his young and sovereign mistress that a great hunting festival was held at Haddon, where all the beauty and high blood of Derbyshire assembled. Lords of distant counties came; for to bend a bow or brittle the deer under the eye of Sir George Vernon was an honour sought for by many. Over the chase of Haddon, over the hill of Stanton, over Bakewell-edge, over Chatsworth hill and Hardwicke plain, and beneath the ancient castle of Bolsover, as far as the edge of the forest of old Sherwood, were the sounds of harquebuss and bowstring heard, and the cry of dogs and the cheering of men. The brown-mouthed and white-footed dogs of Derbyshire were there among the foremost; the snow-white hound and the coal-black, from the Scottish Border and bonny Westmoreland, preserved or augmented their ancient fame; nor were the dappled hounds of old Godfrey Foljambe, of Bakewell Bank, far from the throat of the red deer when they turned at bay, and gored horses and riders. The great hall floor of Haddon was soon covered with the produce of wood and wild.

THE KING OF THE PEAK.

"'Nor were the preparations for feasting this noble hunting party unworthy the reputation for solid hospitality which characterized the ancient King of the Peak. Minstrels had come from distant parts, as far even as the Scottish Border—bold, free-spoken, rude, rough-witted men; "for the selvedge of the web," says the Northern proverb, "is aye the coarsest cloth." But in the larder the skill of man was chiefly employed, and a thousand rarities were prepared for pleasing the eye and appeasing the appetite. In the kitchen, with its huge chimneys and prodigious spits, the menial maidens were flooded nigh ankle-deep in the richness of roasted oxen and deer; and along the passage communicating with the hall of state men might have slided along, because of the fat droppings of that prodigious feast, like a slider on the frozen Wye. The kitchen tables of solid plank groaned and yielded beneath the roasted beeves and the spitted deer; while a stream of rich smoke, massy, and slow, and savoury, sallied out at the grated windows, and sailed round the mansion, like a mist exhaled by the influence of the moon. I tell thee, Dame Foljambe, I call those the golden days of old England.

"'But I wish you had seen the hall prepared for this princely feast. The floor, of hard and solid stone, was strewn deep with rushes and fern; and there lay the dogs of the chase in couples, their mouths still red with the blood of stags, and panting yet from the fervour and length of their pursuit. At the lower end of the hall, where the floor subsided a step, was spread a table for the stewards and other chiefs over the menials. There sat the keeper of the bows, the warder of the chase, and the head-falconer, together with many others of lower degree, but mighty men among the retainers of the noble name of Vernon. Over their heads were hung the horns of stags, the jaws of boars, the skulls of the enormous bisons, and the foreheads of foxes. Nor were there wanting trophies where the contest had been more bloody and obstinate: banners, and shields, and helmets, won in the Civil, and Scottish, and Crusading wars, together with many strange weapons of annoyance or defence, borne in the Norwegian and Saxon broils. Beside them were hung rude paintings of the most renowned of these rustic heroes, all in the picturesque habiliments of the times. Horns, and harquebusses, and swords, and bows, and buff coats, and caps, were thrown in negligent groups all about the floor; while their owners sat in expectation of an immediate and ample feast, which they hoped to wash down with floods of that salutary beverage, the brown blood of barley.

"'At the upper end of the hall, where the floor was elevated exactly as much in respect as it was lowered in submission at the other, there the table for feasting the nobles stood; and well was it worthy of its station. It was one solid plank of white sycamore, shaped from the entire shaft of an enormous tree, and supported on squat columns of oak, ornamented with the arms of the Vernons, and grooved into the stone floor beyond all chance of being upset by human powers. Benches of wood, curiously carved, and covered, in times of more than ordinary ceremony, with cushions of embroidered velvet, surrounded this ample table; while in the recess behind appeared a curious work in arras, consisting of festivals, and processions, and bridals, executed from the ancient poets; and for the more staid and grave a more devout hand had wrought some scenes from the controversial fathers and the monkish legends of the ancient Church. The former employed the white hands of Dora Vernon herself; while the latter were the labours of her sister Margaret, who was of a serious turn, and never happened to be so far in love as to leap from a window.'

"'And now,' said Dame Foljambe, 'I will describe the Knight of Haddon, with his fair daughters and principal guests, myself.' 'A task that will last thee to Doomsday, Dame,' muttered the husbandman. The portress heeded not this ejaculation, but with a particular stateliness of delivery proceeded: 'The silver dinner-bell rang on the summit of Haddon Hall, the warder thrice wound his horn, and straightway the sound of silver spurs was heard in the passage, the folding-door opened, and in marched my own ancestor, Ferrars Foljambe by name. I have heard his dress too often described not to remember it. A buff jerkin with slashed and ornamented sleeves, a mantle of fine Lincoln green fastened round his neck with wolf-claws of pure gold, a pair of gilt spurs on the heels of his brown hunting-boots, garnished above with taslets of silver, and at the square and turned-up toes with links of the same metal, connected with the taslets. On his head was a boarskin cap, on which the white teeth of the boar were set, tipped with gold. At his side was a hunting-horn, called the White Hunting-horn of Tutbury, banded with silver in the middle, belted with black silk at the ends, set with buckles of silver, and bearing the arms of Edmund, the warlike brother of Edward Longshanks. This fair horn descended by marriage to Stanhope of Elvaston, who sold it to Foxlowe of Staveley. The gift of a king and the property of heroes was sold for some paltry pieces of gold.'

"'Dame Foljambe,' said the old man, 'the march of thy tale is like the course of the Wye, seventeen miles of links and windings down a fair valley five miles long. A man might carve thy ancestor's figure in alabaster in the time thou describest him. I must resume my story, Dame; so let thy description of old Ferrars Foljambe stand; and suppose the table filled about with the gallants of the chase and many fair ladies, while at the head sat the King of the Peak himself, his beard descending to his broad girdle, his own natural hair of dark brown—blessings on the head that keeps God's own covering on it, and scorns the curled inventions of man—falling in thick masses on his broad manly shoulders. Nor silver, nor gold, wore he; the natural nobleness of his looks maintained his rank and pre-eminence among men; the step of Sir George Vernon was one that many imitated, but few could attain—at once manly and graceful. I have heard it said that he carried privately in his bosom a small rosary of precious metal, in which his favourite daughter Dora had entwined one of her mother's tresses. The ewer-bearers entered with silver basins full of water; the element came pure and returned red, for the hands of the guests were stained with the blood of the chase. The attendant minstrels vowed that no hands so shapely, nor fingers so taper, and long, and white, and round, as those of the Knight of Haddon, were that day dipped in water.

"'There is wondrous little pleasure in describing a feast of which we have not partaken; so pass we on to the time when the fair dames retired, and the red wine in cups of gold, and the ale in silver flagons, shone and sparkled as they passed from hand to lip beneath the blaze of seven massy lamps. The knights toasted their mistresses, the retainers told their exploits, and the minstrels with harp and tongue made music and song abound. The gentles struck their drinking vessels on the table till they rang again; the menials stamped with the heels of their ponderous boots on the solid floor; while the hounds, imagining they heard the call to the chase, leaped up, and bayed in hoarse but appropriate chorus.

"'The ladies now re-appeared in the side galleries, and overlooked the scene of festivity below. The loveliest of many counties were there; but the fairest was a young maid of middle size, in a dress disencumbered of ornament, and possessed of one of those free and graceful forms which may be met with in other counties, but for which our own Derbyshire alone is famous. Those who admired the grace of her person were no less charmed with her simplicity and natural meekness of deportment. Nature did much for her, and art strove in vain to rival her with others; while health, that handmaid of beauty, supplied her eye and her cheek with the purest light and the freshest roses. Her short and rosy upper-lip was slightly curled, with as much of maiden sanctity, perhaps, as pride; her white high forehead was shaded with locks of sunny brown, while her large and dark hazel eyes beamed with free and unaffected modesty. Those who observed her closely might see her eyes, as she glanced about, sparkling for a moment with other lights, but scarce less holy, than those of devotion and awe. Of all the knights present, it was impossible to say who inspired her with those love-fits of flushing joy and delicious agitation; each hoped himself the happy person, for none could look on Dora Vernon without awe and love. She leaned her white bosom, shining through the veil which shaded it, near one of the minstrels' harps; and, looking round on the presence, her eyes grew brighter as she looked—at least, so vowed the knights, and so sang the minstrels.

"'All the knights arose when Dora Vernon appeared. "Fill all your wine-cups, knights," said Sir Lucas Peverel. "Fill them to the brim," said Sir Henry Avenel. "And drain them out, were they deeper than the Wye," said Sir Godfrey Gernon. "To the health of the Princess of the Peak," said Sir Ralph Cavendish. "To the health of Dora Vernon," said Sir Hugh de Wodensley; "beauty is above titles; she is the loveliest maiden a knight ever looked on, with the sweetest name too." "And yet, Sir Knight," said Peverel, filling his cup, "I know one who thinks so humbly of the fair name of Vernon, as to wish it charmed into that of De Wodensley." "He is not master of a spell so profound," said Avenel. "And yet he is master of his sword," answered De Wodensley, with a darkening brow.

"I counsel him to keep it in its sheath," said Cavendish, "lest it prove a wayward servant." "I will prove its service on thy bosom where and when thou wilt, Lord of Chatsworth," said De Wodensley. "Lord of Darley," answered Cavendish, "it is a tempting moonlight, but there is a charm over Haddon to-night it would be unseemly to dispel. To-morrow I meet Lord John Manners to try whose hawk has the fairer flight and whose love the whiter hand. That can be soon seen; for who has so fair a hand as the love of young Rutland? I shall be found by Durwood Tor when the sun is three hours up, with my sword drawn: there's my hand on't, De Wodensley." And he wrung the knight's hand till the blood seemed starting from beneath his fingernails. "By the saints, Sir Knights," said Sir Godfrey Gernon, "you may as well beard one another about the love of 'some bright particular star, and think to wed it,' as the wild Wizard of Warwick says, as quarrel about this unattainable love. Hearken, minstrels: while we drain our cups to this beauteous lass sing some of you a kindly love strain, wondrously mirthful and melancholy. Here's a cup of Rhenish, and a good gold Harry in the bottom on't, for the minstrel who pleases me." The minstrels laid their hands on the strings, and a sound was heard like the swarming of bees before summer thunder. "Sir Knight," said one, "I will sing ye, 'Cannie Johnnie Armstrong' with all the seventeen variations." "He was hanged for cattle-stealing," answered the Knight; "I'll have none of him." "What say you to 'Dick of the Cow,' or the 'Harper of Lochmaben'?" said another, with something of a tone of diffidence. "What! you Northern knaves, can you sing of nothing but thievery and jail-breaking?" "Perhaps, your knightship," humbly suggested a third, "may have a turn for the supernatural, and I'm thinking the Fairy Legend of young Tamlane is just the thing that suits your fancy." "I like the *naïveté* of the young lady very much," answered the Knight; "but the fair dames of Derbyshire prize the charms of lovers with flesh and blood before the gayest elfin knight that ever ran a course from Carlisle to Caerlaverock." "What would your worship say to 'William of Cloudesley'?" said a Cumberland minstrel. "Or to the 'Friar of Orders Grey'?" said a harper from the halls of the Percys. "Minstrels," said Sir Ralph Cavendish, "the invention of sweet and gentle poesy is dead among you. Every churl in the Peak can chant us these beautiful but common ditties. Have you nothing new for the honour of the sacred calling of verse and the beauty of Dora Vernon? Fellow—harper— what's your name?—you with the long hair and the green mantle," said the Knight, beckoning to a young minstrel who sat with his harp held before him, and his face half-buried in his mantle's fold; "come, touch your strings and sing. I'll wager my gold-hilted sword against that pheasant feather in thy cap that thou hast a new and a gallant strain; for I have seen thee measure more than once the form of fair Dora Vernon with a ballad-maker's eye. Sing, man, sing."

"'The young minstrel, as he bowed his head to this singular mode of request, blushed from brow to bosom; nor were the face and neck of Dora Vernon without an acknowledgment of how deeply she sympathised in his embarrassment. A finer instrument, a truer hand, or a more sweet and manly voice, hardly ever united to lend grace to rhyme.

THE MINSTREL'S SONG.

Last night a proud page came to me:
"Sir Knight," he said, "I greet you free;
The moon is up at midnight hour,
All mute and lonely is the bower:
To rouse the deer my lord is gone,
And his fair daughter's all alone,
As lily fair, and as sweet to see—
Arise, Sir Knight, and follow me."

The stars streamed out, the new-woke moon
O'er Chatsworth Hill gleamed brightly down,
And my love's cheeks, half-seen, half-hid,
With love and joy blushed deeply red:
Short was our time, and chaste our bliss,
A whispered vow and a gentle kiss;
And one of those long looks, which earth
With all its glory is not worth.

The stars beamed lovelier from the sky,
The smiling brook flowed gentlier by;
Life, fly thou on; I'll mind that hour
Of sacred love in greenwood bower;
Let seas between us swell and sound,
Still at her name my heart shall bound;
Her name, which like a spell I'll keep,
To soothe me and to charm my sleep.

"'"Fellow," said Sir Ralph Cavendish, "thou hast not shamed my belief of thy skill; keep that piece of gold, and drink thy cup of wine in quiet, to the health of the lass who inspired thy strain, be she lordly or be she low." The minstrel seated himself, and the interrupted mirth recommenced, which was not long to continue. When the minstrel began to sing the King of the Peak fixed his large and searching eyes on his person with a scrutiny from which nothing could escape, and which called a flush of apprehension to the face of his daughter Dora. Something like a cloud came upon his brow at the first verse, which, darkening down through the second, became as dark as a December night at the close of the third, when, rising, and motioning Sir Ralph Cavendish to follow, he retired into the recess of the southern window. "Sir Knight," said the Lord of Haddon, "thou art the sworn friend of John Manners, and well thou knowest what his presumption dares at, and what are the letts between him and me. *Cavendo tutus!* ponder on thy own motto well. 'Let seas between us swell and sound:' let his song be prophetic; for Derbyshire—for England—has no river deep enough and broad enough to preserve him from a father's sword, whose peace he seeks to wound." "Knight of Haddon," said Sir Ralph, "John Manners is indeed my friend; and the friend of a Cavendish can be no mean person; a braver and a better spirit never aspired after beauty." "Sir Knight," said the King of the Peak, " I court no man's counsel; hearken to my words. Look at the moon's shadow on Haddon-dial; there it is beside the casement; the shadow falls short of twelve. If it darkens the midnight hour, and John Manners be found here, he shall be cast, fettered, neck and heel, into the deepest dungeon of Haddon."

"'All this passed not unobserved of Dora Vernon, whose fears and affections divined immediate mischief from the calm speech and darkened brow of her father. Her heart sank within her when he beckoned her to withdraw; she followed him into the great tapestried room. "My daughter, my love, Dora," said the not idle fears of a father, " wine has done more than its usual good office with the wits of our guests to-night; they look on thee with bolder eyes and speak of thee with a bolder tongue than a father can wish. Retire, therefore, to thy chamber. One of thy wisest attendants shall be thy companion. · Adieu, my love, till sunrise!" He kissed her white temples and white brow; and Dora clung to his neck and sobbed in his bosom, while the secret of her heart rose near her lips. He returned to his guests, and mirth and music and the march of the wine-cup recommenced with a vigour which promised reparation for the late intermission.

"'The chamber, or rather temporary prison, of Dora Vernon was nigh the cross-bow room, and had a window which looked out on the terraced garden and the extensive chase towards the hill of Haddon. All that side of the Hall lay in deep shadow, and the moon, sunk to the very summit of the western heath, threw a level and a farewell beam over river and tower. The young lady of Haddon seated herself in the recessed window, and lent her ear to every sound and her eye to every shadow that flitted over the garden and chase. Her attendant maiden—shrewd, demure, and suspicious, of the ripe age of thirty, yet of a merry, pleasant look, which had its admirers—sat watching every motion with the eye of an owl.

"'It was past midnight, when a foot came gliding along the passage, and a finger gave three slight scratches on the door of the chamber. The maid went out, and after a brief conference suddenly returned, red with blushes from ear to ear. "Oh, my lady!" said the trusty maiden, "oh, my sweet young lady! here's that poor young lad—ye know his name—who gave me three yards of crimson ribbon to trim my peach-bloom mantle, last Bakewell Fair. An honester or a kinder heart never kept a promise; and yet I may not give him the meeting. Oh, my young lady! my sweet young lady! my beautiful young lady! could you not stay here for half an hour by yourself?" Ere her young mistress could answer, the notice of the lover's presence was renewed. The maiden again went, whispers were heard, and the audible salutation of lips; she returned again, more resolute than ever to oblige her lover. "Oh, my lady, my young lady! if ye ever hope to prosper in true love yourself, spare me but one half-hour with this harmless, kind lad. He has come seven long miles to see my fair face, he says; and, oh, my lady! he has a handsome face of his own. Oh, never let it be said that Dora Vernon sundered true lovers! But I see consent written in your own lovely face; so I will run. And oh, my lady! take care of your own sweet handsome self when your faithful Nan's away." And the maiden retired with her lover.

"'It was half an hour after midnight when one of the keepers of the chase, as he lay beneath a holly-bush, listening with a prolonged groan to the audible voice of revelry in the Hall, from which his duty had lately excluded him, happened to observe two forms approaching: one of low stature, a light step, and muffled in a common mantle; the other with the air and in the dress of a forester, a sword at his side and pistols in his belt. The ale and the wine had invaded the keeper's brain and impaired his sight; yet he roused himself up with a hiccup and a "Hilloah," and "Where go ye, my masters?" The lesser form whispered to the other, who immediately said, "Jasper Jugg, is this you? Heaven be praised I have found you so soon. Here's that North-country pedlar, with his beads and blue ribbon—he has come and whistled out pretty Nan Malkin, the lady's favourite and the lord's trusty maid. I left them under the terrace, and came to tell you."

"'The enraged keeper scarce heard this account of the faithlessness of his love to an end; he started off with the swiftness of one of the deer which he watched, making the boughs crash as he forced his way through bush and glade direct for the Hall, vowing desertion to the girl and destruction to the pedlar. "Let us hasten our steps, my love," said the lesser figure, in a sweet voice; and, unmantling as she spoke, turned back to the towers of Haddon the fairest face that ever left them—the face of Dora Vernon herself. "My men and my horses are nigh, my love," said the taller figure; and taking a silver call from his pocket, he imitated the sharp shrill cry of the plover; then turning round, he stood and gazed towards Haddon, scarcely darkened by the setting of the moon, for the festal lights flashed from turret and casement, and the sound of mirth and revelry rang with augmenting din. "Ah, fair and stately Haddon" said Lord John Manners, "little dost thou know thou hast lost thy jewel from thy brow, else thy lights would be dimmed, thy mirth would turn to wailing, and swords would be flashing from thy portals in all the haste of hot pursuit. Farewell, for a while, fair tower—farewell for a while! I shall return, and bless the time I harped among thy menials and sang of my love, and charmed her out of thy little chamber window." Several armed men now came suddenly down from the hill of Haddon, horses richly caparisoned were brought from among the trees of the chase, and the ancestors of the present family of Rutland sought shelter for a time in a a distant land from the wrath of the King of the Peak.'"

THE MOTHER'S DREAM.

She slept—and there was visioned to her eye
A stately mountain, green it seemed, and high;
She sought to climb it—lo! a river dark
Rolled at its foot; there came a gallant bark,
And in the bark were forms the eldest fiend
Had shaped to mock God's image; fierce they leaned
O'er the ship's side, and, seizing her, rushed through
The river wave, which kindled as they flew.
Then to the bank came one and laughed aloud;
Bright robes he wore, stern was his look and proud:
He stretched his arm, and hailed her for his bride;
The shuddering waters washed his robe aside,
And showed a shape the fiend's tormenting flame
Had sorely vexed; she shrieked, and faintness came.
Then shouts she heard, and sound of gladsome song,
And saw a stream of torches flash along.
The feast was spread, the bridal couch prepared,
Dread forms stood round, with naked swords to guard.
Nor looked she long; one whispered in her ear,
"Come, climb thy bed; for lo! the bridegroom's near."
She cried to heaven—at once the wedding joy
Was changed to war-shout and to funeral cry;
Swords in the air, as sunshine, flashed and fell,
Then rose all crimsoned; loud came groan and yell,
And from the middle tumult started out
A form that seized her: blow, and shriek, and shout
Came thick behind. Down to the Solway flood
Fast was she borne—it seemed a sea of blood;
She felt it touch her knees, and with a scream
She started back, and wakened from her dream.
Legend of Lady Beatrice.

Were "The Mother's Dream" a traditionary fiction, and its predictions unfulfilled, gladness would be diffused around many hearths, and the tears wiped away from many matrons' cheeks. It was related to me by a Dumfriesshire lady: her voice was slow and gentle, and possessed that devotional Scottish melody of expression which gives so much antique richness and grace to speech. Under the shade of a long veil she sought to conceal a face where early grief had bleached the roses and impressed a sedate and settled sorrow on a brow particularly white and high. But her eye still retained something of the light of early life, which darkened or brightened as the joys, the sufferings, or the sorrows of wedded and maternal love gave a deeper interest or passion to her story.

"When woman is young," said she, with a sigh, but not of regret, "she loves to walk in the crowded streets and near the dwellings of men; when she becomes wiser, has seen the vanities and drunk of the miseries and woes of life, she chooses her walks in more lonely places, and, seeking converse with her spirit, shuns the joy and the mirth of the world. When sorrow, which misses few, had found me out, and made me a mateless bird, I once walked out to the margin of that beautiful sheet of water, the Ladye's Lowe. It was the heart of summer; the hills in which the lake lay embosomed were bright and green; sheep were scattered upon their sides; shepherds sat on their summits; while the grassy sward, descending to the quiet pure water, gave it so much of its own vernal hue that the eye could not always distinguish where the land and lake met. Its long green water-flags and broad lilies, which lay so flat and so light along the surface, were unmoved, save by the course of a pair of wild swans, which for many years had grazed on the grassy margin or found food in the bottom of the lake.

"This pastoral quietness pertained more to modern than to ancient times. When the summer heat was high, and the waters of the lake low, the remains of a broken but narrow causeway, composed of square stones indented in a frame-work of massy oak, might still be traced, starting from a little bay on the northern side, and diving directly towards the centre of the lake. Tradition, in pursuing the history of this causeway, supplied the lake with an island, the island with a tower, and the tower with narratives of perils and bloodshed, and chivalry and love. These fireside traditions, varying according to the fancy of the peasantry, all concluded in a story too wild for ordinary belief. A battle is invariably described by some grey-headed narrator, fought on the southern side of the lake, and sufficiently perilous and bloody. A lady's voice is heard and a lady's form is seen among the armed men, in the middle of the fight. She is described as borne off towards the causeway by the lord of the tower, while the margin of the water is strewed with dead or dying men. She sees her father, her brother, fall in her defence; her lover, to whom she had been betrothed, and from whom she had been torn, die by her side; and the deep and lasting curse which she denounced against her ravisher, and the tower and the lake which gave him shelter is not forgotten; but it is too awful to mingle with the stories of a grave and a devout people. That night, it is said, a voice was heard as of a spirit running round and round the lake, and pronouncing a curse against it; the waters became agitated, and a shriek was heard at midnight. In the morning the castle of the Ladye's Lowe was sunk, and the waters of the lake slept seven fathoms deep over the copestone.

"They who attach credence to this wild legend are willing to support it by much curious testimony. They tell that when the waters are pure in summer-time, or when the winter's ice lies clear beneath the foot of the curler, the walls of the tower are distinctly seen without a stone displaced; while those who connect tales of wonder with every remarkable place say that once a year the castle arises at midnight from the bosom of the lake, with lights— not like the lights of this world—streaming from loophole and turret; while on the summit, like a banner spread, stands a lady clad in white, holding her hands to heaven, and shrieking. This vision is said to precede, by a night or two, the annual destruction of some person by the waters of the lake. The influence of this superstition has made the Ladye's Lowe a solitary and a desolate place, has preserved its fish, which are both delicious and numerous, from the fisher's net and hook, and its wild swans from the gun of the fowler. The peasantry seldom seek the solitude of its beautiful banks, and avoid bathing in its waters; and when the winter gives its bosom to the curler or the skater, old men look grave and say, 'The Ladye's Lowe will have its yearly victim'; and its yearly victim, tradition tells us, it has ever had since the sinking of the tower.

"I had reached the margin of the lake, and sat looking on its wide pure expanse of water. Here and there the remains of an old tree or a stunted hawthorn broke and beautified the winding line of its border; while cattle, coming to drink and gaze at their shadows, took away from the solitude of the place. As my eye pursued the sinuous line of the lake, it was arrested by the appearance of a form, which seemed that of a human being, stretched motionless on the margin. I rose, and on going nearer I saw it was a man—the face cast upon the earth, and the hands spread. I thought death had been there; and while I was waving my hand for a shepherd, who sat on the hillside, to approach and assist me, I heard a groan and a low and melancholy cry; and presently he started up, and, seating himself on an old tree-root, rested a cheek on the palm of either hand, and gazed intently on the lake. He was a young man, the remains of health and beauty were still about him; but his locks, once curling and long, which maidens loved to look at, were now matted, and wild, and withered; his cheeks were hollow and pale, and his eyes, once the merriest and brightest in the district, shone now with a grey, wild, and unearthly light. As I looked upon this melancholy wreck of youth and strength, the unhappy being put both hands in the lake, and, lifting up water in his palms, scattered it in the air; then dipping both hands again, showered the water about his locks like rain. He continued, during this singular employment, to chant some strange and broken words with a wild tone and a faltering tongue:

SONG OF BENJIE SPEDLANDS.

Cursed be thou, O water, for my sake!
Misery to them who dip their hands in thee!
May the wild fowl forsake thy margin,
The fish leap no more in thy waves;
May the whirlwind scatter thee utterly,
And the lightning scorch thee up;
May the lily bloom no more on thy bosom,
And the white swan fly from thy floods!

Cursed be thou, O water, for my sake!
The babe unborn shall never bless thee;
May the flocks that taste of thee perish;
May the man who bathes in thy flood
Be crossed and cursed with unrequited love,
And go childless down to the grave.
As I curse thee with my delirious tongue,
I will mar thee with my unhappy hands!

As this water, cast on the passing wind,
Shall return to thy bosom no more,
So shall the light of morning forsake thee,
And night-darkness devour thee up.

> As that pebble descends into thy deeps,
> And that feather floats on thy waves,
> So shall the good and the holy curse thee,
> And the madman mar thee with dust.
>
> Cursed mayst thou continue, for my sake,
> For the sake of those thou hast slain ;
> For the father who mourned for his son,
> For the mother who wailed for her child.
> I heard the voice of sorrow on thy banks,
> And a mother mourning by thy waters ;
> I saw her stretch her white hands over thee,
> And weep for her fair-haired son !

"The sound of the song rolled low and melancholy over the surface of the lake. I never heard a sound so dismal. During the third verse the singer took up water in the hollow of his hand, and threw it on the wind. Then he threw a pebble and a feather into the lake; and, gathering up the dust among the margin stones, strewed it over the surface of the water. When he concluded his wild verses he uttered a loud cry, and throwing himself suddenly on his face, spread out his hands, and lay, and quivered, and moaned like one in mortal agony.

"A young woman, in widow's weeds, and with a face still deeper in woe than her mourning dress, now came towards me, along the border of the lake. She had the face and the form of one whom I knew in my youth, the companion of my teens, and the life and love of all who had hearts worth a woman's wish. She was the grace of the preaching, the joy of the dance, through her native valley, and had the kindest and the gayest heart in the wide holms of Annandale. I rode at her wedding, and a gay woman was I ; I danced at her wedding as if sorrow was never to come ; and when I went to the kirking, and saw her so fair, and her husband so handsome, I said, in the simplicity of my heart, they will live long and happy on the earth. When I saw him again he was stretched in his shroud, and she was weeping, with an infant son on her knee, beside the coffin of her husband. Such remembrances can never pass away from the heart, and they came thick upon me as the companion of my early years approached. We had been long separated. I had resided in a distant part, till the loss of all I loved brought me back to seek for happiness in my native place, in the dwellings of departed friends and the haunts of early joys.

"Something of a smile passed over her face when she saw

me, but it darkened suddenly down. We said little for awhile; the histories of our own sorrows were written on our faces; there was no need for speech. 'Alas! alas!' said she, 'a kind husband and three sweet bairns all gone to the green churchyard! But ye were blessed in the departure of your children compared to me. A mother's eye wept over them, a mother's knees nursed them, and a mother's hand did all that a mother's hand could do, till the breath went to Heaven from between their sweet lips. O woman, woman! ye were blessed compared with me!' And she sobbed aloud, and looked upon the lake, which lay clear and unruffled before us. At the sound of her voice the young man raised himself from the ground, gave one wild look at my companion, and uttering a cry, and covering his face with his hands, dropped flat on the earth, and lay mute and without motion.

"'See him, see him!' said she to me. 'His name is Benjie Spedlands; he was once the sweetest youth in the parish, but now the hand of Heaven is heavy upon him, and sore; he is enduring punishment for a season and a time; and heavy as was his trespass, so heavy has been his chastening.' I entreated her to tell me how he had offended, and also how it happened that her appearance gave him such pain, and made him cry and cover his face. 'It is a strange and a mournful story,' she answered; 'but it eases my spirit to relate it. O woman! I was once a merry and a happy creature, with a face as gladsome as the light of day; but for these eight long years I have had nought but cheerless days and joyless nights, sad thoughts and terrible dreams. Sorrow came in a dream to me, but it will not pass from me till I go to the grave.

"'It happened during the summer-time, after I had lost my husband, that I was very down-spirited and lonesome, and my chief and only consolation was to watch over my fatherless son. He was a sweet child; and on the day he was two years old, when I ought to have been glad, and praised Him who had protected the widow and the orphan, I became more than usually melancholy, for evil forebodings kept down my spirits sorely, and caused me to wet the cheeks of my child with tears. You have been a mother, and may have known the tenderness and love which an infant will show her when she is distressed. He hung his little arms round my neck, hid his head in my bosom, and raised up such a murmur and a song of sorrow and sympathy, that I blessed him and smiled, and the bairn smiled, and so we fell asleep. It was about midnight that I dreamed a dream.

"'I dreamed myself seated at my own threshold, dandling my boy in the sun: sleep gives us many joys which are taken from us when we wake, and shadows out to us many woes which are interrupted by sorrow. I thought my husband was beside me; but, though he smiled, his look was more grave than in life, and there seemed a light about him, a purer light than that of day. I thought I saw the sun setting on the green hills before me. I heard the song of the maidens as they returned from the folds; saw the rooks flying in a long black and wavering train towards their customary pines; and beheld first one large star, and then another, arising in the firmament. And I looked again, and saw a little black cloud hanging between heaven and earth; it became larger and darker till it filled all the air, from the sky down to the bosom of the Ladye's Lowe. I wondered what this might mean, when presently the cloud began to move and roll along the earth, coming nearer and nearer, and it covered all the green fields, and shut out the light of heaven. And as it came closer, I thought I beheld shapes of men, and heard voices more shrill than human tongue. And the cloud stood still at the distance of a stone-cast. I grew sore afraid, and clasped my child to my bosom and sought to fly, but I could not move; the form of my husband had fled, and there was no one to comfort me. And I looked again, and lo! the cloud seemed cleft asunder, and I saw a black chariot, drawn by six black steeds, issue from the cloud. And I saw a shadow seated for a driver, and heard a voice say: "I am the bearer of woes to the sons and daughters of men; carry these sorrows abroad, they are in number eight." And all the steeds started forward; and when the chariot came to my threshold, the phantom tarried and said: "A woe and a woe for the son of the widow Rachel." And I rose and beheld in a chariot the coffins of seven children; and their names and their years were written thereon. And there lay another coffin; and as I bent over it I read the name of my son, and his years were numbered six; a tear fell from my cheek, and the letters vanished. And I heard the shadow say: "Woman, what hast thou done? Can thy tears contend with me?"

And I saw a hand pass, as a hand when it writes, over the coffin again. And I looked, and I saw the name of my son, and his years were numbered nine. And a faintness came into my heart and a dimness into mine eye, and I sought to wash the words out with my tears, when the shadow said: "Woman, woman, take forth thy woe and go thy ways; I have houses seven to visit, and may not tarry for thy tears. Three years have I given for thy weeping, and I may give no more."

"'I have often wondered at my own strength, though it was all in a dream. "Vision," I said, "if thy commission is from the Evil One, lash thy fiend-steeds and begone." The shadow darkened as I spoke. "Vision," I said, "if thy mission is from Him who sits on the holy hill—'the Lord giveth and taketh away, blessed be His name'—do thy message and depart." And suddenly the coffin was laid at my door, the steeds and chariot fled, the thick clouds followed, and I beheld him no more. I gazed upon the name, and the years nine; and as I looked it vanished from my sight; and I awoke weeping, and found my locks drenched in sweat, and the band of my bosom burst asunder with the leaping of my heart.

"'And I told my dream, and all the people of the parish wondered; and those who had children waxed sorrowful, and were dismayed. And a woman who dwells by the Rowantree-burn came unto me, and said: "I hear that you have dreamed an evil dream; know ye how ye may eschew it?" And I answered: "I have dreamed an evil dream, and I know not how I may eschew it, save by prayers and humiliation." And the woman said to me: "Marvel not at what I may say: I am old, and the wisdom of ancient times is with me—such wisdom as foolish men formerly accounted evil. Listen to my words. Take the under-garment of thy child, and dip it at midnight in that water called the Ladye's Lowe, and hang it forth to dry in the new moonbeam. Take thy Bible on thy knees, and keep watch beside it; mickle is the courage of a woman when the child that milked her bosom is in danger. And a form, like unto the form of a lady, will arise from the lake, and will seek to turn the garment of thy son; see that ye quail not, but arise and say: 'Spirit, by all the salvation contained between the boards of this book, I order thee to depart and touch not the garment.'"

"'And while this woman spake, there came another woman, the wife of one who had sailed to a distant land, and had left her with two sweet children, and the name of the one was Samuel, and the name of the other John. Now John was a fair and comely child, the image of her husband; but he was not his mother's joy, for she loved Samuel, who bore the image of one she had loved in her youth; and this made her husband sorrowful, and caused him to sail to a far country. And when she came in, she said: "So ye have dreamed a bad dream, and ye have sought this ill woman of the Rowantree-burn to give the interpretation thereof; if evil is threatened, evil is the way you seek to avert it. Now listen unto me; 'the wind bloweth as it listeth'—the ways of God will not be changed by the wisdom of man. Providence may seek thy child for a saint; see that ye cast him not to the fiends by dealing with unholy charms and spells and with graceless hags. I have two fair children; one of them is his father's love, the other is mine. Say, saw ye not the name of John written on one of those visionary coffins? for I hope my Samuel will long be the grace of the green earth before he goes to the dowie mools." And the eyes of the woman of the Rowantree-burn flashed with anger, and she said, "Hearken to the words of this shameless woman! She seeks the destruction of the child of wedlock, and wishes life to the child of wantonness and sin. Lo! I say, hearken unto her. But the evil of her ways shall be to her as sadness, and what has given her joy shall be to the world a hissing and a scorn, to her a scourge and a curse. She will lose the sweet youth John, even as she wishes, but long and full of evil shall be the life of the child she loves." And upon this these two foolish women reproached each other with works of sin and with deeds of darkness; and, waxing wroth with their words, they tore each other's raiment and hair, and smote and bruised one another, and the clamour of their tongues increased exceedingly.

"'Now, in the midst of all this folly there came to my fireside a man cunning in the culture of corn, and versed in the cure of those evils which afflict dumb creatures. And when he saw the strife between the woman of the Rowantree-burn and the mariner's wife he laughed aloud in the fulness of his joy. "Strong may the strife be, and long may it continue," said he, "for pleasant is the feud between the raven and the hooded crow, and the small birds sing when

THE MOTHER'S DREAM.

the hawks of heaven fight. That woman has destroyed the firstlings of the flock, has dried up the udders to the sucking lambs, and lessened the riches of men who live by sweet cheese and fattened herds. She hath also cast her spells over the deep waters of Annan and Ae; the fish have fled, and the nets of the fishermen are dipped in vain. The fowls of heaven, too, have felt the cunning of her hand; the wild swans have left the Ladye's Lowe, the wild geese have fled from the royal lakes of Lochmaben, and the blackcock and the ptarmigan come no more to the snare of the fowler. Let her therefore scream and weep under the strong hand and sharp nails of her bitter enemy. And for the other woman—even she whose husband lives on the deep waters, and to whom she bears children in the image of other men— let her, I say, suffer from the fingers of witchcraft: pleasant is the strife between workers of wickedness; and woe to the wit and sorrow to the hand that seeks to sunder them. Now, touching this singular dream of thine, I have a word to say, and it is this: believe it not—it is the work of the grand architect of human misery, who seeks to draw people to sin in the dreams and shadows of the night. To men whose hearts are warm, and whose blood is young, he descends in soft and voluptuous visions. I have myself beheld a maiden with a languishing look and an eye blue and ensnaring, standing at my bedside, clothed out in a midnight dream with the shadowy beauty of a sleeping imagination; and this appeared, too, on that very night when my inward gifts and graces had raised me from a humble sower of seed-corn to become an elder of our godly kirk— praise be blessed, and may the deed be lauded of men. But it is not alone to the staid and the devout that the enemy appears in dreams; he presents the soldier with imaginary fields of peril and blood, and blesses his ear with the yell and the outcry of battle and the trumpet sound. To the maiden he comes in gallant shapes and costly raiment, with becks and bows, and feet which pace gracefully over the floor to the sound of the flute and dulcimer, and all manner of music. To the sleeping eye of a mother he digs a deep pit for the babe of her bosom, and lays the child that sucks her breast by the side of a fathomless stream. He shows her shrouds and empty coffins, figures stretched in white linen and kirkyard processions, and raises in her ear the wail of the matrons and the lyke-wake song. Heed not dreams therefore ; they are the delusions of him who seeks to sink our souls. But bless thy God, and cherish thy child ; keep his feet from the evil path, and his hand from the evil thing, and his tongue from uttering foolishness; and the boy shall become a stripling, and the stripling a man, wise in all his ways, and renowned in his generation, and thou shalt rejoice with abundance of joy."

"' While this devout person cheered my heart with his counsel, he was not unheard of those two foolish women; they liked not the wisdom of his words, nor his sayings concerning themselves, and they began with a fierce and sudden outcry, "A pretty elder, indeed," said the woman of the Rowantree-burn, "to come here in the shades and darkness of night to expound dreams to a rosy young widow. I'll warrant he would not care if the man-child were at the bottom of the Ladye's Lowe, so long as a full farm, a well-plenished house, and a loving dame in lily-white linen were to the fore. I wish I were a real witch for his sake, he should dree a kittle cast." The words of the mariner's wife chimed in with those of her antagonist. "A pretty elder, truly," said she, smiting her hands together close to his nose; "he'll come here to talk of sinful dreams, and flutes and dulcimers, and shaking of wanton legs, and the smiling of ensnaring eyes. And yet should the bairn of a poor body have a fairer look than ane's ain husband, he will threaten us with kirk censure and session rebuke, though it's weel kenned that mothers cannot command the complexion of their babes nor control the time when it pleases Providence to send them weeping into the world. There was my ain son Samuel; his father had sailed but ten months and a day when the sweet wean came ; where was the marvel of that? If there was not an indulgence, and acts of wondrous bounty and kindness, and blessings in the shape of babes showered upon mariners, sorrowful would their lives be, dwelling so far from their wives in the deep wide waters.'

"'"Woman, woman," said the elder, "I came not hither to hearken to thy confession ; go home and repent, and leave me to admonish the owner of this house, touching the dream with which her spirit is sorely troubled." "Admonish!" said the mariner's spouse, "I dare ye, sir, to use that word of scorn and kirk scandal to the widow of as douce a man as ever stepped in a black-leather shoe. Admonish, indeed ! If ye are so full of the gracious spirit of counsel and admonition, wherefore have ye not come to cheer me in my lonesome home, where all I have is two bairns to keep sadness from my fireside? My husband is sailing on the great deep, and has not blessed my sight these three long years; mickle need have I of some one to soothe my widow-like lot. I could find ye something like Scripture warrant for such kindness which ye wot not of." And the woman went her ways; the man tarried but a little while; and the woman of the Rowantree-burn departed also, admonishing me to remember her words, and do as she had desired.

"' It was on the third evening after I dreamed my dream that I thought on the woman's words; and I debated with myself if such seekings after future events by means of charms and spells were wise and according to the Word. But old beliefs, and legendary stories, and the assurances of many wise and venerable people, have ever proved too hard for the cunning of wisdom and the pure light of the Gospel; and I thought on my grandmother, to whom the person of my grandfather, then in a remote land, was shown in a vision one Hallowmas Eve, and so I went my ways. It was near midnight when I reached the Ladye's Lowe, and, seating myself on the place where I now sit, I looked sadly to the heaven, and sorrowfully to the waters. The moon had arisen with her horns half filled; the stars had gathered around her; the sheep lay white and clustering on the hillsides; the wild swans sailed in pairs along the quiet bosom of the lake; and the only sound I heard was that of the mother-duck, as she led her swarm of yellow young ones to graze on the tender herbage on the margin of the lake. I had wetted, as the woman bade me, the under-garment of my child, and hung it forth to dry on a little bush of broom, and there I sat watching it and ruminating on my lot, on the sorrows and joys of a mother. Midnight came; the lake lay still and beautiful; the wind was heard by fits among the bushes, and gushed gently over the bosom of the water with a sweet and a lulling sound. I looked and thought, and I thought and looked, till mine eyes waxed weary with watching, and I closed them for a time against the dazzling undulation of the water, which swelled and subsided beneath the clear moonlight. As I sat, something came before me as a vision in a dream, and I know not yet whether I slumbered or waked. Summer I thought was changed into winter, the reeds were frozen by the brook, snow lay white and dazzling on the ground, and a sheet of thick and transparent ice was spread over the bosom of the Ladye's Lowe. And, as I looked, the lake became crowded with men; I beheld the faces of many whom I knew, and heard the curling-stones rattle and ring, as they glided along the ice or smote upon one another; and the din and clamour of men flew far and wide. And my son appeared unto me, a child no more, but a stripling tall and fair and graceful, his fair hair curling on his shoulders. My heart leapt with joy.' And seven young men were with him; I knew them all—his school companions; and their seven mothers came, I thought, and stood by my side, and as we looked we talked of our children. As they glided along the ice, they held by each other's hands, and sang a song; above them all I heard the voice of my son, and my heart rejoiced. As the song concluded, I heard a shriek as of many drowning; but I saw nothing, for the ice was fled from the bosom of the lake, and all that was visible was the wild swans with the lesser water-fowl. But all at once I saw my son come from the bottom of the lake; his locks were disordered and drenched, and deadly paleness was in his looks. One bore him out of the water in his arms, and laid him at my feet on the bank. I swooned away; and when I came to myself, I found the morning light approaching, the lake fowl sheltering themselves among the reeds; and, stiff with cold, and with a heavy heart, I returned home.

"'Years passed on: my son grew fair and comely, out-rivalled his comrades at school, and became the joy of the young and the delight of the old. I often thought of my dream as I gazed on the child; and I said, in the fulness of a mother's pride, "Surely it was a vain and an idle vision, coloured into sadness by my fears; for a creature so full of life, and strength, and spirit, cannot pass away from the earth before his prime." Still, at other times the vision pressed on my heart, and I had sore combats with a misgiving mind; but I confided in Him above, and cheered my spirit as well as I might. I went with my son to the kirk, I accompanied him to the market, I walked with him on the green hills and on the banks of the deep rivers; I was with him in the dance, and my heart rejoiced to see him surpass the children of others: wherever he went, a mother's fears and a mother's feet followed him. Some derided my imaginings, and called me the dreaming widow;

while others spoke with joy of his beauty and attainments, and said he was a happy son who had so tender and so prudent a mother.

"'It happened in the seventh year from my dream that a great curling bonspiel was to be played between the youths and the wedded men of the parish; and a controversy arose concerning the lake on which the game should be decided. It was the middle of December; the winter had been open and green; till suddenly the storm set in, and the lakes were frozen equal to bear the weight of a heavy man in the first night's frost. Several sheets of frozen water were mentioned: ancient tale and ancient belief had given a charm to the Ladye's Lowe which few people were willing to break; and the older and graver portion of the peasantry looked on it as a place of evil omen, where many might meet, but few would part. All this was withstood by a vain and froward youth, who despised ancient beliefs as idle superstitions, traditionary legends as the labour of credulous men; and who, in the pride and vanity of human knowledge, made it his boast that he believed nothing. He proposed to play the bonspiel on the Ladye's Lowe; the foolish young men his companions supported his wish; and not a few among the sedater sort consented to dismiss proverbial fears and to play their game on these ominous waters. I thought it was a sad sight to see so many greyheads pass my threshold, and so many young heads following, to sport on so perilous a place; but curiosity could not be restrained—young and old, the dame and the damsel, crowded the banks of the lake to behold the contest; and I heard the mirth of their tongues and the sound of their curling-stones as I sat at my hearth-fire. One of the foremost was Benjie Spedlands.'

"The unhappy mother had proceeded thus far, when the demented youth, who till now had lain silent and motionless by the side of the lake, uttered a groan, and, starting suddenly to his feet, came and stood beside us. He shed back his long and moistened locks from a burning and bewildered brow, and looking steadfastly in her face for a moment, said, 'Rachel, dost thou know me?' She answered only with a flood of tears, and a wave of her hand to be gone. 'Know me! ay, how can ye but know me, since for me that deadly water opened its lips, and swallowed thy darling up. If ye have have a tongue to curse and a heart to scorn me, scorn me then, and curse me; and let me be seen no more on this blessed earth. For the light of day is misery to me, and the cloud of night is full of sorrow and trouble. My reason departs, and I go and sojourn with the beasts of the field: it returns, and I fly from the face of man; but wherever I go, I hear the death-shriek of eight sweet youths in my ear, and the curses of mothers' lips on my name.' 'Young man,' she said, 'I shall not curse thee, though thy folly has made me childless; nor shall I scorn thee, for I may not scorn the image of Him above; but go from my presence, and herd with the brutes that perish, or stay among men, and seek to soothe thy smitten conscience by holy converse and by sincere repentance.' 'Repentance!' he said, with a wildness of eye that made me start: 'of what have I to repent? Did I make that deep lake, and cast thy son, and the sons of seven others, bound into its bosom. Repentance belongs to him who does a deed of evil; sorrow is his who witlessly brings misfortunes on others; and such mishap was mine. Hearken, and ye shall judge.'

"And he sat down by the side of the lake, and, taking up eight smooth stones in his hand, dropped them one by one into the water; then, turning round to us, he said: 'Even as the waters have closed over those eight pebbles, so did I see them close over eight sweet children. The ice crashed, and the children yelled; and as they sunk, one of them, even thy son, put forth his hand, and seizing me by the foot, said, "Oh, Benjie! save me, save me!" But the love of life was too strong in me, for I saw the deep, the fathomless water; and, far below, I beheld the walls of the old tower, and I thought on those doomed yearly to perish in this haunted lake, and I sought to free my foot from the hand of the innocent youth. But he held me fast, and, looking in my face, said, "Oh, Benjie! save me, save me!" And I thought how I had wiled him away from his mother's threshold, and carried him and his seven companions to the middle of the lake, with the promise of showing him the haunted towers and courts of the drowned castle; but the fears for my own life were too strong; so, putting down my hand, I freed my foot, and, escaping over the ice, left him to sink with his seven companions. Brief, brief was his struggle—a crash of the faithless ice, a plunge in the fathomless water, and a sharp shrill shriek of youthful agony, and all was over for him; but for me, broken slumbers, and a burning brain, and a vision that will not pass from me, of eight fair creatures drowning.'

"Ere he had concluded the unhappy mother had leaped to her feet, and stretched forth her hands over him, and, with every feature dilated with agony, gathered up her strength to curse and to confound him. 'Oh! wretched and contemptible creature,' she said, 'were I a man, as I am but a feeble woman, I would tread thee as dust aneath my feet, for thou art unworthy to live. God gave thee his own form, and gave thee hands to save, not to destroy, his fairest handiworks; but what heart, save thine, could have resisted a cry for mercy from one so fair and so innocent? Depart from my presence; crawl—for thou art unworthy to walk like man—crawl as the reptiles do, and let the hills cover thee, or the deeps devour thee; for who can wish thy base existence prolonged? The mother is unblest that bare thee, and hapless is he who owns thy name. Hereafter shall men scorn to count kindred with thee. Thou hast no brother to feel for a brother's shame, no sister to feel for thee a sister's sorrow, no kinsman to mourn for the reproach of kindred blood. Cursed be she who would bear for thee the sacred name of wife. Seven sons would I behold—and I saw one—wae's me!—dragged from the bottom of that fatal lake; see them borne over my threshold, with their long hanks of fair hair wetting the pavement, as the lovely locks of my sweet boy did, and stretch their lily limbs in linen which my own hands had spun for their bridal sheets, even as I stretched my own blessed child—rather than be the mother of such a wretch as thou!' From this fearful malediction, the delirious youth sought not to escape; he threw himself with his face to the earth, spread out his hands on the turf, and renewed his sobbings and his moans, while the sorrowful mother returned to a cheerless home and an empty fireside.

"Such was her fearful dream; and such was its slow, but sure and unhappy, fulfilment. She did not long survive the desolation of her house. Her footsteps were too frequent by the lake, and by the grave of her husband and child, for the peace of her spirit; she faded, and sank away; and now the churchyard grass grows green and long above her. Old people stop by her grave, and relate with a low voice, and many a sigh, her sad and remarkable story. But grass will never grow over the body of Benjie Spedlands. He was shunned by the old and loathed by the young; and the selfish cruelty of his nature met with the singular punishment of a mental alienation, dead to all other feeling save that of agony for the death of the eight children. He wandered into all lonesome places, and sought to escape from the company of all living things. His favourite seat was on a little hill-top, which overlooks the head of the Ladye's Lowe. There he sat watching the water, with an intensity of gaze which nothing could interrupt. Sometimes he was observed to descend with the swiftness of a bird in its flight, and dash into the lake, and snatch and struggle in the water like one saving a creature from drowning. One winter evening, a twelvemonth from the day of the fatal catastrophe on the lake, he was seen to run round its bank like one in agony, stretching out his hands, and shouting to something he imagined he saw in the water. The night grew dark and stormy; the sleet fell, and thick hail came, and the winds augmented. Still his voice was heard at times far shriller than the tempest—old men shuddered at the sound—about midnight it ceased, and was never heard more. His hat was found floating by the side of the water, but he was never more seen nor heard of—his death-lights, glimmering for a season on the lake, told to many that he had found, perhaps sought, a grave in the deepest part of the Ladye's Lowe."

ALLAN-A-MAUT.

Good Allan-a-Maut lay on the rigg,
One called him bear, one called him bigg;
An old dame slipped on her glasses: "Aha!
He'll waken," quoth she, "with joy to us a'."
The sun shone out, down dropped the rain,
He laughed as he came to life again;
And carles and carlins sung who saw't,
Good luck to your rising, Allan-a-Maut.

Good Allan-a-Maut grew green and rank,
With a golden beard and a shapely shank,
And rose sae steeve, and waxed sae stark.
He whomelt the maid, and coupit the clark;
The sick and lame leaped hale and weel,
The faint of heart grew firm as steel,
The douce nae mair called mirth a faut,
Such charms are mine, quoth Allan-a-Maut.

The person who chanted this famous border bousing-rhyme was a tall young man, whose shaggy greatcoat, brass-headed riding whip, and long sharp spurs projecting from behind his massy and iron-heeled boots, might denote him to be a dealer in horses, accoutred for Rosley Hill or Dumfries Fairs. But his inner coat, lined with silk, and studded with silver buttons, a small gold chain round his neck, from which depended a heart of rock crystal, enclosing a tress of nut-brown hair, and half concealed among ruffles of the finest cambric, edged with rich lace, might belong to an opulent and fantastic youth fond of finery, proud of a handsome person, and vain of his influence among the border maidens.

His singular song and remarkable dress attracted instant attention. His character was thus hit off by a demure old dame in a whisper to me, during the applause which followed his song. "He's a frank and a conceited youth, sir; the owner of a fair estate, and well known among the merry maids of Cumberland and Dumfriesshire at fairs and dancings, when his patrimony is showered down among the gay and the cherry-lipped, in the shape of snoods, and ribbons, and gloves. Nor will ye hinder him to reign the chief of chaps in the change-house, when the tale and the strong drink circulate together: who like Lacie Dacre, I should be glad to know, for chanting bousing-ballads and telling merry adventures? He's the wildest of all our border spirits, and his exploits with the brandy-cup and the ale-flagon have obtained him the name of Allan-a-Maut—a scrap of an old-world song, sir, with which young Spend-pelf ever commences and concludes his merriment. I have said my worst of the lad—I believe he's a kind-hearted chield, and as true to his word as the cup is to his lip. And now listen to his story, for I'll warrant it a queer one." And as she concluded, he commenced.

"That song," said the youth, "rude and uncouth though it seems, pitches, as a musician would say, the natural tone or key of the tale I have to tell; it was far from unwise in me to sing it; and so, with this explanation, I will proceed. It happened some summers ago, as I was returning, during the grey of the morning, from a love tryste in a green glen on the banks of Annan water, I fell into a kind of reverie; and what should the subject of it be but the many attachments my heart had formed among the maidens, and the very limited requital the law allows one to make to so many sweet and gentle creatures. My spirit was greatly perturbed, as ye may guess, with this sorrowful subject; and a thick mist, which the coming sun seemed unable to dispel, aided me in totally mistaking my way; and I could not well mistake it further, for I found myself in a region with which I had formed no previous acquaintance: I had wandered into a brown and desolate heath, the mist rolled away in heavy wreaths before me, and followed close on my heels, with the diligence of an evil spirit.

"All hill and woodland mark, our usual country guides, were obscured, and I strayed on till I came to the banks of a moorland brook, stained by the soil through which it passed, till it flowed the colour of the brownest brandy. The tenants of this desert stream partook of the congenial nature of the region; they were not of that swift and silver-speckled sort described by the pastoral-verse-makers, but of a dull and dark mottled kind, and so lean and haggard as to be wholly unworthy of a fisher's bait. I caught one under the mossy bank, and returned it again to the stream as unfit for food.

I saw no living thing in my course across this desert; the heron, that beautiful and solitary bird, rejected it for a haunt; and even the wild moor-fowl, which in the fowler's proverb feeds on the heather-top, sought neither food nor shelter amid the brown and dreary wilderness.

"I came at last to a thick and gloomy plantation of Scotch firs, which, varying the bleak desolation of the moor, gave me the assurance that, some thirty years before, the hand of man had been busied in the region. A fence of loose stone, surmounted by a rude cope or cornice of rough sharp rock, presented an effectual barrier to sheep and even deer. The latter animals will overleap a high wall of firm masonry, but turn back from a very slender impediment which threatens insecure footing.

"The soil had in many places proved ungenial to Scotch firs, the hardiest of all forest trees; they grew in dwarfish and stunted clumps, and exceeded not the altitude of ordinary shrubs. In passing along the side of the fence, I came to a hollow, where the masses of high green bracken betokened a richer soil. Here the trees, striking deep into the mossy loam, towered up into a beautiful and extensive grove, relieved in their gloomy appearance by the wild cherry and mountain ash, at that time covered with bloom. Behind me the moor spread out high and uneven, full of quagmires and pits, out of which the peasants of Annan Vale cut peats for fuel.

"I observed, winding through the field of bracken, a kind of trodden way, resembling a hare-road, which, passing over the fence, by the removal of the cope-stones, dived directly into the bosom of the wood. The path, too, seemed marked with men's feet; and, with the hope of its leading me to some human abode, I entered the plantation. The wood, fair and open at first, became thick and difficult; the road, too, grew sinuous and perplexing; and I was compelled to pull aside the thick masses of boughs, and, gliding gently into the aperture, make the best of my way by sleight and stratagem.

"I had proceeded in this way nearly half a mile, when I came to the foot of one of those vast rocks which tower up so abrupt and unexpectedly on many of the Scottish heaths. It semeed a pile of prodigious stones huddled rudely together in the careless haste of creation, rather than a regular rock. Deep chasms, and openings resembling caves, were visible in many places, shagged round the entrance with heath-berry; and, where the plant that bears this delicious fruit failed to grow, the hardier ivy took root, and with little nourishment shot up into small round masses, called fairy-seats by the peasantry. At the foot of the precipice, some hundreds of high and shivered stones stood on end, like a Druidic grove, but in sevenfold confusion, and here and there a fir inserted in the clefts of the rock struggled for life; while the ivy, shooting its stems to the summit of the crag, shook down a profusion of green tendrils, and crawled along the ground again, till the mossy soil, which bubbled up water at every step, arrested the march of the beautiful evergreen. Around the crag, a circle of spruce firs was planted; while high over the whole the rock rose savage and grey, and gave the eagles, which not infrequently visited its summit, a view over some of the fairest pasture lands in Annandale.

"The desolation of the place was heightened by the absence of living water—the voice of the brook, which lends the tongue of life to many a dreary place. A little puddle of brown moorish water supplied the place of a fountain; around its margin the bones of hares and fowls were strewn; while in a recess in the rock the fox had sought a lair, and heaped it high with wool and feathers. But the proverbial lord of craft and cunning had for some time forsaken this once favourite abode; the presence of man had intruded on his wild domain, and driven him to the neighbouring mountains.

"I climbed to the summit of the rock, and gazed down the vale of Annan as far as the sea of Solway, and westward as far as the green hills of Nithsdale. To enable me more pleasantly to enjoy the beauty of a scene which Turner, or Callcott, or Dewint would love to consecrate, I proceeded to discuss the merits of some ewe-milk cheese, made for me by the lily-white hand of Jessie Johnstone, of Snipeflosh; and the gift of the maiden began to vanish before the sharp-set perseverance of youth. The sun too, dispelling the fog, gleamed over the green heads of the groves in all his summer glory, and I proceeded to examine how I might find out the way to Ae Water, to the dwelling of bonnie Bess Dinwoodie.

"While I sat gazing about me, I observed a thin and curling line of smoke ascending from the base of the crag; it rose up thicker and blacker, and, wafted by the wind, gushed against my face; I never felt a vapour so strange and offensive. As I proceeded to consider the various kinds of exhalations which arise from forest or fen, I saw a large and hungry dog come out of the wood. It uttered a cry of discovery, half howl and half bark, and, coming near, seemed willing to leap at my throat. I threw it a piece of cheese; it caught and devoured it, and renewed its clamour. It was soon joined, to my utter dismay, by a human being. I never beheld a man with a look so startled and threatening. He was tall and strong-built, with hair long and matted, the colour of ashes, while his eyes, large and staring and raw, looked, as Lancie Lauborde the tailor said, 'like scored collops bordered with red plush.'

"He addressed me in a tone that in nowise redeemed his savage appearance. 'Weel met, quoth the wolf to the fox; weel met, my crafty lad. So ye have found out the bonnie bee-byke at last, as the boy said when he thrust his hand into the adder's den. I maun ken more about ye, my lad; so tell me thy tale cleverly; else, I swear by the metal worm through which my precious drink dribbles, I will feast the fox and her five cubs on thy spool-bane. On my conscience, lad, as ye brew, so shall ye drink; and that's o'er fair a law for a gauger.' What this depraved being meant by his mysterious language, and what calling he followed, were alike matters of conjecture; his manner was certainly hostile and threatening. I told him I was passing towards the vale of Ae, and had lost my way in the mist. 'Lost your way in the mist, and found the way ye were seeking for, my wylie lad, I'll warrant; but I shall come at the bare truth presently.' So saying, he laid the flap of his shaggy coat aside, and, showing me a brace of pistols, and the hilt of a dirk stuck in a belt of rough leather, motioned me to follow him.

"Resistance was hopeless; we descended from the rock by a winding and secret way, concealed among the ivy, and the branches of a spreading spruce fir. This brought us to a rude structure, resembling a shepherd's shed, half cavern and half building, and nearly hidden under the involving branches of two luxuriant firs. My guide half pushed me into this unpromising abode; a miserable hovel, loathsome and foul, and filled with a thick and noisome vapour. I was greeted on my entrance by a squat, thick-set, and squalid being, who, starting up from a couch of straw, exclaimed, 'Wha in the fiend's name's this ye have driven into our bit den of refuge in the desert, as ane wad drive a ratton into a trap? Deil drown me in a strong distillation, and that's an enviable death, if this lad's no a stripling exciseman, whelped in our unhappy land by the evil spirits of the government. If he's a gauger, take ye the spade and dig, and I'll take the sword and strike; for he shall never craw day again, else my name's nae mair Jock Mackleg.' And the wretch, as he spoke, proceeded to sharpen an old sword on the strake of a scythe.

"'Hooly, man, hooly with thy bit of rusty airn,' said his companion, 'ye're no sae handy with it when its warse needed, Jock, ye ken. I shall allow the young lad to live, be he devil, or be he gauger, and that's meikle waur, were it only that he might partake of that glorious spirit which I call "stupefy," but which wiser Jock Mackleg christened "heart's blood," and learn of what a princely beverage he would deprive this poor taxed and bleeding land.' It happened well for me that these two wretches, though born for each other's society, like bosom bones, and necessary to each other in their detestable pursuits as the bark is to the bush, chose to be of different opinions respecting the mode of managing me, and thus John Mackleg expressed his dissent from his more moderate as well as powerful associate. 'And so he's to live and to taste of the "heart's blood!"' Deil turn him into our distilling-worm first, that the liquid consolation the gauger tribe seek to deprive us of may run reeking through him. Ah, Mungo Macubin, ye're soft, ye're soft; ye would give the supervisor himself our hain'd drops of distillery dew; and for fear he should drop into a ditch, ye would carry him hame. I'll tell ye what— were ye Mungo Macubin seven times told, I will cease to be longer conjunct and several with you; else may I be whipt through the lang burgh of Lochmaben, with the halter of a gauger's horse.' And still growling out anger, which he dared not more openly express, he threw himself down on a litter bed, while his companion, with a look of scorn, answered: 'Thou predestined blockhead, am I a blind stabber behind backs in the dark, like thyself? Am I to harm the white skin of this young raw haspen of a lad, unless I ken why and wherefore? Spill his sweet life indeed! Faith, if this lad threatened ye with six inches of cauld steel in his hand, though water five fathoms deep and seven mile wide divided ye, ye would be less free of your threats. So lie still there, and put thy bonnet on thy bald scalp, from which whisky has scalded the hair. Ay, that will do. Now sit down, my wandering man of the mist, let me have a look at thee; but first hold this cup of "stupefy" to thy head. Faith, my birkie, if I thought ye kenn'd the might of whisky by mathematical measuring, or any other dangerous government mode of ascertaining spirituous strength, I'd make ye swallow yere gauging sticks. So sit down; else, by the spirit of malt and the heart of corn, I will make thee obedient.'

"I sat down on an empty cask, and holding in my hand a cup full of the hot and untaken-down liquor, which my entertainers were busied in preparing, I could not but give a few hurried glances round this wretched lodge in the wilderness. The cabin itself seemed more the creation of distempered or intoxicated intellects than the work of consideration and sobriety. At the entrance of a kind of cavern in the rock a rude enclosure of stone was raised, the whole covered over with boughs and turf, with an opening in the side capable of admitting one person at a time. The floor was bedded with rushes and bracken, but trodden into mire, and moistened with a liquor of a flavour so detestable that I felt half suffocated; while the steam of a boiling caldron, mingling with the bitter smoke of green firwood, eddied round and round, and then gushed out into the morning air through the aperture by which I entered. In the cavern itself I observed a fire glimmering, and something of the shape of a human being stretched motionless before it. This personage was clad in a garb of rough sheepskin, the wool shorn, or rather singed close, and an old fur-cap slouched over his ears, while his feet, wholly bare, and nearly soot-black, were heated among the warm ashes which he raked from the caldron fire. He lay on his belly, supporting his head with his hands; and about all his person nothing was white but the white of his eye. Beside him stood what seemed an old tobacco-box; he dipped it frequently into a pail of liquor, and each time he carried it to his head a strong smell of whisky was diffused over the place.

"On the right hand of this menial drudge lay the person of John Mackleg: an old Sanquhar rug interposed between him and the foul litter below; a small cask, the spigot of which was worn by frequent use, stood within reach; while a new-drained cup lay at his head, with a crust of bread beside it. On the other side sat Mungo Macubin, on a seat covered with a sheepskin; and compared to his debased and brutish companions he seemed a spirit of light. In spite of his disordered locks, and the habitual intoxication in which his eyes swam, his look was inviting, and even commanding. Something of better days and brighter hopes appeared about him. But in his eye frequently glimmered that transient and equivocal light, suspicious and fierce, which, influenced by drink and inflamed by contradiction, rendered him an insecure companion. A sword lay on a shelf beside him, with several tattered books, a fish-spear, a fishing-rod, and a fowling-piece; and a fiddle, tuned perhaps during the delirium of drink, hung there with its disordered strings. I observed, too, the machinery of a wooden clock, the labour, I afterwards learned, of his knife; together with several spoons and cups of sycamore, which he wanted the patience rather than the skill to finish. The notice which I took of this part of the establishment seemed far from displeasing to the proprietor.

"Around the shealing stood kegs and vessels for containing liquor, all of portable dimensions, such as a man might readily carry; and I wanted not this to convince me that a whisky-still of considerable magnitude was busy in the bosom of this wilderness. In the middle of the floor stood a rude table, the top of which had belonged to some neighbouring orchard, and still threatened in large letters the penalties of traps and guns to nightly depredators. It was swimming with liquor, and strewn with broken cups; and in the midst of the whole lay several of those popular publications which preach up the equality of human intellect and estate, and recommend, along with a general division of worldly goods, a more tolerant system of intercourse between the sexes. No doubt the excellent authors of those works would regard this appearance of their labours amid the Caledonian desert as a certain proof of fame; they would seek more than ever to attract men's affections to a more flexible system of morality; to awaken a kind of devotion which affords more scope to the natural passions of the multitude, and to wean human regard from that austere doctrine which inculcates self-denial, and sundry other such unreasonable matters. On a paper which contained a printed list of rewards given by government to men who had laboured for the good of their country, I observed a calculation of the proceeds of illicit distillations; while on the floor lay the skin of a fat wether recently killed, which still bore the mark of a neighbouring farmer, whose consent to this appropriation my companions, in the full relish of liberty, had not thought it necessary to obtain.

" During this examination the eye of John Mackleg dwelt upon all my motions with increasing jealousy and distrust. At length, when my glance settled on the sheepskin, he exclaimed, in a tone reproving and harsh, 'Deil be in ye, Mungo Macubin; will ye let that fiend's baited hook of a gauger sit quietly there, and take an inventory of the only world's goods the oppression of man has left us? Take tent, lad, take tent; ye think him a bird that means nae mischief in his sang; bide ye a bit, ye may find him worse than a water-adder, and as cunning as lang Sandie Frizel the sautman, who praised the tone of your fiddle and your skill in cup-making, and having proven the excellence of our distillation, sent auld Wylie Metestick, the gauger, to look at our cavern of curiosities!' 'I'll tell ye what, John,' said his companion; 'guide your tongue in a less graceless manner, else it may bring your foreteeth and my right-hand knuckles acquainted. Gauger! What puts it into thy gowk's head that the lad's a gauger? Thinkest thou that a single exciseman, and ane both soft and slim, would have dropped down into the adder's den? But where's the profit of carousing with such a clod of the valley as thee?' Here the chief manager of this illicit establishment rose, and looked out into the wood; returned to his seat; and thus he resumed his conversation.

"'But where's the profit of putting trust in such a capon as thee? When the day comes that we have long looked for, you will put your hand to the full tankard rather than to the sharpened steel. And such a desirable day is not far distant, else let man believe no longer in white paper and black print. What says Ringan Alarum, of the Cowgate, in his strong paper called "Liberty's Lighted Match," which auld Davie Dustyhause, the west-country skin-man, gave us when we sold him our cannily-come-by skins of three mug ewes. Does he not say as much as that the sceptre will soon be more harmless than a shepherd's staff; the mitre as little reverenced as grey hairs or a scone-bonnet; a coronet as empty as a drunkard's drained cup; and that Sunday shall be as Saturday, and Saturday as Sunday; that a silken gown, flounced and furbelowed, will rustle as common in a peasant's sheal as the plaiden kirtle of maid Margery; and that Meg Milligan, in her linsey-woolsey, will be as good and as lordly as our madames with their perfumes and pearlins? Now John, my man, should all these pleasant things come to pass, I will build a whisky-still as big as Wamphray kirk, with a distillation-pipe large enough to pour a flood of pure spirit over the land, in which we might float a revenue cutter.'

"Flooded as the brain of John Mackleg seemed to be with the spirit which his own industry had produced, he had intellect enough remaining to appear visibly delighted with this promised picture of enjoyment. But his natural want of courage withheld him from indulging in his comrade's strain of unguarded rapture. 'O Lord, send it soon and sudden, Mungo! O man, soon and sudden! But I conjure ye, by the pith and power of malt, to speak lowne; O man, speak lowne.' 'Then,' said his comrade, 'await the coming of the blessed time in silence. When it comes we shall have whisky-stills in every kirk, and he that drinks longest shall rule and reign among us. I will choose myself out a warm home in a fertile land. The justice of the peace shall be dumb, and the gauger silent, and his measuring rods regarded no more. Our young men shall drink, and our young maidens dance; the minister of the parish shall fill our cups, and the pulpit and repentance-stool shall hold flagons and mutchkin stoups. I will go to bed with six pint stoups placed at my feet and six at my head; and when I grow doited and dizzy, the sweetest lass in the country-side shall sit and hold my head.' 'And I,' said John Mackleg, in a low and cautious tone, 'shall be the first laird of my whole kin; whisky-brose shall be my breakfast, and my supper shall be the untaken-down spirit, with strength enough to float a pistol-bullet. I shall be the first of the name of Mackleg who owned more land than they measured in the dowie kirkyard.'

"His companion eyed him with a look particularly merry and ironical. 'O thou ambitious knave,' said Mungo Macubin, 'dost thou long to be lord of all the land which thou hast measured with thy drunken carcass? Why, man, thou hast meted out with that genealogical ell-wand half the land 'tween the sea-sand of Caerlaverock and the brown heathy hills of Durisdeer. And so thou thinkest a drunkard's fall on the earth has given thee possession of it? Plague take me, if I give my consent to such a dangerous monopoly.' The perverse being to whom this speech was addressed made light of its irony, and, seizing a large two-eared quaigh, stooped his face into it till nothing remained above the brim save a fleece of sooty uncombed locks, and drained out the liquor at a breath. He hurled the empty cup to the figure before the fire, and, though opposed by violent hiccupings, exclaimed, "More! bring me more! That was delicious. Jock, Jenny Mason's Jock, fill that cog, my man, and hear ye me: come hither and haud it to my head, for I am no sae sicker as I should be, and that whin-stone rock seems as if it would whomble aboon me. And d'ye hear me, Jock Laggengird, let me have none of the dyke-water additions which Mungo Macubin makes to the prime spirit which he drinks. Taxes and stents have made Scotland's crowdie thin, and turned her warm brose into cauld steerie. If ye covet the present length of your lugs, let me have none of your penitential potations.'

"While Jenny Mason's descendant crawled to a cask, and turned a pin from which a pure liquid dribbled drop by drop into the cup, Mungo Macubin took down his fiddle, arranged the disordered strings, played a pleasant air, and accompanied it by singing the following rustic verses, which I have since learned were of his own composition.

MUNGO MACUBIN'S SONG.

Come toom the stoup! Let the merry sun shine
On sculptured cups and the merry man's wine;
Come toom the stoup! From the bearded bear,
And the heart of corn, comes this life-drink dear.
The reap-hook, the sheaf, and the flail for me;
Away with the drink of the slave's vine tree.
The spirit of malt sae free and sae frank,
Is my minted money and bonds in the bank.

Come toom up the stoup! What must be must,
I'm cauld and cankered, and dry as dust;
A simmering stoup of this glorious weet
Gives scaring plumes to Time's leaden feet.
Let yon stately madam, so mim and so shy,
Arch her white neck proud, and sail prouder by;
The spirit of maut, so frank and so free,
Is daintier than midnight madam to me.

Drink fills us with joy and gladness, and soon
Hangs cankered care on the horns of the moon;
Is bed and bedding; and love and mirth
Dip their wings in drink ere they mount from the earth.
Come toom the stoup—it's delightful to see
The world run round, fit to whomel on me;
And yon bonnie bright star, by my sooth it's a shiner,
Ilka drop that I drink it seems glowing diviner.

Away with your lordships of mosses and mools,
With your women, the plague and the plaything of fools;
Away with your crowns, and your sceptres, and mitres;
Lay the parson's back bare to the rod of the smiters;
For wisdom wastes time, and reflection is folly,
Let learning descend to the score and the tally.
Lo! the floor's running round, the roof's swimming in glory,
And I have but breath for to finish my story.

"The arch, and something of a drunken gravity, with which this rhyme was chanted, with the accompanying 'thrum, thrum' on the fiddle, rendered it far from unpleasant. John Mackleg, whether desirous of emulating his companion, or smitten, perhaps, with a wayward desire of song, raised himself up from his lair, and improved the melody of a wild and indecorous rhyme by the hollow sound extracted by means of his drinking quaigh from the head of an empty barrel. I can trust myself with repeating four of the verses only; the others, when the drink is at home and the understanding gone out, may be endured at midnight by the lee-side of a bowl of punch; but I see by the gathering storm in the brow of that sedate dame that I have said enough about the graceless song, yet she will endure a specimen, I have some suspicion.

JOHN MACKLEG'S SONG.

Good evening to thee, madam moon,
 Sing brown barley bree,
Good evening to thee, madam moon,
 Sing bree;
So gladsomely ye're glowering down,
I'u' loth am I to part so soon,
But all the world is running roun'
 With me.

A fair good morrow to thee, sun,
 Sing brown barley bree;
A fair good morrow to thee, sun,
 Sing bree;

> Ye laugh and glory in the fun—
> But look, my stoup is nearly run,
> And, 'las ! my cash is mair than done,
>   With me.
>
> Good morrow to thee, lovesome lass,
>   Sing brown barley bree,
> Good morrow to thee, lovesome lass,
>   Sing bree;
> Who wooes thee on the gowany grass,
> Ere he has cooled him with the tass,
> Should through a threefold penance pass,
>   For me.
>
> Oh, fair's the falcon in his flight,
>   Sing brown barley bree;
> And sweet's a maiden at midnight,
>   Sing bree:
> And welcome is the sweet sunlight,
> But here's a sweeter, blither sight,
> The blood of barley pouring bright,
>   For me.

"Such was a part of the song, and the better part of it. As soon as he had ended his unmelodious chant, he silently raised the quaigh of liquor to his lips, and, laying his head back, the liquid descended into the crevice, as water drops into the chink of a rock. In a moment he started up, with curses murmuring on his lips, and hurling the quaigh, half full of liquor, at the head of the son of Janet Mason, exclaimed: 'Sinner that thou art, thou hast filled my cup out of the barrel of reduced spirit prepared for Andrew Erngrey, the Cameronian. It is as cauld and fizzenless as snow-water, though good enough to cheer the saints at a mountain preaching. I tell ye, my man, if you indulge yourself in such unsonsie pranks, I shall bait Mungo Macubin's fox-trap with your left lug.'

"The drunkard's missile was hurled by a hand which it had helped to render unsteady; it flew over the prostrate descendant of Janet Mason, and, striking against the furnace, poured its contents into the fire. Such was the strength of the liquid, that, subdued as it was for a devout person's use, the moment it touched the fire a sudden and bright flame gushed up to the roof of the shealing, and, kindling the dried grassy turf, flashed along it like gunpowder. I started up, and, seizing the raw sheepskin, fairly smothered and struck out the flame, which would soon have consumed the whole illicit establishment. As I resumed my seat, Mungo Macubin seized my hand, and, nearly wringing it from my wrist, in joy exclaimed, 'By my faith, lad, ye are a rid-handed one, and well do ye deserve a share in the profits of our distillation. Who would have thought that a stolen sheepskin, or rather the skin of a stolen sheep, could have quenched such a furious flame? And now, let me tell you, John Mackleg, if you touch whisky or let whisky touch you, for these four-and-twenty hours, I will surely measure out your inheritance with that scoundrel carcass of yours.' And with a stamp of his foot, and a lour of his brow, he awed his companion into fear and submission.

"I could see that the chief conductor of this wild establishment no longer regarded me with distrust or suspicion. He seated himself between his fiercer comrade and me, as if he dreaded outrage; and, pulling a soiled book from his bosom, appeared to examine it with some attention. It was one of those political labours of the London press, where the author, addressing himself to the multitude, had called in the powerful aid of engraving to render the obscurity of language intelligible. Our southern peasantry, with that love of the simplicity of ancient days which regards instruction as a trick of state, and wishes to reduce the tyranny of learning to the primitive score and tally, have maintained their natural condition in such entire purity, that literature in addressing them is fain to make use of sensible signs and tokens. Of these this book was full; but its owner turned over the leaves with a dissatisfied and disdainful eye, and at last threw it in contempt into the caldron fire. He took up his fiddle again, and, after playing snatches of several serious airs, sang some verses with a tone of bitter sorrow which showed little sympathy with the poetry. I remember several stanzas.

MY MIND TO ME MY KINGDOM IS.

Full thirty winter snows, last yule,
Have fallen on me mid pine and dool;
My clothing scant, my living spare,
I've reckoned kin with woe and care;
I count my days and mete my grave;
While Fortune to some brainless knave
Holds up her strumpet cheek to kiss:
My mind to me my kingdom is.

For faded friendship need I sigh,
Or love's warm raptures long flown by,
When fancy sits and fondly frames
Her angels out of soulless dames?
Sick of ripe lips and sagemen's rules,
The faith of knaves and fash of fools;
And scorning that, and loathing this,
My mind to me my kingdom is.

The Muse with laurel'd brow in vain
Sweeps by me with her visioned train;
I've bowed my head and ruled my hand
Too long beneath her magic wand.
Shall I go shrouded to my hearse,
Full of the folly of vain verse?
I'll court some soberer, surer bliss;
My mind to me my kingdom is.

"Something in the song of Mungo Macubin had awakened a train of thought of a nature too soft for his present hazardous calling; his looks darkened down in a kind of moody sorrow, and I could imagine that retrospection was busy with him. He observed the interest which my looks testified I took in his fate, took me by the hand with much kindness, and said, in a mingled tone of bitterness and sorrow: 'I have often thought that we have less control over our fate than we ought, and that an evil destiny dogs us through life, and pursues us to perdition. Take counsel, I beseech ye, from my words, and warning from my conduct; this shealing contains a being whose fate may be a text for you to preach from till these black locks grow grey. Listen, and then say with the Word, "Surely one vessel is made for honour, and another for dishonour." All I have cherished, or loved, or looked with kindness upon, have passed away, departed, and sunk to death or dishonour; and all I have saved from the stream of destiny is the wretched wreck on which you look. I beheld men of dull and untutorable intellects blessed and doubly blessed. I saw the portion of folly growing as lordly as the inheritance of wisdom, and I said, in the vanity of my heart, shall I not also be beloved and happy? But man's success is not of his own shaping: my cattle died, my crops failed, my means perished, and one I loved dearly forgot me; I could have forgiven that— she forgot herself. I have nothing now to solace or cheer me; I look forward without hope, and the present moment is so miserable that I seek to forget myself in the company of two wretches who are not disturbed with those forebodings which are as a demon to me. This stringed instrument, the carving of these cups, and the making of that wooden timepiece, with that caldron brimful to me of the liquor of oblivion, form the sum of all existing enjoyment. But from them, from this sodded sheal, from this barren spot, and this lonesome desert I shall soon be dragged or driven; for, sorrowful and miserable as I am, my lot is far too happy to last.'

"Never were words more ominously true than the last words of poor Mungo Macubin. Even as he spoke a human shadow darkened the door, another succeeded, and a third and a fourth followed close behind; he saw all this with a composure of face and an alacrity of resource truly surprising. He drew his pistol, he bared his sword, and, at the motion of his hand, the silent and prostrate being at the caldron snatched a piece of blazing fir from the fire, and sought counsel from the conduct or motions of his leader. I heard a sort of suppressed parley at the door, and presently several armed men made a dash through the aperture, exchanging blow and shot with Macubin, who, overthrowing one of the boldest of the officers, forced his way unhurt through all opposition, and disappeared in the thick wood. Meanwhile, his companion applying the fir-torch to the roof, the shealing was filled with smoke, and flame, and human outcry. The fire seized the combustible wood, touched the inflammable spirit, and, wrapping all in a flame, ascended in a high and bright column above the green forest. I escaped into the wood, and never saw that wild spot, nor one of those men, more."

MILES COLVINE,

THE CUMBERLAND MARINER.

WILLIAM GLEN was our captain's name;
He was a bold and a tall young man,
As brave a sailor as e'er sailed the sea,
And he was bound for New Barbarie.

The first of April we spread our sail,
To a low, a sweet, and a pleasant gale;
With a welcome wind on a sunny sea,
Away we sailed for New Barbarie.

We had not sailed more days than two,
Till the sky waxed dark and the tempest blew;
The lightning flashed, and loud roared the sea,
As we were bound for New Barbarie.

Old Ballad.

ON the Cumberland side of the firth of Solway lies a long line of flat and unelevated coast, where the sea-fowl find refuge from the gun of the fowler, and which, save the barren land and the deep sea, presents but one object to our notice —the ruins of a rude cottage, once the residence of Miles Colvine, the Mariner. The person who built this little house of refuge, a seaman, a soldier, a scholar, and a gentleman, suffered shipwreck on the coast; and it was not known for a time that any one else had escaped from the fatal storm. His vessel was from a foreign land, had no merchandise aboard, nor seemed constructed for traffic; and when the tempest drove her along the Allanbay shore, three persons only were visible on deck. Something mysterious hung over the fate of the vessel and crew. The conduct of Miles Colvine was less likely to remove than confirm suspicion; he was a silent and melancholy man; and when the peasantry who saved him from the storm inquired concerning the history of his ship and seamen, he heard them, but answered them not, and seemed anxious to elude all conversation on the subject. As they stood on the beach, looking at the bursting of the billows, and listening to the howling of the storm, the remains of the ship were shivered to pieces, and a large portion of the deck floated ashore at their feet. The planks seemed stained with blood and with wine; and as the peasants hauled it out to the dry land, one of them asked him if it was wet with the blood of beasts or men. "With the blood of both," was the answer. They left the shore, and sought no further intercourse with him.

Where the vessel was wrecked, there he seemed determined to remain; he built a little hut, fenced it round with a wall of loose stone, and lived in it without molestation from any one. He shunned the fishermen of Allanbay and the seamen of Skinverness, nor seemed pleased when the children of the peasantry carried him little presents of food; he sought and found his subsistence in the water. It was the common remark of the fishermen that no man dipped a hook or wetted a net, between Skinverness and Saint Bees, with greater skill and success. In this solitude, exposed to every storm that swept the beach from sea or land, amid much seeming wretchedness and privation, he resided during a summer and autumn: winter, a season of great severity on an unsheltered coast, was expected either to destroy or drive him from his dwelling; but he braved every storm, and resisted all offers of food or raiment.

The first winter of his abode was one of prodigious storm and infinite hardship. The snow lay long and deep on the ground, the ice was thick on lake and pool, and the Solway presented one continual scene of commotion and distress. The shore was covered with the wrecks of ships, the eddies choked with drowned men, and the sea itself so rough and boisterous, that the fishermen suspended their customary labours, and sat with their families at the hearth-fire, listening to the sounding of the surge, and relating tales of maritime disaster and shipwreck. But on Miles Colvine the severe and continued storm seemed to have no influence. He ranged the shore, collecting for his fire the wrecks of ships; he committed his nets and hooks to the sea with his usual skill; and having found a drifted boat, which belonged to some unfortunate vessel, he obtained command over the element most congenial to his heart, and wandered about on the bosom of the waters noon and night, more like a troubled spirit than a human being. When the severity of winter had passed away, and sea-birds laid their eggs in the sand, the mariner remitted his excursions at sea, and commenced a labour which surprised many. The sea-shore, or that portion of the coast which lies between the margin of the sea and the cultivated land—a region of shells, drift sand, and pebbles—has ever been regarded as a kind of common; and the right of suspending nets, hauling boats aground, and constructing huts for the summer residence of the fishermen has never been disputed by the owners of those thriftless domains. It was on this debatable ground, between the barren sea and the cultivated field, that the mariner fixed his abode; but it soon appeared that he wished to extend his possessions and augment his household accommodation. He constructed a larger and more substantial house, with equal attention to durability and neatness; he fenced off the sea by a barrier of large stones, and scattered around his dwelling a few of the common flowers which love to blossom near the sea breeze. The smoke of his chimney, and the unremitting clank of his hammer finishing the interior accommodations, were seen and heard from afar. When all this was concluded, he launched his boat and took to the sea again, and became known from the Mull of Galloway to the foot of Annan Water.

I remember, the first time that ever I saw him was in the market-place of Dumfries: his beard seemed of more than a year's growth; his clothes, once rich and fine, were darned and patched; and over the whole he wore a kind of boat-cloak, which, fastened round his neck, descended nigh the ground; but all this penury could not conceal the step and air of other and better days. He seldom looked in the face of any one; man he seemed to regard with an eye of scorn, and even deadly hatred; but on women he looked with softness and regard; and when he happened to meet a mother and child, he gazed on them with an eye of settled sorrow and affection. He once made a full stop, and gazed on a beautiful girl of four or five years old, who was gathering primroses on the margin of the Nith; the child, alarmed at his uncouth appearance, shrieked, and fell, in its fright, into the deep stream; the mariner made but one spring from the bank into the river, saved the child, replaced it in its mother's bosom, and resumed his journey, apparently unconscious that he had done aught remarkable. Ever after this the children of Dumfries pursued him with the hue and cry, "Eh! come and see the wild bearded man, who saved Mary Lawson."

On another occasion, I was hunting on the Scottish mountain of Criffel, and, having reached its summit, I sat down to look around on the fine prospect of sea and land below me, and take some refreshment. At a little distance I saw something like the figure of a human being, bedded in the heath, and lying looking on the Solway from a projecting rock, so still and motionless that it seemed dead. I went near: it was Miles Colvine. He seemed unconscious of my approach, and, looking steadfastly on the sea, remained fixed, and muttering, as long as I continued on the mountain. Indeed, wherever he went, he talked more like a man holding communion with his own mind than one sharing his thoughts with others; and the general purport of such imperfect sentences as could be heard was that he had doomed many men to perish for some irreparable wrong they had offered to a lady. Sometimes he spoke of the lady as his wife, or his love, and the men he had destroyed as the lawless crew of his own vessel. At other times he addressed his seamen as spirits, whom he had sent to be tortured for wrongs done in the body, and his lady as an angel that still visited his daily dreams and his nightly visions. Through the whole of these wayward musings the cry of revenge, and the sense of deep injury, were heard and understood by all.

When Miles Colvine had fairly finished his new residence, and the flowers and fruits had returned to field and tree, he was observed to launch his boat: this was a common occurrence, but a small lair of seal-skins, a jar of water, and some dried fish called kippered salmon by the Scotch, looked like preparation for a long voyage. The voyage was begun, for he was seen scudding away southward by the light of the stars, and no more was seen or heard of him for some time. Day after day his door continued shut, his chimney ceased to smoke, and his nets hung unemployed. At length the revenue cutter from Saint Bees arrived at Allanbay, to land a cargo of fine Holland gin, which the officers had taken from an Irish smuggler, between Carrickfergus and the Isle of Man. They had been terribly alarmed, they said, on their way, by the appearance, about the third watch of the night, of a visionary boat, navigated by a bearded fiend, which scudded with supernatural

swiftness along the surface of the water. This tale, with all
the variations which a poetical peasantry readily supply,
found its way from cottage to hamlet, and from hamlet to
hall. Old men shook their heads, and talked of the exploits
of the great fiend by sea and land, and wished that good
might happen to Old England from the visit of such a
circumnavigator. Others, who were willing to believe that
the apparition was Miles Colvine on a coasting voyage,
seemed no less ready to confound the maritime recluse with
an evil being, who had murdered a whole ship's crew, sunk
their ship, and dwelt on the coast of "cannie Cumberland,"
for the express purpose of raising storms, shaking corn, and
making unwedded mothers of half the fair damsels between
Sarkfoot and Saint Bees. Several misfortunes of the latter
kind, which happened about this time, confirmed this suspicion, and his departure from the coast was as welcome as
rain to the farmer after a long drought.

About a fortnight after this event, I happened to be on a
moonlight excursion by water, as far as the ruined castle of
Comlongan. I was accompanied by an idle friend or two,
and, on our return, we allowed the receding tide to carry us
along the Cumberland coast, till we came nearly opposite
the cottage of Miles Colvine. As we directed our boat to
the shelter of a small bank, I observed a light glimmering
in the mariner's house; and, landing and approaching
closer, I saw plainly the shadows of two persons, one tall
and manly, the other slim and sylph-like, passing and
repassing on the wall. I soon obtained a fairer view. I
saw the mariner himself; his dress, once rude and sordid,
was replaced by one of the coarsest materials, but remarkably clean; his beard was removed, and his hair, lately
matted and wild, now hung orderly about his neck and
temples. The natural colour was black, but it had been
changed by grief to snow-white; his look was hale, but
sorrowful, and he seemed about forty years of age. The
figure of the creature that accompanied him was much too
tender and beautiful to last long in a situation so rude and
unprotected as the cottage of a fisherman. It was a female,
richly dressed, and of a beauty so exquisite, and a look so
full of sweetness and grace, that the rude scene around was
not wanted to exalt her above all other maidens I had ever
seen. She glided about the cottage, arranging the various
articles of furniture, and passing two white hands, out-

rivalling the fairest creations of the sculptor, over the rude chairs and tables, and every moment giving a glance at the mariner, like one who took delight in pleasing him, and seemed to work for his sake. And he was pleased. I saw him smile, and no one had ever seen him smile before; he passed his hand over the long clustering tresses of the maiden, caused her to sit down beside him, and looked on her face, which, outgrowing the child, had not yet grown into woman, with a look of affection, and reverence, and joy.

I was pondering on what I witnessed, and imagining an interview with the unhappy mariner and his beautiful child, for such his companion was, when I observed the latter take out a small musical instrument from a chest. She touched its well-ordered strings with a light and a ready hand, and played several of the simple and plaintive airs so common among the peasantry of the Scottish and English coasts. After a pause she resumed her music, and, to an air singularly wild and melancholy, sang the following ballad, which relates, no doubt, to the story of her father's and mother's misfortunes; but the minstrel has observed a mystery in his narrative which excites suspicion rather than gratifies curiosity:—

O MARINER, O MARINER.

O mariner, O mariner,
  When will our gallant men
Make our cliffs and woodlands ring
  With their homeward hail agen?
Full fifteen paced the stately deck,
  And fifteen stood below,
And maidens waved them from the shore,
  With hands more white than snow;
All underneath them flashed the wave,
  The sun laughed out aboon,
Will they come bounding homeward
  By the waning of yon moon?

O maid, the moon shines lovely down,
  The stars all brightly burn,
And they may shine till doomsday comes
  Ere your true love return;
O'er his white forehead roll the waves,
  The wind sighs lowne and low,
And the cry the sea-fowl uttereth
  Is one of wail and woe;

So wail they on; I tell thee, maid,
  One of thy tresses dark
Is worth all the souls who perished
  In that good and gallant bark.

O mariner, O mariner,
  It's whispered in the hall,
And sung upon the mountain side
  Among our maidens all,
That the waves which fill the measure
  Of that wide and fatal flood
Cannot cleanse the decks of thy good ship,
  Or wash thy hands from blood;
And sailors meet, and shake their heads,
  And, ere they sunder, say,
God keep us from Miles Colvine
  On the wide and watery way!

And up then spoke he, Miles Colvine,
  His thigh thus smiting soon,
By all that's dark aneath the deep,
  By all that's bright aboon,
By all that's blessèd on the earth,
  Or blessèd on the flood,
And by my sharp and stalwart blade
  That revelled in their blood—
I could not spare them; for there came
  My loved one's spirit nigh,
With a shriek of joy at every stroke
  That doomed her foes to die.

O mariner, O mariner,
  There was a lovely dame,
Went down with thee unto the deep,
  And left her father's hame.
His dark eyes, like a thunder cloud,
  Did rain and lighten fast,
And, oh! his bold and martial face
  All grimly grew and ghast:
I loved her, and those evil men
  Wronged her as far we ranged;
But were ever woman's woes and wrongs
  More fearfully avenged?

The ballad had proceeded thus far, when a band of smugglers, from the coasts of Ireland and Scotland, uniting the reckless desperation of the former with the craft and tact of the latter, attracted by the secure and naked coast, and perhaps by the lonely house, which presented hope of plunder with little appearance of resistance, landed, to the number of seven, and, leaping over the exterior wall, seized the door and shook it violently, calling loudly for admittance. I lay down, with my two companions, behind a small hillock covered with furze, to see the issue of this visit; for at that time I imagined the mariner maintained some mysterious correspondence with these fierce and lawless men.

"Open the door," said one, in a strong Irish accent, "or by the powers, I'll blow your cabin to peelings of potatoes about your ears, my darlings."

"Hout, Patrick, or what's your name," said one of his comrades, in Lowland Scotch, "ye mauna gang that rough way to wark; we maun speak kindly and cannilie, man, till we get in our hand, and then we can take it a' our ain way, like Willie Wilson's sow, when she ran off with the knife in her neck."

The mariner, on hearing this dialogue, prepared himself for resistance, like one perfectly well acquainted with such rencounters. With a sword in one hand, a cocked pistol in the other, and a brace in his belt, he posted himself behind the door, and, in a low voice, admonished his daughter to retire to a little chamber constructed for her accommodation. With a voice which, though quivering with emotion, lost nothing of its native sweetness, the young maiden answered, "Oh, let me be near you!—let me but be near you!"

Her low and gentle voice was drowned in the wild exclamations of one of the smugglers. "Och, my dears, let us break the door, and clap a red turf to the roof, and all to give me light to see to kiss this maiden with the sweet voice. By the holy poker that stirred the turf fire beneath the first potato, I have not been within seven acres broad of a woman since we sailed with Miles Colvine's lady. And, by the bagpiper, she was a bouncer; and a pretty din she made about it, after all, and took it into her head to shriek till the shores rang, and pray till the saints grew deaf. Ah, my hearties, it wouldn't do. What the devil holds this door? Stand by till I show you how handsomely I'll pitch it against the wall. Ah, I wish you had seen me when I upset the house of Ranald Mullagen, in Lurgen, and made the bonniest blaze you ever saw in the wide world, at all, at all."

And, setting his shoulders to the door, he thrust with all his might; but, though seconded by his comrades, who seemed all alike eager for violence, the door resisted his utmost efforts.

"Stand back, my darlings," said the miscreant; "I'll show you a trick worth two of this; I'll teach you how we bring out a bonnie lass from a bolted chamber in little Ireland."

So saying, he proceeded to prime a pistol, having previously hammered the flint with a little steel cross, curiously chased and ornamented, which he took from his bosom. "Ah!" said he, "may the devil cork me up in a stone bottle, and send me to seek out the latitude of the lake of darkness, if I don't carve up that old he-goat into relics! Now, come on, my early boys—my souls of boys! the boy that won't do as I do deserves to be whipped through Purgatory with the tail of St. Patrick's ass. Thack and thunder! Hell's to hinder us when I snap my pistol under the thatch."

In a moment the door opened. Miles Colvine stood on the threshold, a cocked pistol in his right hand, his sword gleaming in his left, his eyes shooting from them a fierce dark light, but his manner perfectly calm and collected. Behind him came the beautiful form of his daughter, with a pistol in her hand, and shuddering from head to foot at the immediate peril which seemed to beset her father. These maritime desperadoes started back at this sudden apparition of an armed man; and even their miscreant leader, forward as he was, recoiled a pace or two. The mariner eyed him for a moment, and said, "Did my sword then do its work slovenly, and did the deep sea not devour thee, thou immeasurable villain? But God has given thee back to earth, to become a warning how sure and how certain just vengeance is." And leaping on him as he spoke, I saw the pistol flash, and the gleam of the descending sword, in almost the same instant. I instantly started up with my companions, and the smugglers, perceiving this reinforcement, carried off their companion, groaning and cursing, and praying; and pushing their boat from the shore, vanished along the misty bosom of the summer sea.

I found Miles Colvine standing on the threshold of his house, and his daughter on her knees beside him. He knew me, for we had often passed each other on the beach and on the sea, and he was aware that I was a friend, for I had endeavoured in vain to oblige him in his forlorn state with little acts of kindness.

"Come hither, sir," said the mariner; "I have to thank

you for aid this night." He paused for a moment, and then said, in a lower tone : " I know your faith is not my faith, and that your life is' not embittered with what has embittered mine. But tell me, sir, tell me—do you believe that the events of our life are ordained? For what hath happened to-night seems of a wise Being's ordering."

"Surely, sir," I said, "God knoweth all things, present and to come; but, whether he permits evil deeds to be wrought, or ordains good ones to be done——"

"Enough, enough," said the mariner. "May Colvine, my love, trim thy father's shealing, and set the supper-table in array, for it is ordained that our deliverers shall rest with us, and break bread at our board; so come in."

And into the mariner's cottage we walked, not unawed by the presence of a being of whose temper and courage we had seen such a proof.

If the exterior of the cottage was rude and unskilfully built, the interior was wonderfully commodious and neat. The floor was laid of drifted ship-timber, and the walls were hung with nets as with tapestry; and fish-spears, and gaff-hooks of steel, sharp and bright, were grouped like weapons for battle in a chieftain's hall of old. The fruits of the fisherman's skill were everywhere visible: the chimney-mantel, a beam of wood which extended from side to side of the cottage, was covered with kippered salmon, large, and red, and savoury, and various kegs were filled with salted fish of the many excellent kinds which the Solway affords. A small bed stood near the chimney, swelled with the feathers of sea-fowl, and hillocked high with quilts and mantles, from beneath which some linen looked out, only rivalled in whiteness by the snow. A very small chamber was constructed at the farther end, into which May Colvine disappeared for a moment to readjust her dress, and, perhaps, add some other of those artificial attractions which women always bring in to the aid of their natural charms. The mariner seated himself, motioned me to a seat, over which a sealskin was thrown, while a lamp, fed plentifully with oil, and suspended from the roof, diffused light over the apartment. Nor was the place devoted to brute comfort alone : several books, among which I observed "Robinson Crusoe," and Homer's " Odyssey" in Greek, with a curious collection of Northern legendary ballads, were scattered about, and a shepherd's pipe and a fiddle were there to bring music to assist in the dissipation of melancholy thought.

May Colvine now came forth from her little chamber, with an increase of loveliness, such as a rose appears when refreshed in dew. She had laid aside the snood of silk and pearl which enclosed her hair, and the curling luxuriance of her ringlets descended over her shoulders, while her white temples, and whiter neck, were seen through the waving fleece which fell so profusely over them. Her father gazed on her like one who recalls the lovely past in the beautiful present; and his thoughts had flitted to other days and remoter climes, for after a brief reverie he said: "Come, my love, the vessel is ready, the mariners aboard, the sails spread to the wind, and we must pass the haunted headland before the moon goes down."

The maiden meanwhile had filled the supper-board with such coarse fare as the cabin afforded, and addressing her father, said: "Sir, the table is prepared, your guests are waiting, and will expect you to bless the fare which is set before them."

The mariner laid his hat aside, and sitting in his place, after the manner of the Presbyterians, said: "Thou who spreadest thy table on the deep waters, and rainest down abundance in the desert places, make this coarse food seem savoury and delicate unto these three men and this tender virgin; but my hands, on which the blood of man yet reeks unatoned for, may not presume to touch blessed food." And spreading the fold of his mantle over his face, and stooping down, he appeared to busy himself in mental devotion, while, tasting the supper set before us, and obeying the mute invitation of the maiden to a glass of water, we complied with all the forms which this extraordinary audience seemed to impose upon us.

After this was past, the young woman took up one of the instruments, and singing as she played, with inexpressible sweetness and grace, her father gradually uncovered his face—his looks began to brighten, and, uttering a deep sigh, he waved his hand, the minstrelsy ceased, and he thus addressed us:

"I was not always an unhappy man—I had fair domains, a stately house, a beauteous wife, and a sweet daughter; but it is not what we have, but what we enjoy, that blesseth man's heart, and makes him as one of the angels. I dwelt on a wild sea-coast, far from here, full of woods and caverns, the haunt of a banditti of smugglers—those fierce and vulgar and intractable spirits who find subsistence in fraud and violence, and from a continued perseverance in hostility to human law, become daily more hardened of heart and fierce of nature. I was young and romantic; and, though I did not approve of the course of these men's lives, there appeared glimpses of generosity and courage and fortitude about them, which shed a halo over a life of immorality and crime. I protected them not, neither did I associate with them; but they soon saw in the passive manner in which I regarded their nocturnal intercourse with the coast, and the ready and delighted ear which I lent to the narratives of their adventures by sea and land, that they had nothing to fear and much to hope. Their confidence increased, and their numbers augmented; and they soon found a leader capable of giving an aim to all their movements, and who brought something like regular craft and ability to their counsels.

"I was reputed rich, and was rich; my treasures were mostly of gold and silver plate, and bars of the former metal, the gain of a relative who had shared with the Buccaneers in the plunder of Panama. I had also been wedded for a number of years, my wife was young and beautiful, and our daughter, an only child, my own May Colvine, here where she sits, was in her thirteenth year, with a frame that seemed much too delicate to survive the disasters she has since been doomed to meet. We were counselled to carry her to warmer climates, and were preparing for our voyage, and my wife was ready to accompany me, when a large smuggling cutter cast anchor in a deep woody bay which belonged to my estate, and, as I sat on the top of my house, looking towards the sea, a person in a naval dress came and accosted me. He was, he said, the captain of the freetrader lying in the bay, with a cargo of choice wine, and his mariners, bold lads and true, had periled themselves freely by land and water, and often experienced the protection of Miles Colvine's bay and the hospitality of his menials. They had heard of my intention to carry my wife and daughter to a more genial climate; and, if we wished to touch at Lisbon, or to go to any of the islands where Europeans seek for health, they would give us a passage, for they honoured us next to commerce without law or restraint.

"But I must tell you that the chief of this band, knowing my love for marvellous tales, hinted that he had men on board who, to the traditionary lore of their maritime ancestors, added their own adventures and deeds; and could, with the romantic ballads of Denmark and Sweden, mingle the Troubadour tales of France, the Moorish legends of Spain, and the singular narratives which survive among the peasantry on my native coast. To soothe and propitiate my wife, he had recourse to another charm; from the pocket of a long boat-cloak he produced a mantle of the most precious fabric, and spreading it out before her, with all its rich variety of colour and Eastern profusion of ornament, offered it as a humble present from himself and his mariners. I need not prolong this part of my narrative; we embarked at twilight, and, standing out of the bay, dropped anchor till morning dawn. The captain sat armed beside us; this excited no suspicion, for he went commonly armed, and related adventures of a daring and remarkable kind which had befallen him on foreign shores, with a liveliness, and a kind of maritime grace, which were perfectly captivating. All night we heard overhead the tramp and the din of sailors passing and repassing, and with the grey of the morning we plucked up our anchor, spread our sails to a shrill wind, shot away seaward, and my native land vanished from my view. All was life and gladness; we danced and we sang on deck, and drained cups of the purest wine, while the breeze favoured us and the sky remained unclouded and serene.

"When the spice groves of one of the Portuguese islands appeared before us, the sun was setting, and it was resolved we should remain at the entrance of a bay till daylight. We were crowded on the deck, looking on the green and beauteous land, and a gentle seaward wind wafted the perfume of the forest about us. My wife was in the bloom of youth and beauty, full of health, and life, and love; and as she stood leaning on my arm, the sailors smoothed their rough looks and refrained from curses, so much were they touched by her beauty; but this awe lasted but a little while. The captain was merry far beyond his usual measure of delight, and drained one wine cup after another to my wife's health and mine; he vowed I was as a god among his men, and that my wife was reverenced as a divinity   'But come,' said he, 'Miles Colvine, I have a curious and a cunning thing to show you, which you alone deserve to see; I got it among the Moors, so come, and come alone.'

"I rose, and followed him, for my curiosity was unbounded; he conducted me below, and, opening a small wicket in the wall of his cabin with a key, ushered me in, and closing it suddenly upon me, locked it; and then I heard him bounding up the stair to the deck. I stood half imagining this to be a jest, or something, at least, of a light nature; but shriek after shriek of my wife, uttered in the piercing agony of anguish and despair, soon undeceived me. I called, I entreated, I used force, and, though I was armed by anger and despair with almost supernatural might, the door withstood all my efforts. But why should I dwell upon a scene of such unutterable misery? What I endured, and what the woman I loved and adored suffered, are fit only to be imagined—not, surely, to be spoken. Her wrongs were remembered, and her shrieks numbered, by a Power far more terrible than man; and a certain doom and deplorable death was pronounced against them, at the moment their joy was fullest.

"The evening passed away, and morning came; and, through a little wicket which looked upon the sea, the light showed me that my chamber was the treasure-room of the pirates, for such they were, as well as smugglers. At the same moment a hole opened above, and a piece of bread and an antique silver cup filled with wine were lowered down. Amid the misery of my situation it seemed but a light evil that I recognized the silver vessel to be part of the treasure I had left at home; and, in seeking for a weapon to force the wicket, I found that my whole riches, in gold as well as silver, had been seized and put on board. I could now measure the extent of my calamity, and prepared myself for a fate, which, among such miscreants, could not be deemed far distant. The morning was not much advanced when the sun dipped at once into a dark and tempestuous ocean of clouds, the wind began to whistle shriller and shriller among our sails, and the sea, upturned by sudden and heavy gusts of wind, showed, as far as the eye could reach, those dark and tremendous furrows so fatal to mariners. The wind was from the land, and I could both see and feel that the vessel was unable to gain the harbour, and had sought security from the approaching tempest by standing out to sea. I heard the wind wax louder, and saw the billows roll, with a joy that arises from the hope of revenge: the sky became darker, the sea flashed over the decks, and the tempest hurried the ship onward with a rapidity which alarmed the sailors, accustomed as they were to the element. The seams of the vessel began to admit the sea, and everywhere symptoms appeared of her immediate destruction.

"I heard a conversation overhead I shall never forget. 'I tell you,' said a voice in Lowland Scotch, 'good can never come of such evil as your captain and you have wrought; had you taken Miles Colvine's gold and silver alone, the sin had been but little, and a grey-headed repentance might have mended all. But the bonnie lady! Her voice has been heard to-day, and tremble all you that touched her sweet body, for here has come an avenging tempest. The sea will soon devour us, and hot hell will hold us; and the mother who bore, and the wife who loved me, and the bonnie babes I have nursed on my knee will behold me no more; and all for being in company with such hell-hounds as you.'

"A voice replied to all this, in a tone too low and suppressed to be audible; and the Scotchman answered again: 'Lo, look! Did ever eyes behold such a sight? All around us the sea is smooth as glass, and other ships pass by us under a gentle breeze, without a wetted sail; but we!—the anger of Heaven has found us, for on us the thick tempest beats, and the evil one is pursuing us to destruction. O thou eternal villain—captain shall I call thee no more—and you! —you fifteen wretches, who shared with him in his crime, make you ready, for that storm will neither leave you, nor forsake you, till you are buried in the ocean.'

"At the very moment when ruin seemed inevitable the tempest ceased, the clouds passed away, and the descending sun shone brightly down, making the shoreless waters sparkle as far as the eye could reach. No bounds were now set to the joy of the crew; they crowded the deck, made a circle round several vessels of wine and baskets of biscuit; and, before the twilight had passed away, a few only were capable of guiding the vessel. The night grew very dark, and, as I sat in utter despair, I heard the same friendly voice that I had so lately heard, say, 'Miles Colvine, put your trust in Him who can still the tempest; thy time is come.'

"In a moment the wicket opened, and the same voice said,

'Take this sword, and come with me. If you have courage to avenge the miseries and the death of your beautiful and wretched wife, come, for the hour is at hand, and, as sure as I hate sin and love immortal happiness, I shall help you.'

"I took the sword, followed in silence, and, coming on deck, I beheld a scene which the hope of sure and immediate revenge rendered inexpressibly sweet. The captain and five sailors, though nearly overcome with wine, were seated on deck; the remainder of the crew had retired below; some shouted, some sang, all blasphemed, and one loud din of cursing and carousal echoed far and wide: the mingled clamour that ascended from this scene of wickedness and debauchery partook of all the evil qualities of debased minds and the most infamous pursuits, and cannot be described. Discord had its full share in the conference on deck between the captain and his confederates; they were debating about their shares in the plunder of my house.

"'Share! By my saul, man,' said a Scottish sailor to the captain, 'your share in Miles Colvine's pure gold can be but small; one hour of his sweet lady, a hundred leagues from land, was worth all the gold that ever shone.'

"'I shall share all fairly,' said the captain, laying his hand on the hilt of his cutlass; 'and first I shall share thy scoundrel carcass among the fishes of the sea, if I hear such a word again. Did I plan the glorious plot of carrying away the fair lady and her lord's treasure, to share either with such a Scotch sawney as thee?'

"The wrath of the Scotchman burnt on his brow far redder than the flush of the wine he had drunk. 'Fiend seethe my saul in his chief caldron, if ye taste na' cauld iron for this!' And out came his cutlass as he spoke.

"'That's my hearty Caledonian,' said one of his comrades; 'give him a touch of the toasting iron. Didn't he give a blow on the head to my mother's own son, this blessed morning, for only playing pluck at the lady's garment. Ah, give him the cold piece of steel, my hearty.'

"A blow from the captain's cutlass was the answer to this; several drunkards drew their swords, and ill-directed blows and ineffectual stabs were given and received in the dark. 'Now,' said my sailor, laying his hand on mine, to stay me till I received his admonition, 'say not one word, for words slay not, but glide in among them like a spirit; thrust your blade, for anger strikes, but revenge stabs.; and I will secure the gangway, and fight along with you.'

"I heard and obeyed, and, gliding among them, thrust one of them through and through; a second and a third dropped, ere they saw who was among them. The captain attempted to draw a pistol, but my sword and my friend's entered at back and bosom; and, though two yet remained unhurt, I struck my sword a second time through the bosom of my mortal enemy, as he lay beneath me, and the last expiring glance of his eye was a look worth remembering. Ere this was accomplished, the other two were both lying with their companions. I have frequently imagined that a firmness and strength more than my own were given me during this desperate encounter. Meanwhile the remainder of the crew below set no bounds to their merriment and shouting, and seemed, as my Scottish friend remarked, ordained to die by my hand, since their clamour, by drowning the groans of their comrades, prevented them from providing for their safety. We fastened the cabin door and barricaded the gangway, keeping watch for many days with pistol and sword, with the hope of seeing some friendly shore, or a compassionate sail; while the vessel, urged onward by a strong wind, scudded with supernatural swiftness through the midnight waters. We had entered the Solway sea, when a storm came on, which, augmenting every moment, carried us rapidly along. When opposite Allanbay, a whirlwind, seizing our ship by the rigging, whirled her fairly round, and dashed her against a sandbank. As the planks sundered, and the waters rushed in, I beheld an armed man, one of the band of wretches from below, rise up before me with a look of fury which a fiend might envy. Our hatred was superior to the tempest and the scene of desolation around, and, drawing our cutlasses, we sought each other's bosom. There is a fate in all things—the planks parted beneath our feet, and the sea broke over us, and he escaped me then, to perish by my hand to-night. Revenge is sweetest when it comes unhoped for. As we sank in the waves, a passing vessel, it seems, saved my sweet May Colvine, while the remainder of the crew went to the bottom, without the chance of swimming for an existence they deserved not to prolong. Such is my story."

Little more is known with certainty of the life of this remarkable man. He forsook his house soon after, and went to another—perhaps his native land. The peasantry and the fishermen, from awe as well as respect to his fortitude and misfortunes, permitted his cottage to remain untouched; and the seamen, as they sailed by, looked with something of a superstitious regard on the residence of Miles Colvine. Many years afterwards, on a summer morning, a peasant went to the sea, to examine his nets and lines. The sun had just risen, and was slanting his first beams over the green hills behind—a few long and narrow lines of dewy light fell across the Solway, and the mountains on the Scottish side were brightened from their summits midway down. He saw a man seated by the door of the mariner's cottage, dressed in a garb resembling that of a pilgrim, and leaning over a staff. He went closer, and addressed him—no answer was returned. The stranger was cold and dead—his hands were clasped together on the head of his staff, and his eyes were wide open, and looking seaward. Some old men came, and said, "A woeful man was Miles Colvine, the Mariner," and interred him among their ancestors in the parish churchyard.

HONEST MAN JOHN OCHILTREE.

A GAY young lad frae Locherben
Came galloping late to our gate en;
He doft his hat, and came bouncing ben,
   Saying, Maiden, I come to wooe.
His brow was brent, his glance was gleg,
A snaw-white skin an' a wanton leg;
A gallant young lad, quo' I, by my feg,
   He's welcome here to wooe.

Aboon the fire upon the bink,
He had bread to eat an' wine to drink,
But ne'er a blithe styme wad he blink
   Till he was warm and fou;
Syne by the hand I have him ta'en,
Ye coldrife lover now get ye gane,
I'd liefer lie a year my lane
   Than lie an hour wi' you.
             Old Scottish Song.

" I WAS not always an old man, with a lank leg and a grey head; there was a time before I began the pleasant trade of cheering the dames and maidens with my merry tales. I was then young, my leg was firm and shapely, my locks were bushy and black; and I could have pitched the bar, or played a fiddle, with the youth of seven parishes. But a sad cough, which I caught among the damp broom on Quarrelwood Hill hearkening a sectarian sermon, plucked strength and spirit down, and drove me to win the bread by my wit, which more favoured men purchase by the sweat of their brow. But the world is an altered world to me since I commenced my calling; it is a white half-crown, a week the worse for the wear; people are grown too wise to be delighted—they laugh not at my wittiest story, nor shed one tear at my saddest. I have seen when ye might have tied seven strong men with a straw, as they shouted and laughed, and lay down and laughed at my narratives; a smile is as hard to earn as a sixpence now, and tears are dried up on the earth. My saddest story would bring red wine out of a rock, or strong drink from a log of Memel fir, sooner than extract one tear from the brightest eye of the present generation.

"But I scatter none of those antique pearls—those tender and touching narratives, before the eyes of the self-sufficient husbandman and the critical mechanic. I steep not my story now in the dark and fathomless stream of superstition: I have seen the time when tales and ballads of fairies and elves, and witches and warlocks, and elve candles and water spunkies, and wraiths and ghosts, and goblins and foul fiends, horned or cloven-footed, would have been to one as food and raiment and white money. But the wisdom of man so much abounds that he is pleased with nought; he laughs at ancient beliefs, and calls for ocular proof, and testimony on oath, and the assurance of many witnesses, for all oral or recorded things. The poetry has departed from story-telling, conjured away by the wand of that sorcerer, education. Not that I mean to aver that all else is as husks and bran, compared to the white and the purified grain. I have had curious adventures of my own, in which the most querulous matter-of-fact man could detect neither superstition nor poetry. These, falling from the lips of one blessed with a natural grace of utterance, might go far to move men to mirth; but I can hope for no such consummation."

The old man adjusted his mantle, stood perpendicularly up, and, combing his white locks with his fingers, commenced his narrative with something of a look and tone at once grave and shrewd.

"The adventures I shall relate commenced with my seventeenth year. I had learned to sing, and also to dance; but Nature, which lavishes so many notable gifts, denied me that ready and familiar grace of address which wins its way to woman's regard. I conversed with the maids whom the music of the fiddle surrendered to my company with such manifest confusion, and even alarm, that they soon reckoned me a creature equally uncouth and ungracious; and I was subjected to abundance of scorn and caprice and wit, when I endeavoured at gallantry. When I led them to the floor, they would examine me from head to foot, with an eye sparkling in malicious wit; and even their grandmothers regarded me with a glance of the most mortifying compassion. It was sometimes a matter of rivalry among the girls to obtain my hand: to dance with such a cutter of uncouth capers, such a marvellous piece of human imperfection as me, was made a matter of boast and a subject for laughter; and any expressions of respect or love which I hazarded were parodied and distorted into all that was absurd and ridiculous by these capricious spirits. They all seemed to possess, for my mortification and sorrow, a talent for humour and ridicule, which broke out on every occasion. I became the most exalted personage in the parish, if my merit might be estimated by the notice I received; and to this 'bad eminence' I was raised by the wit and the fun and folly of women.

"To one of those meetings at the conclusion of harvest, which, taking farewell of autumn, welcome the winter with drinking and dancing and all sorts of rustic festivity, I was about this time invited. I dressed myself out for the occasion in my newest dress, and in the vanity of my heart I counted myself captivating. My aunt assisted me much in this; she possessed an antique taste, and so far back did her intelligence in apparel reach, that she sought to revive, and that on my person, the motley dress of the minstrels at the ancient border tournaments. One mistake was that I had no turn for poetry, so I was soon doomed to endure the malice of verse without the power of inflicting it on others; and another was, that I had nothing of a romantic turn about me, so that the dress sat on me with an evil grace. To the dance, however, I went, waving my right arm gallantly as I marched along, and looking oftentimes back at my shadow in the moonlight; the luminary I could not help thinking neglected to do justice to my form, but that planet is certainly the most capricious of all the lesser lights. I was received with a general stare; and then with a burst of universal and spontaneous mirth. The old men surveyed me with looks in which compassion struggled with curiosity; but the maidens gathered about me, commended the head that imagined my dress, and the hand that fashioned it: the young men joined in this praise with a gravity which I mistook for envy, and the roof rocked and rang to another peal of laughter.

"The fiddler, wholly blind, and seated apart from this scene of merriment and mortification, seemed incensed to think that any one should be the cause of mirth but himself. He stayed his hand, laid down his instrument, and, while he rosined his bow, inquired what all this laughter meant. 'Thy curiosity shall be gratified,' said a wicked young girl;

and, taking my unreluctant hand, she led me up to this producer of sounds, and guided his hand to my person. He felt my dress from head to heel, vowed by his bow he had never touched a garment of such rich device as my coat, swore by his fiddle my bonnet was worth all the money his instrument had ever earned, and hoped I would leave the land before I ruined the mystery of thairms, for there was no need of instrumental mirth where I came. And dismissing me with a suppressed laugh, for open merriment might have diminished his evening's gain, he recommenced his music, and the discontinued dance began.

"My torment now commenced: the lasses danced round me in a ring. I had the misfortune to be so much in request that I was never off the floor : though I danced six-and-thirty reels without let or pause, and though the drops fell from my brows like rain, I saw no end to such perpetual capering. This ridiculous exertion is still remembered among the dames of Annandale; and I lately heard a girl reproach her lover with his listlessness for mirth, saying, 'When will ye dance six-and-thirty reels like daft John Ochiltree?' I grew an inch taller with this proof of my fame. All this was to come to an end. The blind fiddler had been smit in his youth with the disease of tune-making: he had mingled the notes of half a dozen tunes together, from which he extracted a kind of musical square root, and this singular progeny he was desirous of baptizing: much, it seems, depends on having a fine sounding name. At present he was hesitating between 'Prince Charles's Delight' or 'Duke William's Welcome,' when a peasant demanded the tune: 'the new tune, the plague on't—the tune without a name.' 'A tune without a name,' said a girl, 'cannot ye christen it, man? Here, fiddler, play up "Honest Man John Ochiltree."' A shout of laughter succeeded. 'A name, by my faith,' exclaimed many voices at once; and the new name was shouted by a hundred tongues, to the infinite mortification of the fiddler and me: our vanity was wounded. The name of the tune was fixed as unalterably as the laws of the Medes, and from that hour forward it haunted me through life; while the popularity of the air was increased by the noises which a rustic minstrel soon caused to jingle in rude chorus to the air. Thus I got the name of 'Honest Man John Ochiltree,' and the story was a winter's laugh to the parish.

"But there is no sour without its sweet: all this had been witnessed by a farmer's daughter, whom the pursuit of many lovers had not rendered capricious, and who thought she perceived in the patience with which I endured all this musical persecution the materials for making a quiet and tractable husband. She trod on my foot returning from a hill-preaching, and apologized with so much grace that I thought her the fairest maiden of the whole valley; and after touching on the sermon, and quoting the Song of Solomon, we parted with a mutual promise of meeting in her father's barn at midnight. I was punctual to my tryste, and so accurate was the devout maiden that the clock struck twelve as she turned the key in the granary-door. She opened a little wicket, and let in the summer moonlight; and seating ourselves on two inverted bushels, we sat in collateral splendour, side by side, amid the silent light of the luminary.

"I looked at the maiden, who kept looking on the opposite wall with an aspect of demure but arch composure, and seemed to count the stones of which it was built. Had I been afflicted with the cureless evil of verse-making, I had now a matchless opportunity of displaying my gift. The silence of the place—the glow of the moon—the beauty of the maiden, Mary Anderson by name—her white hands, clasped over a whiter bosom—her locks, a glistering and a golden brown, escaping from the comb, descending in ringlets down her left cheek and shoulder, and taking a silvery or a golden hue as they moved to her breath amid the pure moonlight! This was my first attempt at courtship. I trembled much, and the words of love, too, trembled on my tongue. Let no man sit many minutes silent in the presence of his mistress; he will be forgiven for folly, for more serious offences, but never for silence. Had I made my début in darkness, I think I should have spoken, and spoken, too, with much tenderness and true love. But the fault lay with the moon—plague on the capricious planet! I never see her fickle light glimmering through the chink of a barn wall but I think on the time when I lost my first love through her influence. We sat mute for the space of a quarter of an hour; and I had nearly vanquished my aversion to the moon's presence, when an owl rested from her flight on the roof above us for a moment, and, just as the words had assembled on my lips, uttered a long and melancholy 'whoop hoo.' I wished not to pitch the tone of courtship by a sound so ominous, and remained mute. I mustered my resolution again, and the first word (I would give the world to remember what word it was) was actually escaping from my lips, when a sucking calf lowed, perhaps for its dam, in a stall near us, and the voices of the four- and the two-footed animals were blended so curiously in utterance, that a judge of natural music would have found difficulty in awarding to each their own proper notes. This was a sound much more mischievous than the voice of the owl: the maiden, devout as she was, could not suppress a smile, and rising said, 'I think we know enough of one another's minds for one night,' and vanished from my side. So I closed my first night's wooing. I once had the courage to propose to her the endurance of another vigil; she set her hands to her mouth, and 'whooted out whoots three.' We never met again.

"But I was an inextinguishable lover. I disciplined my mind, pampered up my courage, and having, as I hoped, inured myself to the sharp encounter of female wit, boldly resolved to go in quest of an adventure. I have travelled much in the world; but all parts of the earth are surpassed by Scotland in the amorous spirit of its peasantry: there a maiden has many lovers, and a peasant many mistresses; adventures equalling those of romance are encountered; and the effusion of men's blood, as well as maiden's tears, not unfrequently follows those nocturnal excursions. I walked resolutely abroad, and hoped the achievement of some notable adventure. For some time I was without success; but at last a long stream of light from a farmer's window led me up to the casement, within which I observed his eldest daughter, a gay damsel of eighteen, couched on the watch, and waiting the approach of some happy wooer. She opened the window when I appeared, but, seeing a form she had not hoped for, stood holding the sash in her hand, pondering whether she should take the earliest blessing which heaven had sent in human shape.

"At this moment her expected lover appeared, a spruce youth from the neighbouring city, pruned and landered, and scenting the way with musk and frankincense. The maiden wrung her hands with vexation: her wit could not deal with more than one at a time; and as I was never of a quarrelsome nature, and had an aversion to intrude upon true love,

I turned suddenly to retreat. The young man started off too; and, as my road lay the very way he ran, he imagined I pursued him with some sinister intention, so he augmented his speed. I still gained on him. A lake was in the way: I have ever had an affection for running water since it received my rival in its bosom, plump over head and ears, with a dash that startled the wild ducks for a mile round. He swam through like an evil spirit, while I returned to his mistress, and found her holding the casement open, perhaps for the successful lover; so I leaped gaily into the chamber, and, seated by the maiden's side, began to hope I was conquering my fate.

"The night, gloomy before, became tenfold darker now; the wind, accompanied by heavy gushes of rain, shook window and door, and raised in the chimney-top that long and melancholy whine which so many of the peasants reckon ominous. The night waxed wilder and wilder; and, to augment the tempest, the fires flashed and the thunder roared in such rapid succession that the walls of the chamber appeared in continual flame, and the furniture shook and clattered. Now I have heard of lovers who considered a stormy tryste night as a kind gift of fortune, and who could enlist the tempest which 'roared and rustled' around them into the service of love, and compel it to make a pathetic supplication in their behalf to an unmerciful mistress. I never liked these cloudy influences, and instead of making a vassal of elemental commotion, it always made a servant of me; a high wind and a storm, accompanied by thunder and fire, made me quiver and quake. I gave ample proof on this unfortunate night of my submission to the genius of the blast: the maid laid her white arm round my neck, and when she was soothing my terrors with soft words, the door of the chamber opened, and in glided her mother, saying, 'Lassie, are ye waking?' To find a lover in her daughter's chamber was, perhaps, neither uncommon nor unexpected; but to find a new face, to find me, 'Honest Man John Ochiltree,' whose name was doomed to descend to posterity at the top of a ridiculous reel tune, the disclosure was to be dreaded; so the subtle maiden, unloosing a comb from a thick fleece of long auburn hair, threw such a profusion of ringlets over my face as nearly suffocated me, waving her hand at the same time for her mother to retire.

"The prudent mother, however, advanced, saying, 'Bless me, lassie, this is a fearful night to have love-trystes and wooester-daffin in. I have trysted on mony a queer night myself, but on none that equalled this; yet I think nae the waur of the lad who keeps his faith on a night that makes the wide world tremble.' The daughter still waved her hand, but the dame was not to be daunted; and thus she persisted: 'But Jenny, my bonny bairn, when will ye put an end to these dallyings; no that I would have ye to make your election rashly, in the calf-love, as the rude proverb says, for ye're young and no at the end of your teens till the bud be on the bush; but when will ye quit these dallyings, I say, and single out a discreet husband and a devout? Ye have rich lovers, more than one or two, yet set not thy heart on the siller, lass, though I would hardly counsel ye to wed without it. A loving lad in lily-white linen looks weel enough in a fule sang, but give me the lad with bills and bonds, and good set siller, who can fill and fetch mair. Yet make not gowd a god in the choice of thy heart; though to give ye mair for a bridal-tocher than three hundred pounds, and put ye into a fu' farm, is what I wadnae counsel thy father to do.' The daughter still waved her mother to be gone; but the covering of my face excited the good dame's suspicions, and she resolved to see me face to face, though it might diminish the amount of Jenny's admirers.

"No resolution was ever carried more quickly into execution. 'But Jenny, woman, what ails the lad that he hides his face? If he has nae a face worth looking at, he's no a lad for thee. And I ken not a lad in the parish who might wish to hide his head, except that daft chield, Jock Ochiltree; Jock Gomeral would suit him better. His grand-dame was burnt for a witch at the West-bow port of Edinburgh, and if the grandson was burnt for a fool there would be no waste of fuel on the family.' And, removing a handful of her daughter's hair as she spoke, she saw me, and shouted, till her voice fairly exceeded the tempest that still raged without: 'Nay, but the Lord preserve me! His presence be near! Here's that gaping goose, Jock Gowk himself; for my lips I wadnae defile with his name, much less my arms with his person. Oh, to think that ever thy mother's daughter thought of lending credit to such a race, or bearing a bonnie bairn-time to a born gomeral. Out of my house, I say, out of my house; start, else I shall write the notes of thy ain tune on thy face, seven crotchets to the bar.'

"'O mother,' said the submissive daughter, 'turn not the poor lad out on such a night as this: the thunder and fire, the flash and the din, will kill him; for he shakes at every clap like the leaf o' the linn.'

"'Na, worse than all,' shouted the dame, in a tone where scorn was blended with anger; 'na, worse than all. To be but a fool is no such a failing—there's Captain what's his name, whose whole wit lies in feeding capons, and who is hardly fit for watching the worms from the kale, yet he's made a justice o' the peace—but what can one do with a coward? I'm wasting words; I'm whistling a reel tune to a mile-stone: out of my house, I say—I will not defile both window and door with thee, so leap and vanish.' And holding up the casement, I leaped gladly out, happy at escaping from the wicked wagging of her tongue into the more endurable evil of wind and rain and fire.

"This unlucky repulse, with many a mischievous embellishment, flew over the parish; but I was not to be daunted. On the third evening after this mixed adventure of good and evil, I made an excursion beyond the limits of my parish, and entered upon the wild moorlands, where the dwellings are few and far between. A young man finds ready access among marriageable maidens, so I soon found myself seated at a sheep farmer's fire, in company of the good man's only daughter, a maid both ripe and rosy, with her father and mother, and some fifteen sheep dogs, as auditors of our conversation. At first, our talk was of that kind which newspapers call desultory; the weather, with all its variations; the fruits in their season, and the cattle after their kind; and, contracting the circle of our scrutiny as we proceeded, we at last settled upon the cares of a pasture farm. We talked of sheep after their sorts, the Cheviot breed, the auld stock of Tinwald, the lang sheep and the short mug ewes, gimmers, crocks, and dinmans; nor did we fail to discuss the diseases which preyed on this patriarchal wealth—mawks and moorill, rot and leaping-illness; and so extensive was my knowledge in all this, and also on the more mysterious mischief of evil e'en, elf-arrows, and witchcraft, that the old dame grew astonished, and whispered to her husband: 'This lad's words are worth drops of gold; speak him cannilie, Sandie, speak him cannilie.' Her daughter, too, had her own thoughts: she appeared to employ herself with the intricacies of a skein of thread ; but contrived at every motion of her hand to steal a glance at me from beneath a thick mass of natural curls which rivalled in density, and nearly in colour, the fairest fleece of any of her father's flock. Her hand, too, unwittingly paused in its work, and shed back the curls from her ears that she might hear more accurately my ideas of fireside economy and joy. The old man alone seemed slow in entering into the prospect of wedding his daughter's visible wealth to one whose chief substance was speculative. He sat solacing his thoughts with a scheme which had no connection with my happiness. I saw something sinister in his looks ; I heard him utter many a dry and dubious cough as his wife urged his admission of me as a suitor, and perceived, like the half hope of bliss held out by the Puritans, that I might be elected, but should never be chosen.

"At this moment the latch of the door was lifted, and a human figure tottered in, leaning twofold over a staff polished like glass with long use. It was a neighbouring moorland farmer, and a suitor to the maiden. He was dressed, or rather encumbered with clothes, which, in the shape of two coats, a large one and a less, showed the antique skill of cloth-cutting at the time of the Scottish persecution. Over all these a large plaid extended, and a bonnet that nearly overshaded the plaid crowned the whole. He removed this last-mentioned article, and displayed a face as sharp and biting as a northern frost, and a couple of small, keen, and inquisitive grey eyes, which seemed only acquainted with arithmetical calculation. He smoothed back his locks, which seemed to have long rebelled against the comb, and, casting his eyes over us, said with a prefatory cough :

"'Hale be thy heart, goodman, and happy be thine, goodwife, and merry may thine be, Penney, my winsome quean, mair by token I have sold seven score of dinmans, every cloot, and all to buy thee a bridal garment, lass, and a horse to ride on to the kirking, the fellow of whilk ye'll no find from Annan to Nith. But who, in the name of all that's holy, can this strange tyke be?' said this venerable gallant, casting a look of no great delight on me ; 'his dress would scare the sheep, so he can be no shepherd ; and he seems to lack wit to watch the hooded crows from his flock, so he cannot be wealthy;' and with this unceremonious notice of me, he drew in a chair by the side of the maiden, and stroked down her innumerable curls with his hand, which smelled of tar equal to the suffocation of any town damsel. She smiled, for the smell was frankincense to her; the ancient suitor smiled also—a smile rivalling that of a death's-head on a grave-stone—and said, 'Well may ye laugh, lassie; that's the right hand that lays on the tar with mair skill than the proudest man in Tiviotdale, and has more flocks to lay tar on, lassie—seventy score of brood ewes; but why need I brag? A man may ride a summer-day on my farm and no get far over the boundary.'

"I sat confounded at this display of opulence, which I saw had a strong influence on the maiden's heart; while her father, drawing near her, whispered 'Take him, Penney, take him—he's a rich man and well arrayed—he has two tap-coats and a plaid on.'

"The shepherd maiden looked on this antiquated suitor, and she looked on me; but the glow which unrequited love spread over a face of eighteen barely balanced the matter against territorial wealth and its grey-bearded owner. I had no resource save in youth and health; but my adversary came armed in the charms and might of property, and my more modern looks made but a poor battle against the appeal which riches made to maiden vanity. 'Foolish lassie,' said my rival, in a tone which sounded like the first shovelful of churchyard earth thrown on the lid of a coffin—'foolish lassie, why makest thou thy bright een glance from side to side on this stripling and me, as if thou wouldst weigh us in a balance? Who is this raw youth, thinkest thou? The owner of his own proper person, the laird of no-town-brae, as the proverb says, and lord of windy-wa's, as singeth the auld sang. He may wooe you with fine words, but will he drop a bonnet piece of beaten gold in thy lap for every sigh he gives? He may please thee with his face, and, bating that he looks like a fool, his looks are well enough; but can he cast cantraips over ye as I can do? Can he scatter golden spells and paper charms in thy lap, and make ye lady of as mickle land as a hooded crow will fly over when he seeks to prey on the earliest lamb of spring?'

"And as the old man spoke, he produced from the nook-pouch of his plaid a kind of wallet of rough calf-skin, secured with many a strap and string, which he unloosed with a kind of prolonged delight, and then, diving into the bosom of this mouldy sanctuary of Mammon, fished up the remains of an old stocking. 'Haud thy lap, Penney, my woman,' said the owner; and he emptied with a clang into the maiden's lap upwards of a hundred antique pieces of Scottish gold, which avarice had arrested in their circulation before the accession of the house of Stuart. 'There's as mickle as will array thee for the bridal, and here's documents for property which I will give thee the moment the kirk buckles us.' An old piece of leather, which the diligence of the owner had fashioned from a saddle-lap into a pocket-book, supplied him with sundry papers, which he described as he submitted them to her examination. 'That's a haud fast bond on the lands of the laird of Sloken-drouth for seven hundred pounds Scots, a' sure siller; that's the rights of the lands of Knockhoolie, thirty-five pounds yearly, and ye'll be called the dame of Knockhoolie, a bonnie title and weel sounding.'

"But why should I prolong a story of which all who hearken must know the up-shot? I saw the wicked speed that Mammon made in the maiden's affections, and sat dumbfounded and despairing. Her look, which was one of grave consideration at first, gradually brightened and expanded; she looked at the riches and she looked at him, and said, 'But I'm to have the cheese-siller, and the siller for the udder-locks; a riding habit, brown or blue, or one of both; a grey horse and a side saddle. I am to gang to the two fairs of Dumfries, the St. James's fair of Lanark, to the Cameronian sacrament, and to have a dance twice a year—once at Beltane, and once at Hallowmass.'

"'All shall be as thou sayest, Penney, my princess,' said her lover, interrupting, probably, a long list of expected luxuries; 'so name the bridal-day.'

"My vexation now exceeded all bounds of decorum, and I spoke: 'I would counsel ye to name the day soon, for the bridegroom has not an hour to lose; the bridal cups will barely be dry before they're lacked for his lyke wake; he has little time to spare.'

"The bride, as I may safely call her, laughed till her eyes were wet, and said: 'Well spoken, young man; that's the most sensible thing ye have said this blessed night; and so, as there is no time to be lost, ye say, let us be married on Saturday; let the fault fall on the lag end of the week.' For this mention of early joy the bridegroom endeavoured to inflict the penance of a kiss on the lips which uttered it. 'Haud off,' said the damsel, 'filthy body, ye stink of tar. Bide off till the blessing's said, till the meat be consecrated; go home, and nurse your breath, for it's wondrous feeble.'

"I now rose to depart; the bride conducted me to the door, and endeavoured to console me in a departing whisper: 'This is Monday—I'm to be wed on Saturday. Let me see—my father and mother will be frae hame on Thursday, so come owre here in the braw moonlight, and let us have an hour's running round the haystacks, and daffin in the darksome nooks. Auld Worldsworm—Auld Simon Setsiller—him there with the twa tap-coats and the plaid on, wha has not as much breath as would bless his breakfast, he'll ne'er be the wiser on't: what he disnae ken will give him no manner of trouble.' We parted, but we met no more.

"After this unsuccessful inroad on the moorlands, I resolved to push my fortune no farther without some more sensible assurance of success. I was, therefore, on the look out for the young and the handsome: I frequented fairs with the fidelity of a horse dealer, attended all the merry-makings round with the punctuality of a fiddler, and went devoutly to the kirk with the regularity of an ancient maiden whose thoughts had been weaned, by the counsel of aching bones and the eloquence of wrinkles, from free love to religion. But I was doomed to every species of mortification and repulse, and had actually in despair procured a copy of the register of maidens' baptisms in the parish, with the serious resolution of courting them regularly forward according to their seniority of claim, when the wheel of fortune turned up one of her brightest spokes.

"As I sat pondering on my luckless lot, a slender fair-haired girl of fourteen, the daughter of a respectable and opulent farmer, came gliding like a sylph to my side, and, with a manner conscious and sly, said that her father and her mother were gone to a bridal, and that her elder sister, Bess, desired my company to curds and cream, and to help her to while away the fore-night. Now her sister was one of the merriest and rosiest girls in the district; had a dancing foot and a fine ankle, and a voice which lent a grace to old songs which the best of your theatrical quaverers fail to impart. I need not say that her invitation charmed me:

I lavished ribands, as well as thanks, on the bearer of this pleasing news, and passed my hand over her long and curling hair, saying, 'An' thou be spared, some lad will sigh at his supper for thee yet.' She set out a fair chin and a white bosom to the motion of my hand, and seemed perfectly aware, though young now, that she would be older in summer. She tripped to the door, and looking back with an archness of manner, and a roguish glance of her eye, said, 'Ye might have done waur than given me a kiss to carry to my sister, and ane to myself for carrying it;' and, uttering a loud laugh as she saw me rise to follow, away she bounded as light and graceful as a woodland fairy. An old beggar woman looked after her as she fled, and shook her crutch at her: 'Ah, thou young wanton, I heard thy words: they who learn young learn fair, and it's worse to keep the kitten frae the kirn than the auld cat; but see what it all comes to—a lamiter's crutch and an awmous-powk: nought will be a warning!' And the old woman groaned bitterly as she halted along at the memory of merrier days.

"I was true to tryste, and turned my steps to the farmer's residence a little after twilight; the windows were gleaming with light, and the din of merriment resounded far and wide. My fairy messenger met me at the door, and, standing on tiptoe, whispered in my ear: 'Come away, ye have been lang looked for: there's naebody here but Jock Gordon of Goosedub, Rab Robson of Rowantree Burn, and Davie Wilson of Ballacraig: ye ken all the rest except the young laird of Moorbirn and his cousin, whom men call Daunering John.' I entered, and found my knowledge was much more limited than the girl imagined; the farmer's hall was filled with strange faces, for three parishes round had each sent its contribution of youthful flesh and blood.

> 'Ten came east, and ten came west,
>   And ten came rowing o'er the water;
> Twa came down the long dike side,
>   There's twa-and-thirty wooing at her.'

"But if the heroine of Tintock Top rivalled bonnie Bess in the amount of her wooers, I question if she excelled her in the native tact and good management with which she kept in subordination so many fiery and intractable dispositions. We were all seated round a large table, at the head of which the maiden herself presided, distributing her glances among her admirers with an equal and a judicious diligence. Curds and cream, and tea, were in succession handed round—she partook of both, uniting in her own person the pastoral taste of the mountains with the refinement of the vales; songs were sung—she assisted in the strain, and her voice was sweet and delightful; and thus the evening hours flew by. But amid all this show of harmony and good-fellowship, an experienced eye might observe, by the clouding brow and restrained joy of many, that the breeze of love which blew so soft and so balmy would soon burst out into tempest and storm. It is certainly a hazardous policy in such matters to collect a number of admirers face to face: in the silent darkness of a solitary tryst, the lover imagines himself the sole, or at least the favoured, admirer; and after breathing a brief vow, and tasting the joy of a half-yielded kiss, he returns home, leaving his mistress to the nocturnal hardihood and superior address of a more artful lover. But seated with your rivals at your side, your jealousy of affection rises in arms against your peace, and you begin to sum up the hours you have been blessed in her company, and to multiply them by the number of her admirers, conceding in despair a fractional part of affection to yourself, while it is plain your rivals have revelled in round numbers. There is no temper can long endure this; and it seemed plain that my fellow-suitors regarded our meeting as a general field-day—a numbering of the people, that she might wonder over the amount of her admirers and the force of her own charms.

"Conversation began at last to flag, and silence ensued. 'For my own part,' said an upland shepherd, 'I came here for an hour of quiet joy in a dark nook, the darker the better; but here's nought but an assembly of fools from the four winds of heaven, bending their darkening brows at one another, and a young lass sitting to count the strokes they strike, and to reckon every bruised brow a sure sign of her influence among men. Deil have me if I like it; so let short peace and long strife be among ye; and for you, my bonnie dame, the less ye make sport of honest hearts the less sport will evil hearts make of you, and so I leave you.' And away he strode, whistling manfully the tune of the gallant Graemes, in token of defiance. 'Let him go, the rough-footed moorcock, that can clap his wings, but never crow,' said a ploughman from the vale of Ae; 'the smell of tar and tainted mutton is diminished since his departure.' This was touching on a perilous theme—the old feud which exists between the pastoral and agricultural districts. 'I would advise ye lads,' said a youth of moorland descent, 'to eat well of wether mutton and moorcocks afore ye speak lightly of aught that's bred among mosses; ye may need all your strength to maintain unguarded words. Lord, if my cousin of Blackhagg were here, he would make ye eat your own words, though every one were as ill to swallow as a pound of hiplock wool.' The incensed tiller of the holms of Ae started to his feet, his utterance nearly choked with rage: 'Rise, ye moorland coof, ye two-footed tender of four-footed brutes, lacking as much in sense as ye lack in number of limbs; rise this precious moment, else I'll give ye the blow where ye sit.' The man of the moors was not slow in attempting to rise; the brawny arm of a brother shepherd, which clutched his gorget with a grasp equal to the tethering of a bull, alone retarded his rising. 'Let him alone, I say, Sandie; just let him alone,' said the shepherd; 'be civil at a douce man's hearth before his weelfaured daughter: ye ken the auld say, "Be the saint in the hall, and the devil on the greensward"—meaning, nae doubt, that we should carry our mischief out of doors. I'll stretch him as straight as one of his own furrows before an hour blow by, and on the same place too, the lily lea.' The wrath of the husband-man was turned on this doughty auxiliary, and, having a divided aim, it burnt fiercely between them, without harming either. Meantime, other tongues took part in the commotion: parochial nicknames, and family failings, and personal defects were bandied from side to side, with all the keenness of rustic wit and the malice of rivalry; while, on the whole, the maiden sat and looked as one would on a fire burning too fiercely to be quenched.

"It was not my wish to distinguish myself in this strife of tongues, and therefore I sat still, maintaining an expression of face which I hoped would carry me quietly through this stormy tide of contention. I was only deceiving myself.

"'And ye'll sit mute and motionless there, and hear the bonnie green hills of Annandale turned, by the malice of man's wit, into moudie-tammocks,' said a shepherd to me; 'up and speak, for I have spoken till I'm as hoarse as a raven; or rise and fight; if ye have not a tongue in your head, ye may have a soul in your body.'

"All turned their eyes on me at this address, and the uproar subsided for a time to hear my answer to this singular appeal.

"'A soul in his body,' shouted a rustic, in a tone which implied something like a suspicion of my right to the spark immortal, 'have ye not heard the scoffing sang that's ringing from side to side of the country? I wonder the subject of such verses presumed to show his face among sponsible folk.'

"And, to my utter shame and confusion of face, he proceeded to chant the following rude verse, looking all the while on me with an eye sparkling with scorn and derision:

>'Oh, have ye not heard of John Ochiltree?
>That dainty chield John Ochiltree?
>The owl has a voice, and the cat an ee,
>And so has sonsie John Ochiltree.
>An ancient woman wonned in Colean,
>She had never a tooth 'tween her lips but ane,
>She mumbled her meat with a horn spoon,
>Yet she fell in love with a bonnie new tune;
>She bobbed on her crutches so frank and so free,
>To the dainty tune of John Ochiltree.'

"As the verse ended, a laugh burst out which made the roof shake over our heads, to show how fickle men's passions are and the mortification I was doomed to endure. To be the subject of ludicrous rhymes is to have an infection about one equal to the plague. My fellow-suitors shunned me, and the capricious maiden herself assumed an air so haughty and decided that I saw my cause was cureless. All this was witnessed by one who sympathized in my sufferings, and whose ready wit suggested an instant remedy. The milkiness of my nature had already given way to the accumulating reproach; I had started to my feet, and taken one stride towards my rhyming persecutor with a clenched fist, and a face burning in anger, when the young girl who brought me the invitation to this unlucky tryste uttered a scream, and, holding up her hand, laid her ear to the floor like one listening intensely. We all stood mute and motionless: she darted to the door with the rapidity of light, returned in a moment half-breathless, and exclaimed in a voice of seeming despair, 'Oh! Bess, Bess, what will become of ye? Here's Hazelbank—here's our ain father coming up the road. If he sees what I see, he'll burn Solway, be it for him or against him.'

"Like a brood of chickens when the hawk descends, so started, so fluttered, and so flew in all directions this meeting of rivals; the door seemed far too narrow for escape. Seven bounded over the stackyard dike, and three leaped over a quickset hedge six feet high; two ran down the middle of a cornfield, with half the dogs of the place pursuing them; and two, who were strangers, in the haste of escape, fairly leaped into a pond, or small lake, and made good their retreat by swimming to the opposite side. In one minute the clamorous hall of Hazelbank was as mute as a kirk at midnight. As I hastened to retreat with the others, a white hand twitched me cunningly by the sleeve, and pulled me aside into a little closet, where two very warm and ripe lips whispered close in my ear, 'Let the gowks flee, they know not the goose's quack from the eagle's cry; my father's far from home.' And, shutting the chamber-door as she spoke, my bonnie and discreet messenger added, 'My sister Bess is in her grand moods this night; she carries her head o'er high, and winna speak to ye, for the foolery of that silly sang. A pretty thing, to lose a weelfaured lad for the sake of an idle rhyme: sae bide with me; I am almost as tall as Bess is, and I'll be fifteen at midsummer.'

"And now," said this representative of the rustic name of Ochiltree, "I shall stay my narrative; feeling something of the distress of a traveller who comes to the shedlands of sundry roads, and knows not which one to elect; for the adventures which befell me were manifold, and seem in my sight all alike curious and important. But I cannot expect douce grey-headed folk will listen to the idle tales of youthful times. I might have made far more imposing stories of my misadventures among the maidens, for they are not unsusceptible of poetical embellishment; but I despise fictions, and laugh at 'the idly feigned poetic pains' of metre ballad-makers; I abide by the old proverb, 'truth tells aye best.'"

"Truth tells aye best indeed," re-echoed an ancient dame, as she sat by the hall fire, "and yet idle fictions and the embellishments—I think that's the word ye used—of a poetic fancy seem to flow off as glibly as the current of truth itself. Ah! thou auld-farrand ane, dost thou think to pass off the pleasant inventions of thy own fertile brain for the well-known tales of thy early courtship? Ah, my lad"—

and she eyed him with a look where humour and seriousness seemed striving for mastery—"ye are kenned where ye least hope it; far kenned and noted is thy name, as the rhyme-maker said of Satan. And so ye say you are John Ochiltree, and suffered in your youth from maiden's scorn and minstrel's sang? A bonnie tale, indeed! D'ye think I don't know the merry goodman of Dootagen, Simon Rodan by name, whom I have known since he was the height of a pint-stoup. More by token, he plundered my plum-trees when he was a boy, and climbed in at my chamber windows afore the beard was on his chin, and all to woo three of my servant maidens, and my own cousin, bonnie Jeanie Carruthers. Scorned by the lasses, indeed! Mickle scorn have they endured for thee. Ah! thou flatterer and bonnie tale-teller. Many a good advice hast thou received from the parish minister and elders, in full session assembled. A lad the like of Simon Rodan, with all the failings he had, was not to be seen in seven hours' riding. A straighter or a more taper leg never set its foot in a black leather shoe; and it's not much the worse o' the wear yet."

ELPHIN IRVING,

THE FAIRIES' CUPBEARER.

THE lady kilted her kirtle green
  A little aboon her knee,
The lady snooded her yellow hair
  A little aboon her bree,
And she's gane to the good greenwood
  As fast as she could hie.

And first she let the black steed pass,
  And syne she let the brown,
And then she flew to the milk-white steed,
  And pulled the rider down:
Syne out then sang the queen o' the fairies,
  Frae midst a bank of broom,
She that has won him, young Tamlane,
  Has gotten a gallant groom.
                            Old Ballad.

"THE romantic vale of Corriewater, in Annandale, is regarded by the inhabitants, a pastoral and unmingled people, as the last border refuge of those beautiful and capricious beings, the fairies. Many old people yet living imagine they have had intercourse of good words and good deeds with the 'good folk;' and continue to tell that in the ancient of days the fairies danced on the hill, and revelled in the glen, and showed themselves, like the mysterious children of the deity of old, among the sons and daughters of men. Their visits to the earth were periods of joy and mirth to mankind, rather than of sorrow and apprehension. They played on musical instruments of wonderful sweetness and variety of note, spread unexpected feasts, the supernatural flavour of which overpowered on many occasions the religious scruples of the Presbyterian shepherds, performed wonderful deeds of horsemanship, and marched in midnight processions, when the sound of their elfin minstrelsy charmed youths and maidens into love for their persons and pursuits; and more than one family of Corriewater have the fame of augmenting the numbers of the elfin chivalry. Faces of friends and relatives, long since doomed to the battle-trench or the deep sea, have been recognized by those who dared to gaze on the fairy march. The maid has seen her lost lover and the mother her stolen child; and the courage to plan and achieve their deliverance has been possessed by, at least, one border maiden. In the legends of the people of Corrievale there is a singular mixture of elfin and human adventure, and the traditional story of the Cupbearer to the Queen of the Fairies appeals alike to our domestic feelings and imagination.

"In one of the little green loops, or bends, on the banks of Corriewater, mouldered walls, and a few stunted wild plum-trees and vagrant roses, still point out the site of a cottage and garden. A well of pure spring-water leaps out from an old tree-root before the door; and here the shepherds, shading themselves in summer from the influence of the sun, tell to their children the wild tale of Elphin Irving and his sister Phemie; and, singular as the story seems, it has gained full credence among the people where the scene is laid."

"I ken the tale and the place weel," interrupted an old Scottish woman, who, from the predominance of scarlet in her apparel, seemed to have been a follower of the camp; "I ken them weel, and the tale's as true as a bullet to its aim and a spark to powder. Oh, bonnie Corriewater, a thousand times have I pulled gowans on its banks wi' ane that lies stiff and stark on a foreign shore in a bloody grave:" and, sobbing audibly, she drew the remains of a military cloak over her face, and allowed the story to proceed.

"When Elphin Irving and his sister Phemie were in their sixteenth year, for tradition says they were twins, their father was drowned in Corriewater, attempting to save his sheep from a sudden swell, to which all mountain streams are liable; and their mother, on the day of her husband's burial, laid down her head on the pillow, from which, on the seventh day, it was lifted to be dressed for the same grave. The inheritance left to the orphans may be briefly described: seventeen acres of plough and pasture land, seven milk cows, and seven pet sheep (many old people take delight in odd numbers); and to this may be added seven bonnet-pieces of Scottish gold, and a broadsword and spear, which their ancestor had wielded with such strength and courage in the battle of Dryfe Sands, that the minstrel who sang of that deed of arms ranked him only second to the Scotts and Johnstones.

"The youth and his sister grew in stature and in beauty. The brent bright brow, the clear blue eye, and frank and blithe deportment of the former gave him some influence among the young women of the valley; while the latter was no less the admiration of the young men, and at fair and dance, and at bridal, happy was he who touched but her hand or received the benediction of her eye. Like all other Scottish beauties, she was the theme of many a song; and while tradition is yet busy with the singular history of her brother, song has taken all the care that rustic minstrelsy can of the gentleness of her spirit and the charms of her person."

"Now I vow," exclaimed a wandering piper, "by mine own honoured instrument, and by all other instruments that ever yielded music for the joy and delight of mankind that there are more bonnie songs made about fair Phemie Irving than about all other dames of Annandale, and many of them are both high and bonnie. A proud lass maun she be, if her spirit hears; and men say the dust lies not insensible of beautiful verse; for her charms are breathed through a thousand sweet lips, and no farther gone that yestermorn I heard a lass singing on a green hill-side what I shall not readily forget. If ye like to listen, ye shall judge; and it will not stay the story long, nor mar it much, for it is short, and about Phemie Irving." And accordingly he chanted the following rude verses, not unaccompanied by his honoured instrument, as he called his pipe, which chimed in with great effect, and gave richness to a voice which felt better than it could express:

FAIR PHEMIE IRVING.

Gay is thy glen, Corrie,
   With all thy groves flowering;
Green is thy glen, Corrie,
   When July is showering;
And sweet is yon wood where
   The small birds are bowering,
And there dwells the sweet one
   Whom I am adoring.

Her round neck is whiter
   Than winter when snowing;
Her meek voice is milder
   Than Ae in its flowing;

> The glad ground yields music
>   Where she goes by the river;
> One kind glance would charm me
>   For ever and ever.
>
> The proud and the wealthy
>   To Phemie are bowing;
> No looks of love win they
>   With sighing or suing;
> Far away maun I stand
>   With my rude wooing,
> She's a flow'ret too lovely
>   To bloom for my pu'ing.
>
> Oh, were I yon violet,
>   On which she is walking;
> Oh, were I yon small bird,
>   To which she is talking;
> Or yon rose in her hand,
>   With its ripe ruddy blossom;
> Or some pure gentle thought
>   To be blest with her bosom.

This minstrel interruption, while it established Phemie Irving's claim to grace and to beauty, gave me additional confidence to pursue the story.

"But minstrel skill and true love tale seemed to want their usual influence, when they sought to win her attention; she was only observed to pay most respect to those youths who were most beloved by her brother; and the same hour that brought these twins to the world seemed to have breathed through them a sweetness and an affection of heart and mind, which nothing could divide. If, like the virgin queen of the immortal poet, she walked 'in maiden meditation fancy free,' her brother Elphin seemed alike untouched with the charms of the fairest virgins in Corrie. He ploughed his field, he reaped his grain, he leaped, he ran, and wrestled, and danced, and sang, with more skill and life and grace than all other youths of the district; but he had no twilight and stolen interviews: when all other young men had their loves by their side, he was single, though not unsought, and his joy seemed never perfect save when his sister was near him. If he loved to share his time with her, she loved to share her time with him alone, or with the beasts of the field, or the birds of the air. She watched her little flock late, and she tended it early; not for the sordid love of the fleece, unless it was to make mantles for her brother, but with the look of one who had joy in its company. The very wild creatures, the deer and the hares, seldom sought to shun her approach, and the bird forsook not its nest, nor stinted its song, when she drew nigh; such is the confidence which maiden innocence and beauty inspire.

"It happened one summer, about three years after they became orphans, that rain had been for awhile withheld from the earth, the hill-sides began to parch, the grass in the vales to wither, and the stream of Corrie was diminished between its banks to the size of an ordinary rill. The shepherds drove their flocks to moorlands, and marsh and tarn had their reeds invaded by the scythe to supply the cattle with food. The sheep of his sister were Elphin's constant care; he drove them to the moistest pastures during the day, and he often watched them at midnight, when flocks, tempted by the sweet dewy grass, are known to browze eagerly, that he might guard them from the fox, and lead them to the choicest herbage. In these nocturnal watchings he sometimes drove his little flock over the water of Corrie, for the fords were hardly ankle-deep; or permitted his sheep to cool themselves in the stream, and taste the grass which grew along the brink. All this time not a drop of rain fell, nor did a cloud appear in the sky.

"One evening, during her brother's absence with the flock, Phemie sat at her cottage-door, listening to the bleatings of the distant folds and the lessened murmur of the water of Corrie, now scarcely audible beyond its banks. Her eyes, weary with watching along the accustomed line of road for the return of Elphin, were turned on the pool beside her, in which the stars were glimmering fitful and faint. As she looked she imagined the water grew brighter and brighter; a wild illumination presently shone upon the pool, and leaped from bank to bank, and suddenly changing into a human form, ascended the margin, and, passing her, glided swiftly into the cottage. The visionary form was so like her brother in shape and air, that, starting up, she flew into the house, with the hope of finding him in his customary seat. She found him not, and, impressed with the terror which a wraith or apparition seldom fails to inspire, she uttered a shriek so loud and so piercing as to be heard at Johnstone Bank, on the other side of the vale of Corrie."

An old woman now rose suddenly from her seat in the window-sill, the living dread of shepherds, for she travelled the country with a brilliant reputation for witchcraft, and thus she broke in upon the narrative: "I vow, young man, ye tell us the truth upset and down-thrust. I heard my douce grandmother say that on the night when Elphin Irving disappeared—disappeared I shall call it, for the bairn can but be gone for a season, to return to us in his own appointed time—she was seated at the fireside at Johnstone Bank; the laird had laid aside his bonnet to take the book, when a shriek mair loud, believe me, than a mere woman's shriek—and they can shriek loud enough, else they're sair wranged—came over the water of Corrie, so sharp and shrilling, that the pewter plates dinneled on the wall: such a shriek, my douce grandmother said, as rang in her ear till the hour of her death, and she lived till she was aughty-and-aught, forty full ripe years after the event. But there is another matter, which, doubtless, I cannot compel ye to believe: it was the common rumour that Elphin Irving came not into the world like the other sinful creatures of the earth, but was one of the Kane-bairns of the fairies, whilk they had to pay to the enemy of man's salvation every seventh year. The poor lady-fairy—a mother's aye a mother, be she elve's flesh or Eve's flesh—hid her elf son beside the christened flesh in Marion Irving's cradle, and the auld enemy lost his prey for a time. Now, hasten on with your story, which is not a bodle the waur for me. The maiden saw the shape of her brother—fell into a faint, or a trance, and the neighbours came flocking in—gang on with your tale, young man, aud dinna be affronted because an auld woman helped ye wi't."

"It is hardly known," I resumed, "how long Phemie Irving continued in a state of insensibility. The morning was far advanced, when a neighbouring maiden found her seated in an old chair, as white as monumental marble; her hair, about which she had always been solicitous, loosened from its curls, and hanging disordered over her neck and bosom, her hands and forehead. The maiden touched the one, and kissed the other; they were as cold as snow; and her eyes, wide open, were fixed on her brother's empty chair, with the intensity of gaze of one who had witnessed the appearance of a spirit. She seemed insensible of any one's presence, and sat fixed and still and motionless. The maiden, alarmed at her looks, thus addressed her:—' Phemie, lass, Phemie Irving! Dear me, but this be awful! I have come to tell ye that seven of your pet sheep have escaped drowning in the water; for Corrie, sae quiet and sae gentle yestreen, is rolling and dashing frae bank to bank this morning. Dear me, woman, dinna let the loss of the world's gear bereave ye of your senses. I would rather make ye a present of a dozen mug-ewes of the Tinwald brood myself; and now I think on't, if ye'll send over Elphin, I will help him hame with them in the gloaming myself. So, Phemie, woman, be comforted.'

"At the mention of her brother's name she cried out, 'Where is he? Oh, where is he?' gazed wildly round, and, shuddering from head to foot, fell senseless on the floor. Other inhabitants of the valley, alarmed by the sudden swell of the river, which had augmented to a torrent, deep and impassable, now came in to inquire if any loss had been sustained, for numbers of sheep and teds of hay had been observed floating down about the dawn of the morning. They assisted in reclaiming the unhappy maiden from her swoon; but insensibility was joy compared to the sorrow to which she awakened. 'They have ta'en him away, they have ta'en him away,' she chanted, in a tone of delirious pathos; 'him that was whiter and fairer than the lily on Lyddal Lee. They have long sought, and they have long sued, and they had the power to prevail against my prayers at last. They have ta'en him away; the flower is plucked from among the weeds, and the dove is slain amid a flock of ravens. They came with shout, and they came with song, and they spread the charm, and they placed the spell, and the baptized brow has been bowed down to the unbaptized hand. They have ta'en him away, they have ta'en him away; he was too lovely, and too good, and too noble, to bless us with his continuance on earth; for what are the sons of men compared to him?—the light of the moonbeam to the morning sun, the glowworm to the eastern star. They have ta'en him away, the invisible dwellers of the earth. I saw them come on him with shouting and with singing, and they charmed him where he sat, and away they bore him; and the horse he rode was never shod with iron, nor owned before the mastery of human hand. They have ta'en him away over the water, and over the wood, and over the hill. I got but ae look of his bonnie blue ee, but ae, ae look. But as I have endured what never maiden endured, so will I undertake what never maiden undertook, I will win him from them all. I know the invisible ones of the earth; I have heard their wild and wondrous music in the wild woods, and there shall a christened maiden seek him, and achieve his deliverance.' She paused, and glancing around a circle of condoling faces, down which the tears were dropping like rain, said, in a calm and altered but still delirious tone: 'Why do you weep, Mary Halliday? and why do you weep, John Graeme? Ye think that Elphin Irving—oh, it's a bonnie, bonnie name, and dear to many a maiden's heart as well as mine—ye think he is drowned in Corrie, and ye will seek in the deep, deep pools for the bonnie, bonnie corse, that ye may weep over it, as it lies in its last linen, and lay it, amid weeping and wailing, in the dowie kirkyard. Ye may seek, but ye shall never find; so leave me to trim up my hair, and prepare my dwelling, and make myself ready to watch for the hour of his return to upper earth.' And she resumed her household labours with an alacrity which lessened not the sorrow of her friends.

"Meanwhile the rumour flew over the vale that Elphin Irving was drowned in Corriewater. Matron and maid, old man and young, collected suddenly along the banks of the river, which now began to subside to its natural summer limits, and commenced their search; interrupted every now and then by calling from side to side, and from pool to pool, and by exclamations of sorrow for this misfortune. The search was fruitless: five sheep, pertaining to the flock which he conducted to pasture, were found drowned in one of the deep eddies; but the river was still too brown, from the soil of its moorland sources, to enable them to see what its deep shelves, its pools, and its overhanging and hazely banks concealed. They remitted farther search till the stream should become pure; and old man taking old man aside, began to whisper about the mystery of the youth's disappearance; old women laid their lips to the ears of their coevals, and talked of Elphin Irving's fairy parentage, and his having been dropped by an unearthly hand into a Christian cradle. The young men and maids conversed on other themes; they grieved for the loss of the friend and the lover, and while the former thought that a heart so kind and true was not left in the vale, the latter thought, as maidens will, on his handsome person, gentle manners, and merry blue eye, and speculated with a sigh on the time when they might have hoped a return for their love. They were soon joined by others who had heard the wild and delirious language of his sister: the old belief was added to the new assurance, and both again commented upon by minds full of superstitious feeling, and hearts full of supernatural fears, till the youths and maidens of Corrievale held no more love trysts for seven days and nights, lest, like Elphin Irving, they should be carried away to augment the ranks of the unchristened chivalry.

"It was curious to listen to the speculations of the peasantry. 'For my part,' said a youth, "if I were sure that poor Elphin escaped from that perilous water, I would not give the fairies a pound of hiplock wool for their chance of him. There has not been a fairy seen in the land since Donald Cargil, the Cameronian, conjured them into the Solway for playing on their pipes during one of his nocturnal preachings on the hip of the Burnswark hill.'

"'Preserve me, bairn,' said an old woman, justly exasperated at the incredulity of her nephew, 'if ye winna believe what I both heard and saw at the moonlight end of Craigyburnwood on a summer night, rank after rank of the fairy folk, ye'll at least believe a douce man and a ghostly professor, even the late minister of Tinwaldkirk. His only son—I mind the lad weel, with his long yellow locks and his bonnie blue eyes—when I was but a gilpie of a lassie, *he* was stolen away from off the horse at his father's elbow, as they crossed that false and fearsome water, even Locherbriggflow, on the night of the Midsummer fair of Dumfries. Ay, ay— who can doubt the truth of that? Have not the godly inhabitants of Almsfieldtown and Tinwaldkirk seen the sweet youth riding at midnight, in the midst of the unhallowed troop, to the sound of flute and of dulcimer, and though meikle they prayed, naebody tried to achieve his deliverance?'

"'I have heard it said by douce folk and sponsible,' interrupted another, 'that every seven years the elves and fairies pay kane, or make an offering of one of their children, to the grand enemy of salvation, and that they are permitted to purloin one of the children of men to present to the fiend—a more acceptable offering, I'll warrant, than one of their own infernal brood that are Satan's sib allies, and drink a drop of the deil's blood every May morning. And touching this lost lad, ye all ken his mother was a hawk of an uncannie nest, a second cousin of Kate Kimmer, of

Barfloshan, as rank a witch as ever rode on ragwort. Ay, sirs, what's bred in the bone is ill to come out of the flesh.'

"On these and similar topics, which a peasantry full of ancient tradition and enthusiasm and superstition readily associate with the commonest occurrences of life, the people of Corrievale continued to converse till the fall of evening, when each, seeking their home, renewed again the wondrous subject, and illustrated it with all that popular belief and poetic imagination could so abundantly supply.

"The night which followed this melancholy day was wild with wind and rain; the river came down broader and deeper than before, and the lightning, flashing by fits over the green woods of Corrie, showed the ungovernable and perilous flood sweeping above its banks. It happened that a farmer, returning from one of the border fairs, encountered the full swing of the storm; but mounted on an excellent horse, and mantled from chin to heel in a good grey plaid, beneath which he had the farther security of a thick greatcoat, he sat dry in his saddle, and proceeded in the anticipated joy of a subsided tempest and a glowing morning sun. As he entered the long grove, or rather remains of the old Galwegian forest, which lines for some space the banks of the Corriewater, the storm began to abate, the wind sighed milder and milder among the trees; and here and there a star, twinkling momentarily through the sudden rack of the clouds, showed the river raging from bank to brae. As he shook the moisture from his clothes, he was not without a wish that the day would dawn, and that he might be preserved on a road which his imagination beset with greater perils than the raging river; for his superstitious feeling let loose upon his path elf and goblin, and the current traditions of the district supplied very largely to his apprehension the ready materials of fear.

"Just as he emerged from the wood, where a fine sloping bank, covered with short greensward, skirts the limit of the forest, his horse made a full pause, snorted, trembled, and started from side to side, stooped his head, erected his ears, and seemed to scrutinize every tree and bush. The rider, too, it may be imagined, gazed round and round, and peered warily into every suspicious-looking place. His dread of a supernatural visitation was not much allayed when he observed a female shape seated on the ground at the root of a huge old oak-tree, which stood in the centre of one of those patches of verdant sward, known by the name of 'fairy rings,' and avoided by all peasants who wish to prosper. A long thin gleam of eastern daylight enabled him to examine accurately the being who, in this wild place and unusual hour, gave additional terror to this haunted spot. She was dressed in white from the neck to the knees; her arms, long and round and white, were perfectly bare; her head, uncovered, allowed her long hair to descend in ringlet succeeding ringlet, till the half of her person was nearly concealed in the fleece. Amidst the whole, her hands were constantly busy in shedding aside the tresses which interposed between her steady and uninterrupted gaze down a line of old road which winded among the hills to an ancient burial-ground.

"As the traveller continued to gaze, the figure suddenly rose, and, wringing the rain from her long locks, paced round aud round the tree, chanting in a wild and melancholy manner an equally wild and delirious song.

THE FAIRY OAK OF CORRIEWATER.

The small bird's head is under its wing,
    The deer sleeps on the grass;
The moon comes out, and the stars shine down,
    The dew gleams like the glass:
There is no sound in the world so wide,
    Save the sound of the smitten brass,
With the merry cittern and the pipe
    Of the fairies as they pass.
But oh! the fire maun burn and burn,
And the hour is gone, and will never return.

The green hill cleaves, and forth, with a bound,
    Comes elf and elfin steed;
The moon dives down in a golden cloud,
    The stars grow dim with dread;
But a light is running along the earth,
    So of heaven's they have no need:
O'er moor and moss with a shout they pass,
    And the word is spur and speed—
But the fire maun burn, and I maun quake,
And the hour is gone that will never come back.

And when they came to Craigyburnwood,
    The Queen of the Fairies spoke:
"Come, bind your steeds to the rushes so green,
    And dance by the haunted oak:

I found the acorn on Heshbon Hill,
  In the nook of a palmer's poke,
A thousand years since ; here it grows!"
  And they danced till the greenwood shook :
But oh! the fire, the burning fire,
  The longer it burns, it but blazes the higher.

"I have won me a youth," the Elf Queen said,
  "The fairest that earth may see;
This night I have won young Elph Irving
  May cupbearer to be.
His service lasts but for seven sweet years,
  And his wage is a kiss of me."
And merrily, merrily, laughed the wild elves
  Round Corrie's greenwood tree.
But oh! the fire it glows in my brain,
  And the hour is gone, and comes not again.

The Queen she has whispered a secret word,
  "Come hither, my Elphin sweet,
And bring that cup of the charmèd wine,
  Thy lips and mine to weet."
But a brown elf shouted a loud, loud shout,
  "Come, leap on your coursers fleet,
For here comes the smell of some baptized flesh,
  And the sounding of baptized feet."
But oh! the fire that burns, and maun burn;
  For the time that is gone will never return.

On a steed as white as the new-milked milk,
  The Elf Queen leaped with a bound,
And young Elphin a steed like December snow
  'Neath him at the word he found.
But a maiden came, and her christened arms
  She linked her brother around,
And called on God, and the steed with a snort
  Sank into the gaping ground.
But the fire maun burn, and I maun quake,
  And the time that is gone will no more come back.

And she held her brother, and lo! he grew
  A wild bull waked in ire;
And she held her brother, and lo! he changed
  To a river roaring higher;
And she held her brother, and he became
  A flood of the raging fire ;
She shrieked and sank, and the wild elves laughed
  Till the mountain rang and mire.
But oh! the fire yet burns in my brain,
  And the hour is gone, and comes not again.

"O maiden, why waxed thy faith so faint,
  Thy spirit so slack and slaw?
Thy courage kept good till the flame waxed wud,
  Then thy might began to thaw;

Had ye kissed him with thy christened lip,
Ye had wan him frae 'mang us a'.
Now bless the fire, the elfin fire,
That made thee faint and fa';
Now bless the fire, the elfin fire,
The longer it burns it blazes the higher."

"At the close of this unusual strain, the figure sat down on the grass, and proceeded to bind up her long and disordered tresses, gazing along the old and unfrequented road. 'Now God be my helper,' said the traveller, who happened to be the laird of Johnstone Bank, 'can this be a trick of the fiend, or can it be bonnie Phemie Irving, who chants this dolorous sang? Something sad has befallen, that makes her seek her seat in this eerie nook amid the darkness and tempest: through might from aboon I will go on and see.' And the horse, feeling something of the owner's reviving spirit in the application of spur-steel, bore him at once to the foot of the tree. The poor delirious maiden uttered a yell of piercing joy as she beheld him, and, with the swiftness of a creature winged, linked her arms round the rider's waist, and shrieked till the woods rang. 'Oh, I have ye now, Elphin, I have ye now,' and she strained him to her bosom with a convulsive grasp. 'What ails ye, my bonnie lass?' said the laird of Johnstone Bank, his fears of the supernatural vanishing when he beheld her sad and bewildered look. She raised her eyes at the sound, and, seeing a strange face, her arms slipped their hold, and she dropped with a groan on the ground.

"The morning had now fairly broke: the flocks shook the rain from their sides, the shepherds hastened to inspect their charges, and a thin blue smoke began to stream from the cottages of the valley into the brightening air. The laird carried Phemie Irving in his arms, till he observed two shepherds ascending from one of the loops of Corriewater, bearing the lifeless body of her brother. They had found him whirling round and round in one of the numerous eddies, and his hands, clutched and filled with wool, showed that he had lost his life in attempting to save the flock of his sister. A plaid was laid over the body, which, along with the unhappy maiden in a half-lifeless state, was carried into a cottage, and laid in that apartment distinguished among the peasantry by the name of the chamber. While the peasant's wife was left to take care of Phemie, old man and matron and maid had collected around the drowned youth, and each began to relate the circumstances of his death, when the door suddenly opened, and his sister, advancing to the corpse with a look of delirious serenity, broke out into a wild laugh and said: 'Oh, it is wonderful, it's truly wonderful! That bare and death-cold body, dragged from the darkest pool of Corrie, with its hands filled with fine wool, wears the perfect similitude of my own Elphin! I'll tell ye —the spiritual dwellers of the earth, the fairyfolk of oui evening tale, have stolen the living body, and fashioned this cold and inanimate clod to mislead your pursuit. In common eyes this seems all that Elphin Irving would be, had he sunk in Corriewater; but so it seems not to me. Ye have sought the living soul, and ye have found only its garment. But oh, if ye had beheld him, as I beheld him to-night, riding among the elfin troop, the fairest of them all; had you clasped him in your arms, and wrestled for him with spirits and terrible shapes from the other world, till your heart quailed and your flesh was subdued, then would ye yield no credit to the semblance which this cold and apparent flesh bears to my brother. But hearken! On Hallowmass Eve, when the spiritual people are let loose on earth for a season, I will take my stand in the burial-ground of Corrie; and when my Elphin and his unchristened troop come past, with the sound of all their minstrelsy, I will leap on him and win him, or perish for ever.'

"All gazed aghast on the delirious maiden, and many of her auditors gave more credence to her distempered speech than to the visible evidence before them. As she turned to depart, she looked round, and suddenly sunk upon the body, with tears streaming from her eyes, and sobbed out, 'My brother! Oh, my brother!' She was carried out insensible, and again recovered; but relapsed into her ordinary delirium, in which she continued till the Hallow Eve after her brother's burial. She was found seated in the ancient burial-ground, her back against a broken gravestone, her locks white with frost-rime, watching with intensity of look the road to the kirkyard; but the spirit which gave life to the fairest form of all the maids of Annandale was fled for ever."

Such is the singular story which the peasants know by the name of "Elphin Irving, the Fairies' Cupbearer;" and the title, in its fullest and most supernatural sense, still obtains credence among the industrious and virtuous dames of the romantic vale of Corrie.

RICHARD FAULDER, MARINER.

> It's sweet to go with hound and hawk,
>   O'er moor and mountain roamin';
> It's sweeter to walk on the Solway side,
>   With a fair maid at the gloamin';
> But its sweeter to bound o'er the deep green sea,
>   When the flood is chafed and foamin';
> For the seaboy has then the prayer of good men,
>   And the sighing of lovesome woman.
>
> The wind is up, and the sail is spread,
>   And look at the foaming furrow,
> Behind the bark as she shoots away,
>   As fleet as the outlaw's arrow;
> And the tears drop fast from lovely eyes,
>   And hands are wrung in sorrow;
> But when we come back, there is shout and clap,
>   And mirth both night and morrow.
>
> *Old Ballad.*

ON a harvest afternoon, when the ripe grain, which clothed the western slope of the Cumberland hills, had partly submitted to the sickle, a party of reapers were seated on a small green knoll, enjoying the brief luxury of the dinner-hour. The young men lay stretched on the grass; the maidens sat plaiting and arranging their locks into more graceful and seducing ringlets; while three hoary old men sat abreast and upright, looking on the Sea of Solway, which was spread out, with all its romantic variety of headland and rock and bay, below them. The midday sun had been unusually sultry, accompanied with hot and suffocating rushings of wind; and the appearance of a huge and dark cloud, which hung, like a canopy of smoke and flame over a burning city, betokened, to an experienced swain, an approaching storm. One of the old reapers shook his head, and combing the remainder snow over his forehead with his fingers, said, "Woe's me! one token comes, and another token arises, of tempest and wrath on that darkening water.

It comes to my memory like a dream—for I was but a boy then groping trouts in Ellenwater—that it was on such a day, some fifty years ago, that the *Bonnie Babie Allan*, of Saint Bees, was wrecked on that rock, o'er the top of which the tide is whirling and boiling—and the father and three brethren of Richard Faulder were drowned. How can I forget such a sea! It leaped on the shore, among these shells and pebbles, as high as the mast of a brig; and threw its foam as far as the corn-ricks of Walter Selby's stackyard —and that's a good half-mile."

"Ise warrant," interrupted a squat and demure old man, whose speech was a singular mixture of Cumbrian English and Border Scotch—"Ise warrant, Willie, your memory will be rifer o' the loss of the *Lovely Lass*, of Annanwater, who whomel'd, keel upward, on the hip of the Mermaid rock, and spilt her wameful of rare brandy into the thankless Solway. Faith, mickle good liquor has been thrown into that punchbowl; but fiend a drop of grog was ever made out of such a thriftless basin. It will aiblens be long afore such a gudesend comes to our coast again. There was Saunders Macmichael was drunk between yule and yule— forbye——"

"Wae's me, well may I remember that duleful day," interrupted the third bandsman; "it cost me a fair son— my youngest, and my best. I had seven once—alas, what have I now! Three were devoured by that false and unstable water, three perished by the sharp swords of those Highland invaders who slew so many of the gallant Dacres of Clifton and Carlisle; but the Cumberland ravens had their revenge! —I mind the head and lang yellow hair of him who slew my son hanging over the Scottish gate of Carlisle. Ay, I was avenged no doubt. But the son I have left has disgraced for ever our pure blood by wedding a border Gordon, with as mickle gipsy blood in her veins as would make plebeians of all the Howards and the Percies. I would rather have stretched him in the church-ground of Allanbay, with the mark of a Hielandman's brand on his brow, as was the lot of his brave brothers—or gathered his body from among these rocks, as I did those of my other children! But oh, sirs, when did man witness so fearful a coming on as yon dark sky forebodes?"

While this conversation went on, the clouds had assembled on the summits of the Scottish and Cumbrian mountains, and a thick canopy of vapour, which hung over the Isle of Man, waxed more ominous and vast. A light, as of a fierce fire burning, dropped frequent from its bosom, throwing a sort of supernatural flame along the surface of the water, and showing distinctly the haven, and houses, and shipping, and haunted castle of the isle. The old men sat silently gazing on the scene, while cloud succeeded cloud, till the whole congregating vapour, unable to sustain itself longer, stooped suddenly down from the opposing peaks of Criffel and Skiddaw, filling up the mighty space between the mountains, and approaching so close to the bosom of the ocean, as to leave room alone for the visible flight of the seamew and cormorant.

The water-fowl, starting from the sea, flew landward in a flock, fanning the waves with their wings, and uttering that wild and piercing scream which distinguishes them from all other fowl when their haunts are disturbed. The clouds and darkness increased, and the bird on the rock, the cattle in the fold, and the reapers in the field, all looked upward and seaward, expecting the coming of the storm.

"Benjamin Forster," said an old reaper to me, as I approached his side, and stood gazing on the sea, "I counsel thee, youth, to go home, and shelter these young hairs beneath thy mother's roof. The mountains have covered their heads—and hearken, too, that hollow moan running among the cliffs! There is a voice of mourning, my child, goes along the sea-cliffs of Solway before she swallows up the seafaring man. Seven times have I heard that warning voice in one season—and it cries, woe to the wives and the maids of Cumberland!"

On the summit of a knoll, which swelled gently from the margin of a small beck or rivulet, and which was about a dozen yards apart from the main body of the reapers, sat a young Cumbrian maiden, who seemed wholly intent on the arrangement of a profusion of nut-brown locks, which descended, in clustering masses, upon her back and shoulders. This wilderness of ringlets owed, apparently, as much of its curling elegance to nature as to art, and flowed down on all sides with a profusion rivalling the luxuriant tresses of the Madonnas of the Roman painters. Half in coquetry, and half in willingness to restrain her tresses under a small fillet of green silk, her fingers, long, round, and white, continued shedding and disposing this beautiful fleece. At length the locks were fastened under the fillet—a band denoting maidenhood—and her lily-looking hands, dropping across each other in repose from their toil, allowed the eye to admire a smooth and swan-white neck, which presented one of those natural and elegant sinuous lines that sculptors desire so much to communicate to marble. Amid all this sweetness and simplicity there appeared something of rustic archness and coquetry; but it was a kind of natural and born vanity, a little of which gives a grace and joyousness to beauty. Those pure creations of female simplicity, which shine in pastoral speculations, are unknown among the ruddy and buxom damsels of Cumberland. The maritime nymphs of Allanbay are not unconscious of their charms, or careless about their preservation; and to this sweet maiden Nature had given so much female tact as enabled her to know that a beautiful face and large dark hazel eyes have some influence among men. When she had wreathed up her tresses to her own satisfaction, she began to cast around her such glances—suddenly shot, and as suddenly withdrawn—as would have been dangerous concentrated on one object, but which, divided with care, even to the fractional part of a glance, among several hinds, infused a sort of limited joy without exciting hope. Indeed, this was the work of the maiden's eyes alone, for her heart was employed about its own peculiar care, and its concern was fixed on a distant and different object. She pulled from her bosom a silken case, curiously wrought with the needle. A youth sat on the figured prow of a bark, and beneath him a mermaid swam on the green silken sea, waving back her long tresses with one hand and supplicating the young seaman with the other. This singular production seemed the sanctuary of her triumphs over the hearts of men. She began to empty out its contents in her lap; and the jealousy of many a Cumbrian maiden, from Allanbay to Saint Bees Head, would have been excited by learning whose loves these emblems represented. There were letters expressing the ardour of rustic affection—locks of hair, both black and brown, tied up in shreds of silk—and keepsakes, from the magnitude of a simple brass pin, watered with gold, to a massy brooch of price and beauty. She arranged these primitive treasures, and seemed to ponder over the vicissitudes of her youthful affections. Her eyes, after lending a brief scrutiny to each keepsake and symbol, finally fixed their attention upon a brooch of pure gold: as she gazed on it, she gave a sigh, and looked seaward, with a glance which showed that her eye was following in the train of her affections. The maiden's brow saddened at once, as she beheld the thick gathering of the clouds; and, depositing her treasure in her bosom, she continued to gaze on the darkening sea, with a look of increasing emotion.

The experienced mariners on the Scottish and Cumbrian coasts appeared busy mooring, and double mooring, their vessels. Some sought a securer haven; and those who allowed their barks to remain prepared them, with all their skill, for the encounter of a storm, which no one reckoned distant. Something now appeared in the space between the sea and the cloud, and, emerging more fully, and keeping the centre of the sea, it was soon known to be a heavily laden ship, apparently making for the haven of Allanbay. When the cry of "A ship! a ship!" arose among the reapers, one of the old men, whose eyes were something faded, after gazing intently, said, with a tone of sympathy, "It *is* a ship indeed—and woe's me but the path it is in be perilous in a moment like this!"

"She'll never pass the sunken rocks of Saint Bees' Head," said one old man. "Nor weather the headland of Barnhouric and the caverns of Colvend," said another. "And should she pass both," said a third, "the coming tempest, which now heaves up the sea within a cable's length of her stern, will devour her ere she finds shelter in kindly Allanbay!"

"Gude send," said he of the mixed brood of Cumberland and Caledonia—"since she maun be wrecked, that she spills nae her treasure on the thankless shores of Galloway! These northerns be a keen people, with a ready hand, and a clutch like steel: besides, she seems a Cumberland bark, and its meet that we have our ane fish-guts to our ane seamaws."

"Oh, see, see!" said the old man, three of whose children had perished when the *Bonnie Babie Allan* sank—"see how the waves are beginning to be lifted up! Hearken how deep calls to deep; and hear and see how the winds and the windows of heaven are loosened! Save thy servants— even those seafaring men—should there be but one righteous person on board!" And the old reaper rose, and stretched out his hands in supplication as he spoke.

The ship came boldly down the middle of the bay, the masts bending and quivering, and the small deck crowded with busy men, who looked wistfully to the coast of Cumberland.

"She is the *Lady Johnstone*, of Annanwater," said one, "coming with wood from Norway."

"She is the *Buxom Bess*, of Allanbay," said another, "laden with the best of West India rum."

"And I," said the third old man, "would have thought her the *Mermaid*, of Richard Faulder—but," added he, in a lower tone, "the *Mermaid* has not been heard of, nor seen, for many months—and the Faulders are a doomed race: his bonny brig and he are in the bottom of the sea, and with them sleeps the pride of Cumberland, Frank Forster of Derwentwater."

The subject of their conversation approached within a couple of miles, turned her head for Allanbay, and, though the darkness almost covered her as a shroud, there seemed every chance that she would reach the port ere the tempest burst. But just as she turned for the Cumbrian shore, a rush of wind shot across the bay, furrowing the sea as hollow as the deepest glen, and heaving it up masthead high. The cloud, too, dropped down upon the surface of the sea; the winds, loosened at once, lifted the waves in multitudes against the cliffs; and the foam fell upon the reapers, like a shower of snow. The loud chafing of the waters on the rocks prevented the peasants from hearing the cries of men whom they had given up to destruction. At length the wind, which came in whirlwind gusts, becoming silent for a little while, the voice of a person singing was heard from the sea, far above the turbulence of the waves. Old William Dacre uttered a shout, and said:

"That is the voice of Richard Faulder, if ever I heard it in a body. He is a fearful man, and never sings in the hour of gladness, but in the hour of danger—terror and death are beside him when he lifts his voice to sing. This is the third time I have listened to his melody, and many mothers will weep, and maidens too, if his song have the same ending as of old."

The voice waxed bolder, and approached the shore: and as nothing could be discerned, so thick was the darkness, the song was impressive, and even awful.

THE SONG OF RICHARD FAULDER.

It's merry, it's merry, among the moonlight,
    When the pipe and the cittern are sounding,
To rein, like a war-steed, my shallop, and go
    O'er the bright waters merrily bounding.
It's merry, it's merry, when fair Allanbay,
    With its bridal candles is glancing,
To spread the white sails of my vessel, and go
    Among the wild sea-waters dancing.

And it's blithesomer still, when the storm is come on,
    And the Solway's wild waves are ascending
In huge and dark curls, and the shaven masts groan,
    And the canvas to ribbons is rending;
When the dark heaven stoops down unto the dark deep,
    And the thunder speaks 'mid the commotion,
Awaken and see, ye who slumber and sleep,
    The might of the Lord on the ocean!

This frail bark, so late growing green in the wood
    Where the roebuck is joyously ranging—
Now doomed for to roam o'er the wild fishy flood,
    When the wind to all quarters is changing—
Is as safe to thy feet as the proud palace floor,
    And as firm as green Skiddaw below thee;
For God has come down to the ocean's dread deeps,
    His might and his mercy to show thee.

As the voice ceased, the ship appeared, through the cloud, approaching the coast in full swing; her sails rent, and the wave and foam flashing over her, midmast high. The maiden, who has already been introduced to the affection of the reader, gazed on the ship, and, half suppressing a shriek of joy, flew down to the shore, where the cliffs, sloping backwards from the sea, presented a ready landing-place when the waves were more tranquil than now. Her fellow-reapers came crowding to her side, and looked on the address and hardihood of the crew, who, with great skill and success, navigated their little bark through and among the sandbanks and sunken rocks, which make the Solway so perilous and fatal to seamen. At last they obtained the shelter of a huge cliff, which, stretching like a promontory into the sea, broke the impetuosity of the waves, and afforded them hopes of communicating with their friends, who, with ropes and horses, were seen hastening to the shore.

But although Richard Faulder and his *Mermaid* were

now little more than a cable-length distant from the land, the peril of their situation seemed little lessened. The winds had greatly abated; but the sea, with that impulse communicated by the storm, threw itself against the rocks, elevating its waters high over the summits of the highest cliffs, and leaping and foaming around the bark, with a force that made her reel and quiver, and threatened to stave her to pieces. The old and skilful mariner himself was observed amid the confusion and danger, as collected and self-possessed as if he had been entering the bay in the tranquillity of a summer evening, with a hundred hands waving and welcoming his return. His spirit and deliberation seemed more or less communicated to his little crew; but chiefly to Frank Forster, who, in the ardent buoyancy of youth, moved as he moved, thought as. he thought, and acted from his looks alone, as if they had been both informed with one soul. In those times, the benevolence of individuals had not been turned to multiply the means of preserving seamen's lives; and the mariner, in the hour of peril, owed his life to chance, his own endeavours, or the intrepid exertions of the humane peasantry.

The extreme agitation of the sea rendered it difficult to moor or abandon the bark with safety; and several young men ventured fearlessly into the flood on horseback, but could not reach the rope which the crew threw out to form a communication with the land. Young Forster, whose eye seemed to have singled out some object of regard on shore, seized the rope; then leaping with a plunge into the sea, he made the waters flash! Though for a moment he seemed swallowed up, he emerged from the billows like a waterfowl, and swam shoreward with unexpected agility and strength. The old mariner gazed after him with a look of deep concern; but none seemed more alarmed than the maiden with many keepsakes. As he seized the rope, the lily suddenly chased the rose from her cheek, and uttering a loud scream, and crying out, "Oh, help him, save him!" she flew down to the shore, and plunged into the water, holding out her arms, while the flood burst against her, breast high.

"God guide me, Maud Marchbank," cried William Dacre, "ye'll drown the poor lad out of pure love. I think," continued he, stepping back, and shaking the brine from his clothes, "I am the mad person myself—a caress and a kiss from young Frank of Derwentwater is making her comfortable enough. Alas! but youth be easily pleased—it is as the Northern song says:

> Contented wi' little and cantie wi' mair;

but old age is a delightless time!"

To moor the bark was the labour of a few moments; and fathers and mothers and sisters and sweethearts welcomed the youths they had long reckoned among the dead with affection and tears. All had some friendly hand and eye to welcome and rejoice in them, save the brave old mariner, Richard Faulder alone. To him no one spoke, on him no eye was turned; all seemed desirous of shunning communication with a man to whom common belief attributed endowments and powers, which came not as knowledge and might come to other men; and whose wisdom was of that kind against which the most prudent divines and the most skilful legislators, directed the rebuke of church and law. I remember hearing my father say, that when Richard Faulder, who was equally skilful in horsemanship and navigation, offered to stand on his grey horse's bare back, and gallop down the street of Allanbay, he was prevented from betting against the accomplishment of this equestrian vaunt by a wary Scotchman, who, in the brief manner of his country, said, "Dinna wager, Thomas—God guide your wits—that man's no cannie!" At that time, though a stripling of seventeen, and possessed strongly with the belief of the mariner's singular powers, I could not avoid sympathizing with his fortune and the forlorn look with which he stood on the deck while his companions were welcomed and caressed on shore. Nothing, indeed, could equal the joy which fathers and mothers manifested towards their children but the affection and tenderness with which they were hailed by the bright eyes of the Cumbrian maidens.

"His name be praised!" said one old man, to whose bosom a son had been unexpectedly delivered from the waves.

"And blessed be the hour ye were saved from the salt sea and that fearful man," said a maiden, whose blushing cheek and brightening eye indicated more than common sympathy.

"And oh! Stephen Porter, my son," resumed the father, "never set foot on shipboard with that mariner more!"

In another group stood a young seaman with his sister's arms linked round his neck, receiving the blessings and the admonitions which female lips shower so vainly upon the sterner sex: "This is the third time, Giles, thou hast sailed with Richard Faulder, and every time my alarm and thy perils increase. Many a fair face he has witnessed the fate of, and many a fair ship has he survived the wreck of: think of the sea, since think of it thou must, but never more think of it with such a companion."

In another group a young woman stood gazing on a sailor's face, and in her looks fear and love held equal mastery. "Oh! William Rowanberry," said she, and her hand trembled with affection in his while she spoke, " I would have held my heart widowed for one year and a day, in memory of thee; and though there be fair lads in Ullswater, and fairer still in Allanbay, I'll no say they would have prevailed against my regard for thee before the summer. But I warn thee," and she whispered, waving her hand seaward to give importance to her words, "never be found on the great deep with that man again!"

Meanwhile, the subject of this singular conversation kept pacing from stem to stern of the *Mermaid;* gazing, now and then, wistfully shoreward, though he saw not a soul with whom he might share his affections. His grey hair, and his melancholy look, won their way to my youthful regard, while his hale and stalwart frame could not fail of making an impression on one not wholly insensible to the merits of the exterior person. A powerful mind should in poetical justice have a noble place of abode. I detached myself a little from the mass of people that filled the shore, and, seeming to busy myself with some drift wood, which the storm had brought to the hollow of a small rock, I had an opportunity of hearing the old mariner chant, as he paced to and fro, the fragment of an old maritime ballad, part of which is still current among the seamen of Solway, along with many other singular rhymes full of marine superstition and adventure.

SIR RICHARD'S VOYAGE.

Sir Richard shot swift from the shore, and sailed
  Till he reached Barnhourie's steep,
And a voice came to him from the green land,
  And one from the barren deep.
The green sea shuddered, and he did shake,
  For the words were those which no mortals make.

Away he sailed—and the lightning came,
    And streamed from the top of his mast ;
Away he sailed, and the thunder came,
    And spoke from the depth of the blast :
"O God!" he said, and his tresses so hoar
Shone bright i' the flame, as he shot from the shore.

Away he sailed—and the green isles smiled,
    And the sea-birds sang around :
He sought to land—and down sank the shores
    With a loud and a murmuring sound ;
And where the greenwood and the sweet sod should be
There tumbled a wild and a shoreless sea.

Away he sailed—and the moon looked out,
    With one large star by her side—
Down shot the star, and up sprang the sea-fowl
    With a shriek—and roared the tide !
The bark, with a leap, seemed the stars to sweep,
And then to dive in the hollowest deep.

Criffel's green mountain towered on his right—
    Upon his left, Saint Bees—
Behind, Caerlaverock's charmed ground—
    Before, the wild wide seas :
And there a witch-fire, broad and bright,
Shed far a wild unworldly light !

A lady sat high on Saint Bees' Head,
    With her pale cheek on her hand ;
She gazed forth on the troubled sea,
    And on the troubled land ;
She lifted her hands to heaven—her eyes
Rained down bright tears—still the shallop flies.

The shallop shoulders the surge and flies,
    But at that lady's prayer
The charmed wind fell mute, nor stirred
    The rings of her golden hair :
And over the sea there passed a breath
From heaven—the sea lay mute as death.

And the shallop sunders the gentle flood,
    No breathing wind is near :
And the shallop sunders the gentle flood,
    And the flood lies still with fear—
And the ocean, the earth, and the heaven smile sweet
As Sir Richard kneels low at that lady's feet !

While the old mariner chanted this maritime rhyme, he looked upon me from time to time, and perhaps felt pleased in exciting the interest of a youthful mind, and obtaining a regard which had been but sparingly bestowed in his native land. He loosed a little skiff, and, stepping into it, pushed through the surge to the place where I stood, and was in a moment beside me. I could not help gazing, with an eye reflecting wonder and respect, on a face—bold, mournful, and martial, as his was—which had braved so long "the battle and the breeze." He threw across my shoulders a mantle of leopard skin, and said, as he walked towards his little cottage on the rock: "Youth, I promised that mantle to the first one who welcomed me from a voyage of great peril. Take it, and be happier than the giver—and glad am I to be welcomed by the son of my old captain, Randal Forster."

Such were the circumstances under which I became acquainted with Richard Faulder of Allanbay. At his lonely hearth I was afterwards a frequent and welcome guest, and an attentive and wondering auditor to his wild maritime legends, gathered on many an isle and mainland coast; but none of all his stories made a deeper impression on my memory than the tale of "The Last Lord of Helvellyn."

THE LAST LORD OF HELVELLYN.

"An ancient curse still clings to their name."

"IT was, I think, in the year seventeen hundred and thirty-three, that, one fine summer evening, I sat on the summit of Rosefoster Cliff, gazing on the multitudes of waves which, swelled by the breeze and whitened by the moonlight, undulated as far as the eye could reach. The many lights, gleaming from Allanbay, were extinguished one by one; the twinklings of remote Saint Bees glimmered fainter and fainter on the Solway; while the villages and mansions on the Scottish coast, from Annand to Kirkcudbright, were perfectly silent and dark, as beseemed their devout and frugal inhabitants. As I sat and thought on the perils I had encountered and braved on the great deep, I observed a low dark mist arise from the middle of the Solway; which, swelling out, suddenly came rolling huge and sable towards the Cumberland shore. Nor was fear or fancy long in supplying this exhalation with sails and pennons, and the busy hum and murmur of mariners. As it approached the cliff on which I had seated myself, it was not without dismay that I observed it become more dark, and assume more distinctly the shape of a barge, with a shroud for a sail. It left the sea, and settled on the beach within sea-mark, maintaining still its form, and still sending forth the merry din of mariners. In a moment the voices were changed from mirth to sorrow; and I heard a sound and outcry like the shriek of a ship's company whom the sea is swallowing. The cloud dissolved away, and in its place I beheld, as it were, the forms of seven men, shaped from the cloud, and stretched black on the beach; even as corses are prepared for the coffin. I was then young, and not conversant with the ways in which He above reveals and shadows out approaching sorrow to man. I went down to the beach, and though the moon, nigh the full and in mid-heaven, threw down an unbroken light—rendering visible mountain and headland and sea, so that I might count the pebbles and shells on the shore—the seven black shadows of men had not departed, and there appeared a space in the middle, like room measured out for an eighth. A strange terror came upon me, and I began to dread that this vision was sent for my warning; for, be assured, Heaven hath many and singular revelations for the welfare and instruction of man. I prayed, and, while I, prayed, the seven shadows began to move—filling up the space prepared for another; then they waxed dimmer and dimmer, and then wholly vanished!

"I was much moved; and, deeming it the revelation of approaching sorrow, in which I was to be a sharer, it was past midnight before I could fall asleep. The sun had been some time risen when I was awakened by Simon Forester, who, coming to my bedside, said, 'Richard Faulder, arise, for young Lord William of Helvellyn Hall has launched his new barge on the Solway, and seven of the best and boldest mariners of Allanbay must bear him company to bring his fair bride from Preston Hall—even at the foot of the mountain Criffel; hasten and come, for he sails not, be sure, without Richard Faulder!'

"It was a gallant sight to see a shallop, with her halsers and sails of silk, covered with streamers, and damasked with gold, pushing gaily from the bay. It was gallant, too, to behold the lordly bridegroom, as he stood on the prow, looking towards his true-love's land; not heeding the shout and the song and the music swell with which his departure was hailed. It was gallant to see the maids and the matrons of Cumberland, standing in crowds, on headland and cliff, waving their white hands seaward, as we spread our sails to the wind, and shot away into the Solway, with our streamers dancing and fluttering like the mane of a steed as he gallops against the wind. Proud of our charge, and glorying in our skill, we made the good ship go through the surge as we willed; and every turn we made, and every time we wetted her silken sails, there came shout and trumpet-sound from the shore, applauding the seven merry mariners of Allanbay.

"Helvellyn Hall, of which there is now no stone standing, save an old sun-dial around which herdsmen gather at noonday to hear of old marvels of the Foresters, was an extensive mansion, built in the times when perils from the pirate and the Scot were dreaded, and stood on a swelling knoll, encompassed with wood, visible from afar to mariners. In the centre was a tower, and on the summit of the tower was a seat, and in that seat tradition will yet tell you that the good Lord Walter Forester sat for a certain time, in every day of the year, looking on the sea. The swallows and other birds which made their nests and their roosts on the castle-top became so accustomed to his presence, that they built and sang and brought forth their young beside him; and old men, as they beheld him, shook their heads, and muttered over the ancient prophecy, which a saint, who suffered from persecution, had uttered againt the house of Helvellyn:

> 'Let the Lord of Helvellyn look long on the sea—
> For a sound shall he hear, and a sight shall he see;
> The sight he shall see is a bonnie ship sailing,
> The sound he shall hear is of weeping and wailing;
> A sight shall he see on the green Solway shore,
> And no Lord of Helvellyn shall ever see more.'

"As we scudded swiftly through the water, I looked towards the shore of Cumberland, stretching far and near, with all its winding outline, interrupted with woody promontories; and there I beheld the old Lord Walter of Helvellyn, seated on the topmost tower of his castle, looking towards the Scottish shore. I thought on the dying man's rhyme, and thought on the vision of last night; and I counted the mariners, and looked again on the castle and Lord Walter, and I saw that the fulfilling of the prophecy and the vision was approaching. Though deeply affected, I managed the barge with my customary skill, and she flew across the bay, leaving a long furrow of foam behind. Michael Halmer, an old mariner of Allanbay, afterwards told me he never beheld a fairer sight than the barge that day, breasting the billows; and he stood, warding off the sun with his hands from his fading eyes, till we reached the middle of the bay. At that time, he said, he beheld something like a ship formed of a black cloud, sailing beside us, which moved as we moved, and tacked as we tacked; had the semblance of the same number of mariners, and in every way appeared like the bridegroom's barge! He trembled with dismay, for he knew the spectre shallop of Solway, which always sails by the side of the ship which the sea is about to swallow. It was not my fortune to behold fully this fearful vision; but, while I gazed towards Helvellyn Hall, I felt a dread, and although I saw nothing on which ny fears could fix, I remember that a kind of haze or exhalaton, resembling the thin shooting of a distant light, floated through the air at our side, which I could not long endure to look upon. The old lord still preserved his position on the tower, and sat gazing towards us, as still and motionless as a marble statue, and with an intensity of gaze like one who is watching the coming of destiny.

'The acclamations which greeted our departure from Cumberland were exceeded by those which welcomed us to the Scottish shore. The romantic and mountainous coast of Colvend and Siddick was crowded with shepherd and matron and maid, who stood as motionless as their native rocks, and as silent too till we approached within reach of their voices, and then such a shout arose as startled the gulls and cormorants from rock and cavern for a full mile. The Scotch are a demure, a careful, and a singular people; and, amid much homeliness of manner, have something of a poetical way of displaying their affections, which they treasure, too, for great occasions, or, as they say, 'daimen times.' There are certain of their rustics much given to the composition of song and of ballad, in which a natural elegance occasionally glimmers among their antique and liquid dialect. I have been told the Lowland language of Scotland is more soft and persuasive than even that of England; and assuredly there was Martin Robson, a mariner of mine in the *Mermaid*, whose wily Scotch tongue made the hearts of half the damsels of Cumberland dance to their lips. But many of their ballads are of a barbarous jingle, and can only be admired because the names of those whom their authors love and hate, and the names of hill and dale and coast and stream, are interwoven with a ready ease unknown among the rustic rhymes of any other people.

"Preston Hall—the plough has long since passed over its foundation-stones!—was long the residence of a branch of the powerful and ancient name of Maxwell; and such was its fame for generosity that the beggar or pilgrim who went in at the eastern gate empty always came out at the western gate full, and blessing the bounty of the proprietor. It stood at the bottom of a deep and beautiful bay, at the entrance of which two knolls, slow in their swell from the land and abrupt in their rise from the sea, seemed almost to shut out all approach. In former times they had been crowned with slight towers of defence. It was a fairy nook for beauty;

and tradition, which loves to embellish the scenes on which Nature has been lavish of her bounty, asserted that the twin hillocks of Preston Bay were formerly one green hill, till a wizard, whose name has not yet ceased to work marvels, cleft the knoll asunder with his wand, and poured the sea into the aperture, laying, at the same time, the foundation-stone of Preston Hall with his own hand.* On the sides and summits of these small hills stood two crowds of peasants, who welcomed the coming of Lord William with the sounding of instruments of no remarkable harmony. As this clamorous hail ceased, the melody of maidens' tongues made ample amends for the instrumental discord. They greeted us as we passed with this poetical welcome, after the manner of their country:

THE MAIDENS' SONG.

Maids of Colvend.

Ye maidens of Allanbay, sore may ye mourn,
For your lover is gone, and will wedded return;
His white sail is filled, and the barge cannot stay,
Wide flashes the water—she shoots through the bay.
Weep, maidens of Cumberland, shower your tears salter,
The priest is prepared and the bride's at the altar!

Maids of Siddick.

The bride she is gone to the altar, and far
And in wrath flies gay Gordon of green Lochinvar;
Young Maxwell of Munshes, thy gold spur is dyed
In thy steed, and thy heart leaps in anguish and pride;
The bold men of Annand and proud Niddisdale
Have lost her they loved, and may join in the wail.

Maids of Colvend.

Lord William is come; and the bird on the pine,
The leaf on the tree, and the ship on the brine,

---

* Scotland is rife with the labours of wizard and witch. The beautiful green mountain of Criffel, and its lesser and immediate companions, were created by a singular disaster which befell Dame Ailie Gunson. This noted and malignant witch had sustained an insult from the sea of Solway, as she crossed it in her wizard shallop, formed from a cast-off slipper; she, therefore, gathered a huge creelful of earth and rock, and, stride after stride, was advancing to close up for ever the entrance of that beautiful bay. An old and devout mariner who witnessed her approach thrice blessed himself, and at each time a small mountain fell out of the witch's creel; the last was the largest, and formed the mountain Criffel, which certain rustic antiquarians say is softened from "creel fell," for the witch dropped earth and creel in despair.

The blue heaven above, and below the green earth,
Seem proud of his presence, and burst into mirth.
Then come, thou proud fair one, in meek modest mood—
The bridal bed's ready—unloosen thy snood !

Maids of Siddick.
The bridal bed's ready ; but hearken, high lord !
Though strong be thy right arm, and sharp be thy sword,
Mock not Beatrice Maxwell ! else there shall be sorrow
Through Helvellyn's valleys, ere sunrise to morrow :
Away, haste away ! Can a gallant groom falter
When the bridal wine's poured and the bride's at the altar !

"During this minstrel salutation the barge floated into the bosom of Preston Bay ; and through all its woody links and greenwood nooks the song sounded mellow and more mellow, as it was flung from point to point over the sunny water. The barge soon approached the greensward, which, sloping downwards from the Hall, bordering with its livelier hue the dull deep green of the ocean, presented a ready landing-place. When we were within a lance's length of the shore there appeared, coming towards us from a deep grove of holly, a female figure, attired in the manner of the farmer matrons of Scotland—with a small plaid, or mantle, fastened over her grey lint-and-woollen gown, and a white cap, or mutch, surmounting, rather than covering, a profusion of lyart locks which came over her brow and neck, like remains of winter snow. She aided her steps with a staff, and descending to the prow of the barge, till the sea touched her feet, stretched her staff seaward, and said, with a deep voice and an unembarrassed tone : 'What wouldest thou, William Forster, the doomed son of a doomed house, with Beatrice Maxwell, the blessed child of a house whose name shall live, and whose children shall breathe, while green woods grow and clear streams run ? Return as thou camest, nor touch a shore hostile to thee and thine. 'If thy foot displaces but one blade of grass, thy life will be as brief as the endurance of thy name, which that giddy boy is even now writing on the sand within sea-mark—the next tide will pass over thee, and blot it out for ever and for ever ! Thy father, even now watching thy course from his castle-top, shall soon cease to be the warder of his house's destiny ; and the Cumberland boor, as he gazes into the bosom of the Solway, shall sigh for the ancient and valiant name of Forster.'

"While this singular speech was uttering I gazed on the

person of the speaker, from whom no one who once looked could well withdraw his eyes. She seemed some seventy years old, but unbowed or unbroken by age, and had that kind of commanding look which common spirits dread. Lord William listened to her words with a look of kindness and respect. 'Margery Forsythe,' he said, 'thou couldest have prophesied more fortunately and wisely hadst thou wished it; but thou art a faithful friend and servant to my Beatrice—accept this broad piece of gold, and imagine a more pleasant tale when, with the evening tide, I return with my love to Helvellyn.'

"The gold fell at the old woman's feet, but it lay glittering and untouched among the grass, for her mind and eye seemed intent on matters connected with the glory of her master's house.

"'Friend am I to Beatrice Maxwell, but no servant,' said Margery, in a haughty tone, 'though it's sweet to serve a face so beautiful. Touch not this shore, I say again, William Forster; but it's vain to forbid—the thing that must be must; we are fore-ordained to run our course, and this is the last course of the gallant house of Forster.'

"She then stepped aside, opposing Lord William no longer, who, impatient at her opposition, was preparing to leap ashore. Dipping her staff in the water as a fisher dips his rod, she held it dripping towards the Solway, to which she now addressed herself:—'False and fathomless sea, slumbering now in the sweet summer sun like a new-lulled babe, I have lived by thy side for years of sin that I shall not sum; and every year hast thou craved and yearned for thy morsel, and made the maids and matrons wail in green Galloway and Nithsdale. When wilt thou be satisfied, thou hungry sea? Even now, sunny and sweet as thou seemest, dost thou crave for the mouthful ordained to thee by ancient prophecy, and the fair and the dainty morsel is at hand.'

"Her eyes, dim and spiritless at first, became filled, while she uttered this apostrophe to the sea, with a wild and agitated light—her stature seemed to augment, and her face to dilate with more of grief than joy; and her locks, snowy and sapless with age, writhed on her forehead and temples, as if possessed with a distinct life of their own. Throwing her staff into the sea, she then went into the grove of holly, and disappeared.

"'May I be buried beyond the plummet sound,' said Sam Dacre of Skiddawbeck, 'if I fail to prove if that dame's tartan kirtle will flatten swan-shot,—I never listened to such unblessed language;' and he presented his carbine after her, while William Macgowan, a Galloway sailor, laid his hand on the muzzle, and said:

"'I'll tell thee what, Margery Forsythe has mair forecast in the concerns o' the great deep than a wise mariner ought to despise. Swan-shot, man! She would shake it off her charmed calimanco kirtle as a swan shakes snow from its wings. I see ye're scantly acquaint with the uncannie pranks of our Colvend dame. But gang up to the Boran Point, and down to Barnhourie Bank, and if the crews of two bonnie ships, buried under fifteen fathom of quicksand and running water, winna waken and tell ye whose uncannie skill sunk them there, the simplest hind will whisper ye that Margery Forsythe kens mair about it than a God-fearing woman should. So ye see, Lord William Forster, I would even counsel ye to make yere presence scarce on this kittle coast—just wyse yersel warily owre the salt water again. And true-love's no like a new-killed kid in summer; it will keep, ye see; it will keep. This cross cummer will grow kindly, and we shall come snoring back in our barge, some bonnie moonlight summer night, and carry away my young lady with a sweeping oar and a wetted sail. For if we persist when she resists we shall have wet sarks and droukit hair. Sae ye laugh and listen not? Aweel, aweel, them that will to Couper will to Couper! A doomed man's easily drowned! The thing that maun be maun be! and sic things shall be if we sell ale!'

"These predestinating exclamations were abridged by a long train of bridal guests hurrying from the Hall to receive the bridegroom, who, disregarding all admonition, leaped gaily ashore, and was welcomed with trumpet flourish and the continued sound of the Lowland pipe. He was followed by six of his seven mariners; I alone remained, overawed by the vision I had beheld on the preceding night, by the prophetic words of the sorceress of Siddick, and by that boding forecast of disaster which the wise would do well to regard.

"On all sides people were seated on the rising grounds: the tree-tops, the immemorial resting-places of ravens and rooks, were filled with young men, anxious to see the procession to the chapel of Preston and to hearken the bridal joy; and even the rough and dizzy cliff of Barnhourie Burn, which overlooks the Solway for many miles, had the possession of its summit disputed with its native cormorants and eagles by some venturous schoolboys, who thus showed that love of adventure which belongs to the children of the sea-coast. The sun was in noon when we landed in Preston Bay, and its edge was touching the grassy tops of the western hills of Galloway, when shout above shout, from wood and eminence, the waving of white hands from field and knoll, and the sudden awakening of all manner of clamorous and mirthful melody announced the coming of the bridal crowd. The gates of Preston Hall burst suddenly open; out upon the level lawn gushed an inundation of youths and maidens clad in their richest dresses, and the living stream flowed down to the Solway side. As they approached, a shallop, covered from the masthead to the water with streamers and pennons and garlands, came suddenly from a small anchorage scooped out of the bosom of the garden, making the coming tide gleam to a distance with the gold and silver lavished in its decoration. But my admiration of this beautiful shallop was soon interrupted by the appearance of a lady, who, standing on the ground by the prow of the bride's barge, looked earnestly seaward, and trembled so much that the white satin dress which covered her from bosom to heel, studded and sown and flowered with the most costly stones and metals, shook as if touched by an ungentle wind. Her long tresses, of raven black hair, and which, in the boast of maidenhood of my early days, descended till she could sit upon them, partook of her agitation. Her eyes alone, large and bright, and fringed with long lashes of a black still deeper than that of her hair, were calm and contemplative, and seemed with her mind meditating on some perilous thing. While she stood thus a maiden came to her side, and, casting a long white veil, a present from the bridegroom, over her head, shrouded her to the feet; but the elegance of her form and the deep dark glance of her expressive eyes triumphed over the costly gift, though the fringe was of diamonds and the disastrous tale of the youth who perished swimming over the Solway to his love was wrought, or rather damasked, in the middle. I could have gazed from that hour till this on this beautiful vision; but while I looked there came slowly from the wood a figure of a woman, bent with age or distress to the ground, and entirely covered in a black mantle: she approached the bride unperceived, and lay down at her feet, as a footstool on which she must tread before she could enter the shallop. This was unheeded of many, or of all; for the blessings showered by all ranks on the departing pair, the bustle of the mariners preparing to sail with the tide, which now filled Preston Bay, the sounding of bugle and pipe, and the unremitting rivalry in song and ballad between the mariners in the barges of the bridegroom and bride, successively filled every mind save mine, overclouded then, and as it has ever since been, before some coming calamity. Ballad and song passed over my memory without leaving a verse behind; one song alone, sung by a mariner of Allanbay, and which has long been popular on the coast, interested me much, more I confess from the dark and mysterious manner in which it figured or shadowed forth our catastrophe than from its poetical merit, the last verse alone approaching to the true tone of the lyric.

MICHAEL HALMER'S SONG.

Upon the bonnie mountain side,
  Upon the leafy trees,
Upon the rich and golden fields,
  Upon the deep green seas,
The wind comes breathing freshly forth
  Ho! pluck up from the sand
Our anchor, and go shooting as
  A winged shaft from the land!
The sheep love Skiddaw's lonesome top,
  The shepherd loves his hill,
The throstle loves the budding bush,
  Sweet woman loves her will;
The lark loves heaven for visiting,
  But green earth for her home;
And I love the good ship, singing
Through the billows in their foam.

"My son," a grey-haired peasant said,
  "Leap on the grassy land,
And deeper than five fathom sink
  Thine anchor in the sand,
And meek and humble make thy heart,
  For ere yon bright'ning moon
Lifts her wondrous lamp above the wave
  Amid night's lonely noon,
There shall be shriekings heard at sea,
  Lamentings heard ashore—
My son, go pluck thy mainsail down,
  And tempt the heav'n no more.

Come forth and weep, come forth and pray,
  Grey dame and hoary swain—
All ye who have got sons to-night
  Upon the faithless main."

"And wherefore, old man, should I turn?
  Dost hear the merry pipe,
The harvest bugle winding
  Among Scotland's cornfields ripe—
And see her dark-eyed maidens dance,
  Whose willing arms alway
Are open for the merry lads
  Of bonnie Allanbay?"
Full sore the old man sighed, and said,
  "Go bid the mountain wind
Breathe softer, and the deep waves hear
  The prayers of frail mankind,
And mar the whirlwind in his might."
  His hoary head he shook,
Gazed on the youth and on the sea,
  And sadder waxed his look.

"Lo! look! here comes our lovely bride!
  Breathes there a wind so rude
As chafe the billows when she goes
  In beauty o'er the flood—
The raven fleece that dances
  On her round and swan-white neck—
The white foot that wakes music
  On the smooth and shaven deck—
The white hand that goes waving thus,
  As if it told the brine,
'Be gentle in your ministry,
  O'er you I rule and reign'—
The eye that looks so lovely,
  Yet so lofty in its sway?
Old man, the sea adores them—
  So adieu, sweet Allanbay!"

"During the continuance of this song, an old gentleman of the house of Maxwell, advancing through the press to the barges, said aloud: 'A challenge, ye gallants, a challenge! Let the bridegroom take his merry mariners of England—let the bride take her mariners of old Galloway—push the barges from Preston Bay as the signal-pipe sounds; and a pipe of blood-red wine to a cupful of cold water that *we* reach Allanbay first.' As the old man finished his challenge hundreds of hats, and bonnets too, were thrown into the air, and the bridegroom, with a smile, took his offered hand and said: 'What! Sir Marmaduke Maxwell, wilt thou brave us too? A pipe of the richest wine to a drink of the saltest brine in the centre of Solway, that the merry lads of Allanbay exceed thee at least by ten strokes of the oar.' The English mariners replied, as is their wont, with a shout, threw aside their jackets and caps, and prepared gladly for the coming contest; nor were the mariners of Siddick and Colvend slow in preparing: they made themselves ready with that silent and sedate alacrity peculiar to that singular people. 'May I never see Skiddaw again,' said William Selby of Derwent, 'nor taste Nancy Grogson's grog, or her pretty daughter's lips, if the fresh-water lads of Barnhourie surpass the salt-water lads of Allanbay!'

"'And for my part,' said Charles Carson, 'in answer to my comrade's vow, may I be turned into a sheldrake, and doomed to swim to doomsday in the lang black lake of Loughmaben, if the powkpuds of Skiddaw surpass the cannie lads of green Galloway!' And both parties, matched in numbers, in strength—of equal years and of similar ability —stood with looks askance on each other, ready to start, and willing to win the bridal boast, and the bride or bridegroom's favour.

"'And now, my sweet bride,' said Lord William, 'shall I help thee into thy barge? Loth am I that thy kinsman's vaunt causes a brief separation. Now guide thy barge wisely and warily,' said he to her helmsman; 'I would rather pay the wine for thy mistress ten thousand-fold than one lock of her raven hair should be put in jeopardy. If thou bringest her harmless into Allanbay, I will give a hundred pieces of gold to thee and thy mates. Shouldst thou peril her in thy folly, come before my face no more.'

"'Peril Beatrice Maxwell, Lord William!' said the Scottish helmsman, with a look of proud scorn; 'my fathers have fought to the saddle-laps in English blood for the men of the house of Maxwell, and I would rather see all who own the surname of Forster sinking in the Solway without one to help them than be the cause of the fair maiden of Preston soiling slipper or snood. I see ye dinna ken the Howatsons of Glenhowan.'

"'I know nought of the Howatsons of Glenhowan,' said the bridegroom, 'but what I am proud and pleased with; therefore ply the oar and manage the sail, for I have men with me who will put you to your might in both.'

"To this conciliating speech the maritime representative of the ancient Howatsons of Glenhowan returned no answer, but, busying himself in his vocation, chanted, as was his wont on going upon any important mission, some fragments of an old ballad, made by one of the minstrels of the house of Maxwell when its glory was at the fullest.

> "Give the sail to the south wind, thou mariner bold,
>   Keep the vessel all stately and steady,
> And sever the green grassy sward with her prow,
>   Where yon lances gleam level and ready."
> "An ominous star sits above the bright moon,
>   And the vessel goes faster and faster ;
> And see ! the changed planet, so lovely e'en now,
>   Glows like blood, and betokens disaster."
> "The moon, thou coward churl—lo ! see the swift shafts
>   All as fleet as the winter snow flying,
> And hearken the war-steed ! he neighs in his strength,
>   And tramples the dead and the dying."
> And the bark smote the ground, and ashore they all leapt,
>   With war-shout, and pipe-note, and clangour
> Of two-handed claymore and hauberk—and soon
>   Their foes they consumed in their anger.
>
> All on yon fair shore, where the cowslips bloom thick
>   And the sea-waves so brightly are leaping,
> The sun saw in gladness—the moon saw in death
>   Three hundred proud Foresters sleeping :
> And long shall the Cumberland damosels weep,
>   Where the sweet Ellenwater is flowan,
> The hour the gay lads of Helvellyn were slain
>   By Lord Maxwell and gallant Glenhowan.

"Ere the song had ceased the bride proceeded to enter the barge, when she perceived at her feet a figure in a black mantle, and scarce refrained from shrieking. 'Margery, what wouldst thou with me, Margery?' she said; 'the cottage thou livest in I have given thee.'

"'Worlds, wealth, and creature comforts are no cares of mine,' said the old domestic of the house of Maxwell. 'I laid me down here, that ere Beatrice Maxwell departs with one of a doomed house she should step over my grey hairs. Have I not said—have I not prayed?'

"'Margery, Margery,' said the bride, 'be silent and be wise.'

"'Are we to stand here, and listen to the idle words of a crazed menial?' said one of the house of Maxwell. 'Aboard, ye gallants, aboard!' And, placing the bride on deck, the barges, urged by oar and sail, darted out of the bay of Preston, while the shout and song of clamouring multitudes followed us far into the ocean.

"The wind of the summer twilight, gentle and dewy, went curling the surface of the water; before us the green mountains of Cumberland rose; behind us we beheld the huge outline of the Scottish hills, while, a full stonecast asunder, the barges pursued their way, and the crews, silent and anxious, had each their hopes of conquering in the contest. As we went scudding away I looked toward the Hall of Helvellyn, and there I beheld on its summit the old lord, with his grey hair, his hands clasped, and his eyes turned intent on the barge which contained his son. I thought on the prophecy and on the vision of the preceding evening, and looked towards the hills of Scotland, now fast diminishing in the distance. At first I thought I saw the waters agitated in the track we had pursued, and, continuing to gaze, I observed the sea, furrowed into a tremendous hollow, following the sinuous course of the barge. I now knew this to be a whirlwind, and, dreading that it would fasten on our sails, I tacked northward—the whirlwind followed also. I tacked southward, and to the south veered the whirlwind, increasing in violence as it came. The last sight I beheld was the sea at our stern, whirling round in fearful undulations. The wind at once seized our sails, turned us thrice about, and down went the barge, headforemost, in the centre of Solway. I was stunned, and felt the cold brine bubbling in my ears, as, emerging from the flood, I tried to swim. Barge, bridegroom, and mariners were all gone. The bride's barge came in a moment to my side, and saved me, and, standing for the coast of Cumberland, spread the tale of sorrow along the shore, where crowds had assembled to welcome us. The old Lord of Helvellyn remained on the castle-top after he had witnessed the loss of his son; and, when his favourite servant ventured to approach, he was found seated in his chair, his hands clasped more in resignation than agony, his face turned to the Solway and his eyes gazing with the deepest intensity, and stiff and dead. The morning tide threw the body of Lord William and those of his six mariners ashore; and when I walked down at day-dawn to the beach I found them stretched in a row on the very spot where the vision had revealed their fate to me so darkly and so surely. Such a tale as this will be often told you among the sea-coast cottages of Cumberland. Young man, be wise, and weigh well the mysterious ways of Providence."

JUDITH MACRONE,

THE PROPHETESS.

> BUT I am haunted by a fearful shape—
> Some hated thing which sharp fear forms of shadows;
> Something which takes no known form, yet alarms
> Me worse than my worst foeman armed in proof;
> Something which haunts my slumbers—finds me out
> In my deep dreams—in fiercest strife, when blood
> Runs rife as rivulet water—in quiet peace,
> When rustic songs abound—in silent prayer,
> For prayer, too, have I tried—still is it there;
> Now—now—the dismal shadow stalks before me,
> More visible than ever!

THE whole course of Annanwater, in Dumfriesshire, is beautiful; from where it arises among the upland pastures, in the vicinity of the sources of the Clyde and the Tweed, and winding its way by old churchyard, decayed castle, Roman encampment, and battle-field, through fine natural groves and well-cultivated grounds, finally unites its waters with the sea of Solway, after conferring its name on the pretty little borough of Annan. The interior of the district, it is true, presents a singular mixture of desolate nature and rich cultivation; but the immediate banks of the river itself are of a varied and romantic character. At every turn we take we come to nooks of secluded and fairy beauty—groves of fine ancient trees, coeval with the ruined towers they embosom—clumps of the most beautiful holly, skirted with *rones* or irregular rows of hazel, wild cherry, and wild plum—remains of military or feudal greatness, dismantled keeps or peels, and repeated vestiges of broad Roman roads and ample camps, with many of those massive and squat structures, vaulted and secured with double iron doors, for the protection of cattle, in former times, from reavers and forayers. The river itself has attractions of its own: its inconsiderable waters are pure, and the pebbles may be numbered in the deepest pools, save when the stream is augmented by rains; and for the net, the liester, and the fly-hook, it produces abundance of salmon, grilses, herlings, and trouts.

The peasantry are as varied in their character as the district they inhabit. Agriculture and pasturage claim an equal share in the pursuits of almost every individual; and they are distinguished from the people of many other Lowland districts by superior strength, agility, and courage: the free mountain air, gentle labour, and variety of pursuits give a health and activity which fit them for martial exercises, and they have, perhaps, more of a military air about them than the inhabitants of any of the neighbouring vales. Many strange, romantic, and martial stories linger among them; and those who have the good fortune to be admitted to their friendship or their fireside may have their condescension richly repaid by curious oral communications, in which history, true and fabulous, and poetry and superstition, are strangely blended together. The tale of the spirit which for many generations has haunted the castle of Spedlans will have its narrative of ordinary horror accompanied by fairy legends and traditions more romantic in their origin, and more deeply steeped in the dews of superstition.

One fine September morning, for the combined purpose of angling, gathering nuts, and exploring the strongholds of the ancient heroes of Annandale—the Hallidays, the Jardines, the Carlyles, the Bells, and the Irvings—I proceeded up the river bank, and employed my fish-rod with a success which drove me in despair to nut-gathering. It was past midday when I arrived at a fine bold sweep of the stream, where the shade of the bordering groves was invitingly cool and the greensward fresh, soft, and untrodden. The sun was, to use the expression of a Scottish poet, "wading 'mang the mist," or, as a fastidious Englishman would say, "struggling amid drizzly rain," which abated the heat of the luminary, and rendered the grass blade cool and moist. A large oak-tree or two, set down in the random beauty of Nature, adorned the narrow holm, or bordering of greensward, between the wood and the water; while at the extremity of the walk, where the stream was limited by projecting rocks, stood the remains of one of those square peels, or towers of refuge, already alluded to. The building was roofless, and the walls had been lessened in their height by military violence; while from its interior ascended a thin blue smoke, which, curling away among the straight stems of the trees, escaped into the free air through the upper boughs of the grove. Between the tower and the river lay many webs of fine linen, bleaching on the grass; while from the ruin itself came the uninterrupted merriment of some country maidens—a singular medley of open laughter, fragments of song, and taunts about courtship and sarcasms on the lack of lovers.

"Lads!" said a shrill voice, "I never saw such soulless coofs! Ane would think we had ne'er a tooth in our heads, or a pair o' lips for the kissing."

"Kissing, indeed!" said another; "ane would think our lips were made for nought save supping curds or croudy, and that we were suspected of witchcraft. Here we have been daidling in this den of woe and dool from blessed sunrise, and deil a creature with hair on its lip has mistaken its road and come near us. I think ancient spunk and glee be dead and gone from merry Annanwater."

"Ah, my bonnie lasses," interrupted an old woman, half-choked with a churchyard cough, "I mind weel in the blessed year fifteen, we had a bonnie bleaching in this very place. There was Jeany Bell, and Kate Bell, her cousin, who had a misfortune at forty, and was made an honest woman at fifty-eight; and there was Bell Irving and me. Lads! we had the choice of the parish; ye might have heard the caressing o' our lips as far as the Wyliehole; and what would ye think—Pate Irving, now a douce man and a godly, was the wantonest of all. Ah, my bonnie kimmers, that was a night."

This description of departed joys seemed to infuse its spirit into the younger branches of the establishment; for while I pondered how I might introduce myself to these water-nymphs with discretion and humility, I observed a young rosy face, ornamented with a profusion of glistering nut-brown locks, projected past the porch, and reconnoitring me very steadfastly. A forehead with dark eyes and raven hair instantly assisted in the scrutiny, and presently the head of the ancient dame herself appeared, obtruded beyond them both—like Care looking out between Mirth and Joy, in a modern allegory. A tartan nightcap endeavoured in vain to restrain her matted and withered air, which the comb had not for a long while sought to shed or the scissors to abridge; her cheeks were channeled, and a pair of spectacles perched on a nose something of the colour and shape of a lobster's claw assisted her in drawing conclusions from the appearance of a stranger.

I heard the tittering and whispering of the maidens; but the voice of the old woman aspired to something more elevated than a whisper, and mingled counsel and scolding in equal quantities.

"A fisher, indeed!" responded the sibyl to the queries of one of her greener companions; "and what's he come to fish?—a snow-white web from the bottom of our caldron? Ay, ay, 'cause he has ae handsome leg, and something of a merry ee—mind ye, I say na twa—ye christen his calling honest. He's a long black fallow with a tinker look, and I'll warrant there's no his marrow from Longtown to Lochmaben for robbing hen-roosts; and yet I shouldna wonder, Mysie Dinwoodie, if ye held tryst with that strange lad for a whole night with no witness save the blessed moon."

"Hout now, Prudence Caird," said the fair-haired girl, "ye are thinking on the mistake ye made with Pate Johnstone of Dargavel, and how ye failed to mend it with Dick Bell o' Cowfloshan."

The secret history of the old woman's unhappy loves was interrupted by the appearance of a very handsome girl, who, bearing refreshments for her menials, glided through the grove, with a foot so light and white, a look so sweet, a high white forehead, shaded with locks clustering over the temples, and with eyes so large, so bright, and blue—that she seemed a personification of the shepherd maidens of Scottish song. Two fine moorland dogs accompanied her: they sat as she sat, stood as she stood, and moved as she moved. She withdrew from her companions, and approached where I stood, with a look at once so sweet and demure, that, trespasser as I imagined myself to be, I was emboldened to abide a rebuke, which I hoped would come softened from such sweet lips. Though apparently examining the progress of her linen towards perfect whiteness, and approaching me rather by a sidelong than a direct step, I observed, by a quick glance of her eye, that I was included in her calculations. I was saved the confusion which a bashful person feels in addressing a stranger by a voice from the river bank, which, ascending from a small knoll of green willows, sang with singular wildness some snatches of an old ballad.

O Annan runs smoothly atween its green banks,
  The ear may scarce listen its flowing:
Ye may see 'tween the ranks of the lofty green trees
  The golden harvest glowing,
And hear the horn wound, see the husbandman's bands
Fall on with their sharp sickles bright in their hands.
I have seen by thy deep and romantic stream
  The sword of the warrior flashing;
I have seen through thy deep and thy crystal stream
  The barbed war-steeds dashing:
There grows not a green tree, there stands not a stone,
But the fall of the valiant and noble has known.

When the song ceased I observed two hands shedding apart the thick willows, while an eye glanced for a moment through the aperture on the young maiden and me. A song of a gentler nature instantly followed, and I could not help imagining that my companion felt a particular interest in the minstrel's story. The time and the place contributed to the charm of the sweet voice and the rustic poetry.

BONNIE MARY HALLIDAY.

Bonnie Mary Halliday,
  Turn again, I call you;
If you go to the dewy wood
  Sorrow will befall you:
The ringdove from the dewy wood
  Is wailing sore and calling,
And Annanwater, 'tween its banks,
  Is foaming far and falling.

Gentle Mary Halliday,
  Come, my bonnie lady;
Upon the river's woody bank
  My steed is saddled ready;
And for thy haughty kinsmen's threats,
  My faith shall never falter;
The bridal banquet's ready made,
  The priest is at the altar.

Gentle Mary Halliday,
  The towers of merry Preston
Have bridal candles gleaming bright,
  So busk thee, love, and hasten;
Come, busk thee, love, and bowne thee
  Through Tinwald and green Mouswal;
Come, be the grace and be the charm
  To the proud towers of Machusel.

Bonnie Mary Halliday,
  Turn again, I tell you:
For wit, an' grace, an' loveliness,
  What maidens may excel you?

Though Annan has its beauteous dames,
  And Corrie many a fair one,
We canna want thee from our sight,
  Thou lovely and thou rare one.

Bonnie Mary Halliday,
  When the cittern's sounding,
We'll miss thy lightsome lily foot,
  Amang the blithe lads bounding ;
The summer sun shall freeze our veins,
  The winter moon shall warm us,
Ere the like of thee shall come again,
  To cheer us and to charm us.

During the song I walked unconsciously down to the river bank, and stood on a small promontory which projected into the stream; it was bordered with willows and wild flowers, and the summit, nibbled by some pet sheep, was as smooth as the softest velvet. Here I obtained a full view of this singular songstress. She was seated among the willows, on the indented bank, with her bare feet in the stream: a slouched straw hat, filled with withered flowers and blackcock and peacock feathers, lay at her side ; and its removal allowed a fine fleece of hazel-coloured hair to fall down on all sides, till it curled on the grass. She wore a bodice of green tarnished silk ; her lower garments were kilted in the thrifty fashion of the country maidens of Caledonia ; and round her neck and arm she wore, as much, it is true, for a charm as an ornament, several bracelets of the hard, round, and bitter berries of the mountain-ash, or witch-tree.

"It is poor Judith Macrone, sir," said the maiden, who, with the privilege of a listener, had come close to my side ; "she has found her bed in the wild woods for some weeks, living on nuts and plums : I wish the poor demented maiden would come and taste some of my curds and cream."

Judith rose suddenly from her seat, and, scattering some handfuls of wild flowers in the stream, exclaimed, with something of a scream of recognition "Aha, bonnie Mary Halliday, lass, ye wear the snood of singleness yet, for a' yere gentle blood and yere weel-filled farms. But wha's this ye have got with ye? May I love to lie on wet straw wi' a cold sack above me if it is not Francis Forster, all the way from bonnie Derwentwater. Alake, my bonnie lass, for such a wooer ! He could nae say seven words of saft, sappy, loving Scotch t'ye, did every word bring for its dower the

H

bonnie lands of Lochwood, which your forefathers lost.
No, no, Mary Halliday, take a bonnie Annanwater lad, and
let the Southron gang."

> There's bonnie lads on fairy Nith,
>   And cannie lads on Dee,
> And stately lads on Kinnel side,
>   And by Dalgonar tree:
> The Nithsdale lads are frank and kind,
>   But lack the bright blue ee
> Of the bonnie Annanwater lads,
>   The wale of lads for me.
>
> There's Willie Watson of Witchstone,
>   Dick Irving of Gowktree,
> Frank Forest of the Houlet-ha,
>   Jock Bell of Lillylea;
> But give to me a Halliday,
>   The witty, bauld, and free,
> The frackest lads of Annanbank,
>   The Hallidays for me.
>
> The Johnstone is a noble name,
>   The Jardine is a free,
> The Bells are bauld, the Irvings good,
>   The Carlyles bear the gree,
> Till the gallant Hallidays come in
>   With minstrel, mirth, and glee,
> Then hey! the lads of Annanbank,
>   The Hallidays for me.

This old rude rhyme was sung with considerable archness and effect: the songstress then came towards the place where we stood, not with a regular direct step, but a sidelong hop and skip, waving, as she came, her bonnet and feathers from side to side, accompanying every motion with a line of an old song. Old Prudence Caird seemed scandalized at the extravagant demeanour of the poor girl, and, advancing towards her, waving her hands to be gone, exclaimed:

"In the name of all aboon, what are ye skipping and skirling there for, ye born gowk and sworn gomeral? Ye'll fall belly-flaught, breadth and length, on the lily-white linen that has cost such a cleansing. Away to the woods like another gowk, away, else I'se kirsen ye with a cupful of scalding water, my sooth shall I;" and, partly suiting the action to the word, she came forward with a cupful of water in her hand.

The singular person to whom these bitter words were

addressed heard them with a loud laugh of utter contempt and scorn; and, with a thousand fantastic twirls and freaks, she threaded, with great dexterity, the whole maze of linen webs, and confronted old Prudence. She looked her full in the face, she eyed her on one side and eyed her on another, she stooped down and she stood on tiptoe, examining her all the while with an eye of simple but crafty scrutiny.

"Protect us, sirs!" said the wandering maiden, "what wicked liars these two blue een o' mine are—I'll ne'er credit them again; and yet, believe me, but it's like her. Hech be't, she's sore changed since that merry time—it cannot be her. Harkee, my douce decent-looking dame, d'ye ken if Prudence Caird be living yet?"

"And what hast thou to say to Prudence Caird?" said the old woman, growing blacker with anger, and clutching, as she spoke, the long sharp fingers of her right hand, portending hostility to the blue eyes of Judith.

"Say to Prudence Caird?" said the maiden; "a bonnie question, indeed! What advice could a poor bewildered creature like me give to a douce person who has had twice the benefit of the counsel of the minister and kirk session?"

And, with unexpected agility, away Judith danced and leaped and laughed, eluding the indignation of her less active antagonist.

I could not help feeling anxious to learn something of the history of Judith; and while I was expressing this to Mary Halliday, the poor girl approached and received a bowl of curds and cream, which she acknowledged with abundance of fantastic bows and becks.

"Look at her now," said my companion, "but say not a word."

Judith seated herself on the margin of the river; and, throwing a spoonful of the curds into the stream, said: "There, taste that, thou sweet and gentle water; and when I bathe my burning brow in thy flood, or wade through thee, and through thee, on the warm moonlight evenings of summer, mind who fed yere bonnie mottled trouts and yere lang silver eels, and no drown me as ye did my bonnie sister Peggy and her young bridegroom." In a small thicket beside her, a bird or two, confiding in the harmlessness of a creature with whom they were well acquainted, continued to pour forth their uninterrupted strain of song. "Ye wee daft things," said Judith, changing from a tone of sadness to one of the most giddy gaiety, "what sit ye lilting there for, on the broad green bough—wasting yere sweetest songs on a fool quean like me : but ye shall not go unrewarded." So saying, she scattered a spoonful of curds beside her on the grass, and said, with some abatement of her mirth : "Come, and peckle at my hand, my poor feathered innocents—ilka bird of the forest, save the raven and the hooded crow, is a sister to me." A redbreast as she spoke, with an audacity which that lover of the human face seldom displays save when the snow is on the ground, came boldly to her elbow, and began to obey her invitation. "Aha, Rabin, my red-bosomed lover, are ye there? Ye'll find me stiff and streekit under the greenwood bough some morning, and ye mauna stint to deck me out daintily with green leaves, my bonnie man ;" and, throwing the bird some more curds, she proceeded to sup the remainder herself, indulging between every mouthful in much bewildered talk.

The interest I took in the poor girl, a few handfuls of nuts—and, above all, a few pleasant glances from one, who (though old and bent and withered now) was once twenty-one, had a handsome leg, and mirth in his eye—obtained me the good graces of the nymphs of Annanwater. Our conversation turned upon poor Judith Macrone.

"She is a poor innocent," said Mary Halliday, "as wild and as harmless as the birds she is feeding. She was ever a singular girl, and wit and folly seem to keep alternate sway over her mind."

"She an innocent!" said Prudence Caird; "she's a cunning and a crafty quean, with a wicked memory and a malicious tongue. It sets her weel to wag her fool tongue at me, and say a word that is nae to my credit."

"Hoot, toot, woman," said one of the fair-haired menials; "we can scarce keep our balance with all the wit we have— what can ye expect o' such an adder cap as crazy Jude? But of all the queans of Annanbank, she is the quean for old-world stories. Set her on a sunny hillside, give her her own will—and, wise or daft, who likes na that?—and she'll clatter ye into a dead sleep, with tales of spirits and apparitions, and the dead who have not peace in the grave and walk the earth for a season. I heard douce John Stroudwater, the Cameronian elder, say that assuredly an evil spirit has filled her head with fool songs and queer lang-sin-syne ballads, by and attour a foreknowledge of coming evil. It's well known that she foretold the drowning of her sister and her bridegroom, in that black pool before us, where poor Jude now sits so sorrowful."

"Troth and atweel, and that's too true," said Prudence Caird, "and I was unwise to grow cankered with such a kittle customer. She tried my patience sore, but I never heard of any one's luck who crossed her—that one never did good that she wished harm to yet; I hope she'll wish no kittle wish to me."

"I know not," said Mary Halliday, with more than ordinary gravity, and in a tone something between hesitation and belief; "I know not how Judith is informed of evil fortune; but her foreknowledge of human calamity, whether it comes from a good or an evil source, is of no use but to be wondered at, and perhaps sorrowed for. What is foredoomed will surely come to pass, and cannot be guarded against; and, therefore, I deem all warning of the event to be vain and useless. But touching her skill in minstrel lore —with her each oak-tree has its tale, each loop of Annanwater its tradition, and every green knowe or holly-bush its ballad of true-love or song of knightly bravery."

"But the story of her sister's bridal," said one of the menials, "is the best of all the tales told of idle Jude; it is said to be sorrowful—ye may pick sorrow out of aught as weel as ye may pick mirth, and some cry for what others laugh at—but I know this, that lang Tam Southeranairn, the tinker, told me that, save the drowning of the bride and bridegroom in the mirkest pool of Annanwater, shame fall of aught saw he to sorrow for; and he would not have such a duck again as he had that blessed night for all the tuphorns of Dryfesdale and the heads they grow upon."

"I had better, without farther clipping and cutting of the bridal tale, relate it at once," said Mary Halliday; "it is a strange story, and soon told. The marriage of Margaret, the sister of Judith, happened in the very lap of winter—the snow lay deep on the ground, the ice was thick on the river, and the wheel of her father's mill had not turned round for full forty days. The bride was a sweet and a kind-hearted beautiful girl; and there was not a cleverer lad than her bridegroom, David Carlyle, from the head to the foot of Annanwater. I heard the minister of the parish say, after he had joined their hands together, that fifty years he had been a marrier of loving hearts, but he had never married a fairer pair. The bridegroom's mother was a proud dame, of the ancient house of Morison. She took it sore to heart that her son should marry a miller's daughter; she forbade him, under pain of the mother's curse —and a woman's curse, they say, is a sore one—to bed with his bride under a churl's roof-tree, and, as he wished to be happy, to bring her home to his father's house on the night of the wedding.

"Now, ye will consider that the house of the bride stood on one hillside, and the home of the bridegroom on another; while between them, in the bosom of the valley, lay no less a water than the Annan, with its bank knee-deep in snow, and its surface plated with ice. The mirk winter night and the mother's scorn did not prevent one of the blithesomest bridals from taking place that ever a piper played to or a maiden danced in. Ye have never seen, sir, one of our inland merry-makings, and seen the lads and the lasses moving merrily to the sound of the fiddle and the harpstring, else ye might have some notion of the mirth at Margaret's bridal. The young were loudest in their joy, but the old were blither at the heart; and men forgot their white heads and women that they were granddames, and who so glad as they? An old man, one of the frank-hearted Bells of Middlebee, wiped his brow as he sat down from a reel, and said: 'Aweel, Mary, my bonnie lass, there are just three things which intoxicate the heart of man: first, there is strong drink; secondly, there is music; and thirdly, there is the company of beautiful women, when they move to the sound of dulcimer and flute. Blest be the Maker, for they are the most wonderful of all His works.'

"But the merriest, as well as the fairest, was the bride herself: she danced with unequalled life and grace—her feet gave the tone, rather than took it, from the fiddle; and the old men said the melody of her feet, as they moved on the floor, would do more mischief among men's hearts than her eyes, and her eyes were wondrous bright ones. Many stayed from dancing themselves, and stood in a circle round the place where she danced. I listened to their remarks, which the catastrophe of the evening impressed on my memory. 'I think,' said William Johnstone of Chapelknowe, 'our bonnie bride's possessed; I never saw her look so sweet or dance so delightfully. It's no sonsie to look so smiling on her wedding-night; a grave bride's best, owre blithe a bride is seldom a blest one.' 'There's no a sweeter or more modest maid on Annanbank,' said John Stroudwater, the Cameronian, who, scorning to mingle in the dance himself, yet could endure to be a witness of youthful folly where the liquor was plenty; 'she's a bonnie quean; yet I cannot say I like to see the light which comes from her eyes, as if it were shed from two stars; nor love I to hearken the vain and wanton sound which she causeth the planed floor to utter, as she directeth her steps to the strange outcry of that man's instrument of wood, called by the profane a fiddle.' Nor were the women without their remarks on the bride's mirth on this unhappy night. ' I protest,' said an old dame in a black hood, 'against all this profane minstrelsy and dancing; it is more sinful in its nature than strong drink—I wish good may come of it!' and she paused to moisten her lips with a cup of brandy, to which a piece of sugar and a single teaspoonful of water had communicated the lady-like name of cordial. 'I wish, I say, good may come of it: I have not danced these thirty years and three, but the bride is dancing as if this night was her last. I fear she is fey.'

" If the bride and bridegroom were blithe, there was another sad enough: even poor Judith, who, retiring from the mirth and the dancing, went to her father's mill-door, and seating herself on a broken mill-stone, and loosing her locks from the comb, let them fall like a shroud around her, while she gazed intent and silent upon Annanwater, which lay still and clear in the setting light of the moon. I had an early regard for this unhappy maid—we were school-fellows and play-fellows; and, though her temper was wayward, and her mind, equal to the hardest task one week, was unequal for any kind of learning another; yet, from the frequency of these remarkable fits of impulse and ability, she became one of the finest scholars in Annandale. So I went out into the open air, and found her sitting silent and melancholy, and looking with a fixed and undeviating gaze on the river, which glittered a good half-mile distant. I stood beside her, and sought rather to learn what oppressed her spirit, from her actions and her looks, than by questioning her. It has been remarked that on ordinary occasions, though she is talkative and fond of singing snatches of songs, yet, when the secret of any coming calamity is communicated to her spirit, she becomes at once silent and gloomy, and seeks to acquaint mankind with the disaster awaiting them by sensible signs and tokens—a kind of hieroglyphic mode of communication which she has invented to avoid the misery, perhaps, of open speech. She seemed scarcely aware of my presence.

"At last she threw back her long hair from her face, that nothing might intercept her steady gaze at the river; and, plucking a silver bodkin from her bosom, she proceeded to describe on the ground two small and coffin-shaped holes— one something longer than the other. I could not help shuddering while I looked on these symbols of certain fate; and my fears instantly connected what I saw with the wedding and the bride and bridegroom. I seized her by the arm, and, snatching the bodkin from her, said: 'Judith, thou art an evil foreboder, and I shall cast this bodkin of thine, which has been made under no good influence, into the blackest pool of Annanwater.' At other times I was an overmatch for her in strength; but when the time of her sorrow came she seemed to obtain supernatural strength in body as well as in mind, and on this occasion she proved it by leaping swiftly to her feet and wresting the bodkin from me. She resumed her seat; and, taking the bride and bridegroom's ribands from her bosom, she put the latter into the larger grave and the former in the less, and wrung her hands, threw her hair wildly over her face, and wept and sobbed aloud.

"All this had not passed unobserved of others. 'Mercy on us!' cried the Laird of Gooseplat, 'but the young witch is casting cantraips, and making the figures of graves, and dooming to the bedral's spade and the parish mortcloth the quick instead of the dead. I'se tell thee what, my cannie lass, two red peats and a tar-barrel would make a warm conclusion to these unsonsie spells ye are casting; and may I be choked with a thimbleful of brandy if ye should want a cross on the brow as deep as the bone if I had my whittle.' Other spectators came to more charitable conclusions. 'Red peats and sharp whittles!' muttered William Graeme of Cummerlair; 'I'se tell ye what, laird, if ye lay a hand of harm on the poor demented lassie, I'se lend ye a Lockerby lick to take home with ye. Eh, sirs, but this be fearful to look upon—she is showing us by dumb looks, and sure nods, and sad signs, and awful symbols, the coming of wrath and woe. There are two graves, and the bridal ribands laid like corses in them—he that runs may read.'

"While this passed out of doors, the dancing and bridal mirth abounded more than ever. It was now ten o'clock, and as the bridal chamber lay a mile distant the bride and bridegroom prepared to depart, accompanied by a sure friend or two, to witness the conclusion of the marriage. 'Let them go,' said more voices than one; 'we shall make the fiddle-strings chirp and shake our legs till the small hours of the morning. Come, Tom Macthairm, play us up something wily and wanton: who can leap rafter-high to a sorrowful psalm tune like that?' The fiddler complied, and wall and rafter quivered and shook to the reviving merriment. The young couple now stood on the threshold and looked towards their future habitation, in which the lights of preparation were shining. 'An' I were you, bridegroom,' said one adviser, 'I would go by the bridge—I have heard oftener than once to-night the soughing of the west wind and the roaring of the linns. The Annan is a fair water in summer-time, but I would not trust such a bonnie lass as the bride on its fickle bosom on a winter night.' 'An' I were you, bridegroom,' said another counsellor, 'I would lippen to the old proverb, "The nearest road to the bride's bed's the best." The bosom of the Annanwater is bound in ice as hard and as firm as iron—ye might drive Burnswark Hill over its deepest pools, providing it had four feet. So dauner away down the edge of the wood, and cross at the Deadman's Plump; and if ye give me a shout and the bride a kiss when ye cross over't, it will give pleasure to us both.'

"The bride herself came forward to bid farewell to her sister, not unconscious that the time of sorrow had come over her spirit, and that whispers of the import of her predictions were circulated among the bridal guests. She stood before Judith with a cheek flushed with dancing and parting benedictions from rustic lips, and her eyes gleaming with a wild and unusual light—which has often since been noticed by the tellers of her melancholy tale, as a light too unlike that of earthly eyes to be given for her good. 'Graves!' said the bride, with a laugh, which had something of a shriek in it; 'is this all you have as an apology for your fear? Where's your sight, if your senses be wandering? My sister has only made the bridal beds, and strewed them with bridal favours.' She turned round to depart: Judith uttered a piercing shriek, and, throwing her arms about her sister, clung to her, giving one convulsive sob after another; and finally, throwing herself between her and the river, strove, but still strove in silence, to impress her with a sense of danger. It was in vain; the bride and bridegroom departed; while Judith, covering, or rather shrouding herself in her mantle, and turning her face from the river, sat as mute and as still as a statue; a slight convulsive shudder was from time to time visible.

"The young pair reached the Annan, and attempted to pass over the pool called the Deadman's Plump; the dancing and merriment, which had sustained a brief remission, had recommenced, when, far above the din of the dance and the music, one shriek, and then another, was heard in the direction of the river. 'Hearken the shout!' said one rustic; 'the bridegroom is fairly over the water now—then, hey, play up "The Runaway Bride."' 'Alas!' answered another peasant, 'yon is not the cry of pleasure, but the shriek of agony. My kale-yard to the Johnstone's land, but they are fallen into the Deadman's Plump, and Judith's prophecy's true.' The hall-door seemed much too narrow for the multitude who rushed to get out. The shrieks were repeated, and, mingling with the shrieks, and at last o'ermastering them, was heard the downward dash of Annanwater, which, swollen suddenly with distant rains, descended from the hills with all its increase of waters, lifting the ice before it, and heaving it on the banks with a crash that resounded far and wide. The unhappy pair were seen struggling together against the overpowering element, which, encumbered with ice and trees, filled the channel from bank to bank, and rushed down six feet deep abreast. No effort could be made to save them; and, when the river subsided n the morning, they were found in a distant eddy, the bridegroom's left hand round his bride's waist, and his right hand held out like one in the act of swimming. They lie buried together in the old kirkyard of Dryfesdale. I have often seen Judith sitting weeping on their grave."

THE GHOST WITH THE GOLDEN CASKET.

> Is my soul tamed
> And baby-rid with the thought that flood or field
> Can render back, to scare men and the moon,
> The airy shapes of the corses they enwomb?
> And what if 'tis so—shall I lose the crown
> Of my most golden hope, 'cause its fair circle
> Is haunted by a shadow?

FROM the coast of Cumberland the beautiful old Castle of Caerlaverock is seen standing on the point of a fine green promontory, bounded by the river Nith on one side, by the deep sea on another, by the almost impassable morass of Solway on a third; while, far beyond, you observe the three spires of Dumfries and the high green hills of Dalswinton and Keir. It was formerly the residence of the almost princely names of Douglas, Seaton, Kirkpatrick, and Maxwell: it is now the dwelling-place of the hawk and the owl, its courts are a lair for cattle, and its walls afford a midnight shelter to the passing smuggler, or, like those of the city doomed in Scripture, are places for the fishermen to dry their nets. Between this fine old ruin and the banks of the Nith, at the foot of a grove of pines, and within a stonecast of tide-mark, the remains of a rude cottage are yet visible to the curious eye; the bramble and the wild plum have in vain tried to triumph over the huge grey granite blocks which composed the foundations of its walls. The vestiges of a small garden may still be traced, more particularly in summer, when roses and lilies, and other relics of its former beauty, begin to open their bloom, clinging, amid the neglect and desolation of the place, with something like human affection, to the soil. This rustic ruin presents no attractions to the eye of the profound antiquary, compared to those of its more stately companion, Caerlaverock Castle; but with this rude cottage and its garden tradition connects a tale so wild and so moving as to elevate it, in the contemplation of the peasantry, above all the princely feasts and feudal atrocities of its neighbour.

It is now some fifty years since I visited the parish of Caerlaverock; but the memory of its people, its scenery, and the story of "The Ghost with the Golden Casket" are as fresh with me as matters of yesterday. I had walked out to the river bank one sweet afternoon of July, when the fishermen were hastening to dip their nets in the coming tide, and the broad waters of the Solway sea were swelling and leaping against bank and cliff as far as the eye could reach. It was studded over with boats, and its more unfrequented bays were white with water-fowl. I sat down on a small grassy mound between the cottage ruins and the old garden plat, and gazed, with all the hitherto untasted pleasure of a stranger, on the beautiful scene before me. On the right, and beyond the river, the mouldering relics of the ancient religion of Scotland ascended, in unassimilating beauty, above the humble kirk of New Abbey and its squalid village; farther to the south rose the white sharp cliffs of Barnhourie, while on the left stood the ancient keeps of Cumlongan and Torthorald and the Castle of Caerlaverock. Over the whole looked the stately green mountain of Criffel, confronting its more stately but less beautiful neighbour, Skiddaw, while between them flowed the deep wide sea of Solway, hemmed with cliff and castle and town.

As I sat looking on the increasing multitudes of waters, and watching the success of the fishermen, I became aware of the approach of an old man, leading, as one will conduct a dog in a string, a fine young milch cow, in a halter of twisted hair, which, passing through the ends of two pieces of flat wood fitted to the animal's cheekbones, pressed her nose, and gave her great pain whenever she became disobedient. The cow seemed willing to enjoy the luxury of a browze on the rich pasture which surrounded the little ruined cottage, but in this humble wish she was not to be indulged, for the aged owner, coiling up the tether, and seizing her closely by the head, conducted her past the tempting herbage, towards a small and close-cropped hillock, a good stone-cast distant. In this piece of self-denial the animal seemed reluctant to sympathize; she snuffed the fresh green pasture, and plunged and startled, and nearly broke away. What the old man's strength seemed nearly unequal to was accomplished by speech:

"Bonnie lady, bonnie lady," said he, in a soothing tone, "it canna be, it mauna be—hinnie! hinnie! What would become of my three bonnie grandbairns, made fatherless and mitherless by that false flood afore us, if they supped milk and tasted butter that came from the greensward of this doomed and unblessed spot?"

The animal appeared to comprehend something in her own way from the speech of her owner; she abated her resistance, and, indulging only in a passing glance at the rich deep herbage, passed on to her destined pasture.

I had often heard of the singular superstitions of the Scottish peasantry, and that every hillock had its song, every hill its ballad, and every valley its tale. I followed with my eye the old man and his cow; he went but a little way, till, seating himself on the ground, retaining still the tether in his hand, he said: "Now, bonnie lady, feast thy fill on this good greensward—it is halesome and holy compared to the sward at the doomed cottage of auld Gibbie Gyrape. Leave that to smugglers' nags: Willie o' Brandyburn and Roaring Jock o' Kempstane will ca' the haunted ha' a hained bit—they are godless fearnoughts." I looked at the person of the peasant: he was a stout hale old man, with a weather-beaten face, furrowed something by time, and perhaps by sorrow. Though summer was at its warmest he wore a broad chequered mantle, fastened at the bosom with a skewer of steel, a broad bonnet, from beneath the circumference of which straggled a few thin locks as white as driven snow, shining like amber and softer than the finest flax, while his legs were warmly cased in blue-ribbed boot-hose. Having laid his charge to the grass, he looked leisurely around him, and espying me—a stranger, and dressed above the manner of the peasantry—he acknowledged my presence by touching his bonnet; and, as if willing to communicate something of importance, he struck the tether stake in the ground and came to the old garden fence.

Wishing to know the peasant's reasons for avoiding the ruins, I thus addressed him : "This is a pretty spot, my aged friend, and the herbage looks so fresh and abundant that I would advise thee to bring thy charge hither ; and while she continued to browze I would gladly listen to the history of thy white locks, for they seem to have been bleached in many tempests."

"Ay, ay," said the peasant, shaking his white head

with a grave smile, "they have braved sundry tempests between sixteen and sixty; but, touching this pasture, sir, I know nobody who would like their cows to crop it—the aged cattle shun the place, the bushes bloom but bear no fruit, the birds never build in the branches, the children never come near to play, and the aged never choose it for a resting-place; but pointing it out, as they pass, to the young, tell them the story of its desolation. Sae ye see, sir, having nae goodwill to such a spot of earth myself, I like little to see a stranger sitting in such an unblessed place; and I would as good as advise ye to come owre with me to the cowslip knoll; there are reasons mony that an honest man should nae sit there."

I arose at once, and, seating myself beside the peasant on the cowslip knoll, desired to know something of the history of the spot from which he had just warned me. The Caledonian looked on me with an air of embarrassment.

"I am just thinking," said he, "that as ye are an Englishman I should nae acquaint ye with such a story. Ye'll make it, I'm doubting, a matter of reproach and vaunt when ye gae hame how Willie Borlan o' Caerlaverock told ye a tale of Scottish iniquity that cowed all the stories in Southron book or history."

This unexpected obstacle was soon removed. "My sage and considerate friend," I said, "I have the blood in my bosom will keep me from revealing such a tale to the scoffer and scorner. I am something of a Caerlaverock man, the grandson of Marion Stobie of Dookdub."

The peasant seized my hand. "Marion Stobie! bonnie Marion Stobie o' Dookdub, whom I wooed sae sair and loved sae lang! Man, I love ye for her sake; and well was it for her braw English bridegroom that William Borlan— frail and faded now, but strong and in manhood then—was a thousand miles from Caerlaverock, rolling on the salt sea, when she was brided. Ye have the glance of her ee; I could ken't yet amang ten thousand, grey as my head is. I will tell the grandson of bonnie Marion Stobie ony tale he likes to ask for, and the story of 'The Ghost and the Gowd Casket' shall be foremost.

"You may imagine, then," said the old Caerlaverock peasant, rising at once with the commencement of his story from his native dialect into very passable English—"you may imagine these ruined walls raised again in their beauty

—whitened, and covered with a coating of green broom; that garden, now desolate, filled with herbs in their season, and with flowers, hemmed round with a fence of cherry and plum-trees; and the whole possessed by a young fisherman, who won a fair subsistence for his wife and children from the waters of the Solway sea; you may imagine it, too, as far from the present time as fifty years. There are only two persons living now who remember when the *Bonne-Homme-Richard*, the first ship ever Richard Faulder commanded, was wrecked on the Pellock sand; one of these persons now addresses you, the other is the fisherman who once owned that cottage—whose name ought never to be named, and whose life seems lengthened as a warning to the earth how fierce God's judgments are. Life changes—all breathing things have their time and their season; but the Solway flows in the same beauty—Criffel rises in the same majesty—the light of morning comes and the full moon arises now as they did then. But this moralizing matters little. It was about the middle of harvest—I remember the day well; it had been sultry and suffocating, accompanied by rushings of wind, sudden convulsions of the water, and cloudings of the sun—I heard my father sigh, and say, 'Dool—dool to them found on the deep sea to-night; there will happen strong storm and fearful tempest.' The day closed and the moon came over Skiddaw: all was perfectly clear and still—frequent dashings and whirling agitations of the sea were soon heard mingling with the hasty clang of the water-fowls' wings as they forsook the waves and sought shelter among the hollows of the rocks. The storm was nigh. The sky darkened down at once—clap after clap of thunder followed, and lightning flashed so vividly and so frequent that the wide and agitated expanse of Solway was visible from side to side—from St. Bees to Barnhourie. A very heavy rain, mingled with hail, succeeded; and a wind accompanied it so fierce and so high that the white foam of the sea was showered as thick as snow on the summit of Caerlaverock Castle.

"Through this perilous sea, and amid this darkness and tempest, a bark was observed coming swiftly down the middle of the sea, her sails rent and her decks crowded with people. The carry, as it is called, of the tempest, was direct from St. Bees to Caerlaverock; and experienced swains could see that the bark would be driven full on the fatal shoals of the Scottish side; but the lightning was so fierce that few dared venture to look on the approaching vessel or take measures for endeavouring to preserve the lives of the unfortunate mariners. My father stood on the threshold of his door, and beheld all that passed in the bosom of the sea. The bark approached fast—her canvas rent to threads, her masts nearly levelled with the deck, and the sea foaming over her so deep and so strong as to threaten to sweep the remains of her crew from the little refuge the broken masts and splintered beams still afforded them. She now seemed within half a mile of the shore when a strong flash of lightning, that appeared to hang over the bark for a moment, showed the figure of a lady, richly dressed, clinging to a youth who was pressing her to his bosom. My father exclaimed, 'Saddle me my black horse and saddle me my grey, and bring them down to the Deadman's Bank;' and, swift in action as he was in resolve, he hastened to the shore, his servants following with his horses. The shore of Solway presented then, as it does now, the same varying line of coast; and the house of my father stood in the bosom of a little bay, nearly a mile from where we sit. The remains of an old forest interposed between the bay at Deadman's Bank and the bay at our feet; and mariners had learned to wish that, if it were their doom to be wrecked, it might be in the bay of douce William Borlan rather than that of Gilbert Gyrape, the proprietor of that ruined cottage. But human wishes are vanities, wished either by sea or land. I have heard my father say he could never forget the cries of the mariners as the bark smote on the Pellock Bank, and the flood rushed through the chasms made by the concussion; but he would far less forget the agony of a lady—the loveliest that could be looked upon— and the calm and affectionate courage of the young man who supported her, and endeavoured to save her from destruction. Richard Faulder, the only man who survived, has often sat at my fireside, and sung me a very rude, but a very moving ballad, which he made on this young and unhappy pair; and the old mariner assured me he had only added rhymes, and a descriptive line or two, to the language in which Sir William Musgrave endeavoured to soothe and support his wife."

It seemed a thing truly singular that at this very moment two young fishermen, who sat on the margin of the sea below us, watching their halve-nets, should sing, and with much sweetness, the very song the old man had described. They warbled verse and verse alternately, and rock and bay seemed to retain and then release the sound. Nothing is so sweet as a song by the sea-side on a tranquil evening.

SIR WILLIAM MUSGRAVE.

First Fisherman.

"O lady, lady, why do you weep?
Though the wind be loosed on the raging deep,
Though the heaven be mirker than mirk may be,
And our frail bark ships a fearful sea—
Yet thou art safe, as on that sweet night
When our bridal candles gleamed far and bright."—
There came a shriek, and there came a sound,
And the Solway roared, and the ship spun round.

Second Fisherman.

"O lady, lady, why do you cry?
Though the waves be flashing topmast high,
Though our frail bark yields to the dashing brine,
And heaven and earth show no saving sign,
There is One who comes in the time of need,
And curbs the waves as we curb a steed."—
The lightning came with the whirlwind blast,
And cleaved the prow, and smote down the mast.

First Fisherman.

"O lady, lady, weep not, nor wail,
Though the sea runs howe as Dalswinton vale,
Then flashes high as Barnhourie brave,
And yawns for thee like the yearning grave—
Though 'twixt thee and the ravening flood
There is but my arm, and this splintering wood,
The fell quicksand, or the famished brine,
Can ne'er harm a face so fair as thine."

Both.

"O lady, lady, be bold and brave,
Spread thy white breast to the fearful wave,
And cling to me with that white right hand,
And I'll set thee safe on the good dry land."—
A lightning flash on the shallop strook,
The Solway roared, and Caerlaverock shook:
From the sinking ship there were shriekings cast,
That were heard above the tempest's blast.

The young fishermen having concluded their song, my companion proceeded: "The lightning still flashed vivid and fast, and the storm raged with unabated fury; for between the ship and the shore the sea broke in frightful undulation, and leaped on the greensward several fathoms deep abreast. My father, mounted on one horse, and holding another in his hand, stood prepared to give all the aid that a brave man could to the unhappy mariners; but neither horse nor man could endure the onset of that tremendous surge. The bark bore for a time the fury of the element; but a strong eastern wind came suddenly upon her, and crushing her between the wave and the freestone bank, drove her from the entrance of my father's little bay towards the dwelling of Gibbie Gyrape, and the thick forest intervening, she was out of sight in a moment. My father saw, for the last time, the lady and her husband looking shoreward from the side of the vessel, as she drifted along; and, as he galloped round the head of the forest, he heard for the last time the outcry of some, and the wail and intercession of others. When he came before the fisherman's house, a fearful sight presented itself—the ship, dashed to atoms, covered the shore with its wreck and with the bodies of the mariners—not a living soul escaped, save Richard Faulder, whom the fiend who guides the spectre-shallop of Solway had rendered proof to perils on the deep. The fisherman himself came suddenly from his cottage, all dripping and drenched, and my father addressed him:—'Oh, Gilbert, Gilbert, what a fearful sight is this!—has Heaven blessed thee with making thee the means of saving a human soul!' 'Nor soul nor body have I saved,' said the fisherman, doggedly: 'I have done my best—the storm proved too stark, and the lightning too fierce for me; their boat alone came near with a lady and a casket of gold, but she was swallowed up with the surge.' My father confessed afterwards that he was touched with the tone in which these words were delivered, and made answer: 'If thou hast done thy best to save souls to-night, a bright reward will be thine; if thou hast been fonder for gain than for working the mariners' redemption, thou hast much to answer for.' As he uttered these words, an immense wave rolled landward as far as the place where they stood—it almost left its foam on their faces—and suddenly receding, deposited at their feet the dead body of the lady. As my father lifted her in his arms, he observed that the jewels which had adorned her hair, at that time worn long, had been forcibly rent away—the diamonds and gold that enclosed her neck, and ornamented the bosom of her rich satin dress, had been torn off—the rings removed from her fingers; and on her neck, lately so lily-white and pure, there appeared the marks of hands—not laid there in love and gentleness, but with a fierce and deadly grasp.

"The lady was buried with the body of her husband, side by side, in Caerlaverock burial-ground. My father never openly accused Gilbert the fisherman of having murdered the lady for her riches as she reached the shore, preserved, as was supposed, from sinking by her long, wide, and stiff satin robes; but from that hour till the hour of his death my father never broke bread with him—never shook him or his by the hand, nor spoke with them in wrath or in love. The fisherman from that time, too, waxed rich and prosperous, and from being the needy proprietor of a halve-net, and the tenant at will of a rude cottage, he became, by purchase, lord of a handsome inheritance, proceeded to build a bonny mansion, and called it Gyrape-ha'; and became a leading man in a flock of a purer kind of Presbyterians—and a precept and example to the community.

"'Though the portioner of Gyrape-ha' prospered wondrously, his claims to parochial distinction, and the continuance of his fortune, were treated with scorn by many, and with doubt by all: though nothing open or direct was said—looks, more cutting at times than the keenest speech, and actions still more expressive, showed that the hearts of honest men were alienated—the cause was left to his own interpretation. The peasant scrupled to become his servant —sailors hesitated to receive his grain on board, lest perils should find them on the deep—the beggar ceased to solicit alms—the drover and horse-couper, an unscrupling generation, found out a more distant mode of concluding bargains than by shaking his hand—his daughters, handsome and blue-eyed, were neither wooed nor married—no maiden would hold tryste with his sons—though maidens were then as little loth as they are now; and the aged peasant, as he passed his new mansion, would shake his head and say, 'The voice of spilt blood will be lifted up against thee—and a spirit shall come up from the waters will make the corner-stone of thy habitation tremble and quake.'

"It happened, during the summer which succeeded this unfortunate shipwreck, that I accompanied my father to the

Solway, to examine his nets. It was near midnight—the tide was making, and I sat down by his side, and watched the coming of the waters. The shore was glittering in starlight as far as the eye could reach. Gilbert the fisherman had that morning removed from his cottage to his new mansion—the former was, therefore, untenanted; and the latter, from its vantage-ground on the crest of the hill, threw down to us the sound of mirth and music and dancing, a revelry common in Scotland on taking possession of a new house. As we lay quietly looking on the swelling sea, and observing the water-fowl swimming and ducking in the increasing waters, the sound of the merriment became more audible. My father listened to the mirth, looked to the sea, looked to the deserted cottage, and then to the new mansion, and said: 'My son, I have a counsel to give thee—treasure it in thy heart, and practise it in thy life—the daughters of *him* of Gyrape-ha' are fair, and have an eye that would wile away the wits of the wisest; their father has wealth—I say nought of the way he came by it—they will have golden portions doubtless. But I would rather lay thy head aneath the gowans in Caerlaverock kirkyard, and son have I none beside thee, than see thee lay it on the bridal pillow with the begotten of that man, though she had Nithsdale for her dowry. Let not my words be as seed sown on the ocean—I may not now tell thee why this warning is given. Before that fatal shipwreck, I would have said Prudence Gyrape, in her kirtle, was a better bride than some who have golden dowers. I have long thought some one would see a sight—and often, while holding my halve-net in the midnight tide, have I looked for something to appear—for where blood is shed, there doth the spirit haunt for a time, and give warning to man. May I be strengthened to endure the sight!'

"I answered not, being accustomed to regard my father's counsel as a matter not to be debated, as a solemn command: we heard something like the rustling of wings on the water, accompanied by a slight curling motion of the tide. 'God haud his right hand about us!' said my father, breathing thick with emotion and awe, and looking on the sea with a gaze so intense that his eyes seemed to dilate, and the hair of his forehead to project forward and bristle into life. I looked, but observed nothing, save a long line of thin and quivering light, dancing along the surface of the sea: it ascended the bank, on which it seemed to linger for a moment, and then entering the fisherman's cottage, made roof and rafter gleam with a sudden illumination. 'I'll tell thee what, Gibbie Gyrape,' said my father, 'I wouldna be the owner of thy heart, and the proprietor of thy right hand, for all the treasures in earth and ocean.' A loud and piercing scream from the cottage made us thrill with fear, and in a moment the figures of three human beings rushed into the open air, and ran towards us with a swiftness which supernatural dread alone could inspire. We instantly knew them to be three noted smugglers, who infested the country; and rallying when they found my father maintain his ground, they thus mingled their fears and the secrets of their trade— for terror fairly overpowered their habitual caution.

"'I vow by the night tide, and the crooked timber,' said Willie Weethause, 'I never beheld sic a light as yon since our distillation pipe took fire, and made a burnt instead of a drink-offering of our spirits; I'll uphold it comes for nae good—a warning may be—sae ye may gang on, Wattie Bouseaway, wi' yere wickedness; as for me, I'se gae hame and repent.' 'Saulless bodie!' said his companion, whose natural hardihood was considerably supported by his communion with the brandy-cup—'saulless bodie, for a flaff o' fire and a maiden's shadow would ye forswear the gallant trade? Saul to gude! but auld Miller Morison shall turn yere thrapple into a drain-pipe to wyse the waste water from his mill, if ye turn back now, and help us nae through with as strong an importation as ever cheered the throat, and cheeped in the crapin. Confound the fizzenless bodie! he glowers as if this fine starlight were something frae the warst side of the world, and thae staring een o' his are busy shaping heaven's sweetest and balmiest air into the figures of wraiths and goblins.' 'Robert Telfer,' said my father, addressing the third smuggler, 'tell me nought of the secrets of your perilous craft, but tell me what you have seen, and why ye uttered that fearful scream, that made the wood-doves start from Caerlaverock pines.' 'I'll tell ye what, goodman,' said the mariner, 'I have seen the fires o' heaven running as thick along the sky, and on the surface of the ocean, as ye ever saw the blaze on a bowl o' punch at a merry-making, and neither quaked nor screamed; but ye'll mind the light that came to that cottage to-night was one for some fearful purport, which let the wise expound; sae it lessened nae one's courage to quail for sic an apparition.

Od! if I thought living soul would ever make the start I gied an upcast to me, I'll drill his breast-bane wi' my dirk like a turnip lantern.'

"My father mollified the wrath of this maritime desperado, by assuring him he beheld the light go from the sea to the cottage, and that he shook with terror, for it seemed no common light. 'Ou God! then,' said hopeful Robin, 'since it was one o' our ain cannie sea apparitions, I care less about it. I took it for some landward sprite! and now I think on't, where were my een? Did it no stand amang its ain light, with its long hanks of hair dripping and drenched; with a casket of gold in ae hand, and the other guarding its throat? I'll be bound it's the ghost o' some sonsie lass that has had her neck nipped for her gold; and had she stayed till I emptied the bicker o' brandy, I would have ask'd a cannie question or twae.' Willie Weethause had now fairly overcome his consternation, and began to feel all his love for the gallant trade, as his comrade called it, return. 'The tide serves, lads! the tide serves: let us slip our drap o' brandy into the bit bonnie boat, and tottle away amang the sweet starlight as far as the Kingholm or the town quarry— ye ken we have to meet Bailie Gardevine, and Laird Soukaway o' Ladlemouth.' They returned, not without hesitation and fear, to the old cottage; carried their brandy to the boat; and, as my father and I went home, we heard the dipping of their oars in the Nith, along the banks of which they sold their liquor, and told their tale of fear, magnifying its horror at every step, and introducing abundance of variations.

"The story of 'The Ghost with the Golden Casket' flew over the country-side with all its variations, and with many comments: some said they saw her, and some thought they saw her; and those who had the hardihood to keep watch on the beach at midnight, had their tales to tell of terrible lights and strange visions. With one who delighted in the marvellous, the spectre was decked in attributes that made the circle of auditors tighten round the hearth; while others, who allowed to a ghost only a certain quantity of thin air to clothe itself in, reduced it in their description to a very unpoetic shadow, or a kind of better sort of will-o'-the-wisp, that could for its own amusement counterfeit the human shape. There were many who, like my father, beheld the singular illumination appear at midnight on the coast; saw also something sailing along with it in the form of a lady in bright garments, her hair long and wet, and shining in diamonds; and heard a struggle, and the shriek as of a creature drowning.

"The belief of the peasantry did not long confine the apparition to the sea-coast; it was seen sometimes late at night far inland, and following Gilbert the fisherman, like a human shadow—like a pure light—like a white garment— and often in the shape, and with the attributes, in which it disturbed the carousal of the smugglers. I heard douce Davie Haining—a God-fearing man, and an elder of the Burgher congregation, and on whose word I could well lippen, when drink was kept from his head—I heard him say that as he rode home late from the Roodfair of Dumfries—the night was dark, there lay a dusting of snow on the ground, and no one appeared on the road but himself— he was lilting and singing the cannie end of the auld sang, 'There's a cuttie stool in our kirk,' which was made on some foolish quean's misfortune, when he heard the sound of horses' feet behind him at full gallop, and ere he could look round, who should flee past, urging his horse with whip and spur, but Gilbert the fisherman! 'Little wonder that he galloped,' said the elder, 'for a fearful form hovered around him, making many a clutch at him, and with every clutch uttering a shriek most piercing to hear.' But why should I make a long story of a common tale? The curse of spilt blood fell on him, and on his children, and on all he possessed; his sons and daughters died; his flocks perished; his grain grew, but never filled the ear; and fire came from heaven, or rose from hell, and consumed his house, and all that was therein. He is now a man of ninety years—a fugitive and a vagabond on the earth, without a house to put his white head in, with the unexpiated curse still clinging to him."

While my companion was making this summary of human wretchedness, I observed the figure of a man, stooping to the earth with extreme age, gliding through among the bushes of the ruined cottage, and approaching the advancing tide. He wore a loose great-coat, patched to the ground, and fastened round his waist by a belt and buckle; the remains of stockings and shoes were on his feet; a kind of fisherman's cap surmounted some remaining white hairs, while a long peeled stick supported him as he went.

companion gave an involuntary shudder when he saw him—"Lo, and behold, now, here comes Gilbert the fisherman! once every twenty-four hours doth he come, let the wind and the rain be as they will, to the nightly tide, to work o'er again, in imagination, his auld tragedy of unrighteousness. See how he waves his hand, as if he welcomed some one from sea—he raises his voice, too, as if something in the water required his counsel; and see how he dashes up to the middle, and grapples with the water as if he clutched a human being!"

I looked on the old man, and heard him call, in a hollow and broken voice: "O hoy! the ship, O hoy,—turn your boat's head ashore! And, my bonnie lady, keep haud o' yere casket. Hech be't! that wave would have sunk a three-decker, let be a slender boat. See—see, an' she binna sailing aboon the water like a wild swan!" And, wading deeper in the tide as he spoke, he seemed to clutch at something with both hands, and struggle with it in the water.

"Na! na! dinna haud your white hands to me—ye wear owre mickle gowd in your hair, and o'er many diamonds on your bosom, to 'scape drowning. There's as mickle gowd in this casket as would have sunk thee seventy fathom deep." And he continued to hold his hands under the water, muttering all the while.

"She's half gane now—and I'll be a braw laird, and build a bonnie house, and gang crousely to kirk and market; now I may let the waves work their will—my work will be ta'en for theirs."

He turned to wade to the shore, but a large and heavy wave came full dash on him, and bore him off his feet, and ere any assistance reached him, all human aid was too late; for nature was so exhausted with the fulness of years, and with his exertions, that a spoonful of water would have drowned him. The body of this miserable old man was interred, after some opposition from the peasantry, beneath the wall of the kirkyard; and from that time, the Ghost with the Golden Casket was seen no more, and only continued to haunt the evening tale of the hind and the farmer.

THE HAUNTED SHIPS.

> THOUGH my mind's not
> Hoodwinked with rustic marvels, I do think
> There are more things in the grove, the air, the flood,
> Yea, and the charnelled earth, than what wise man,
> Who walks so proud as if his form alone
> Filled the wide temple of the universe,
> Will let a frail mind say. I'd write i' the creed
> O' the sagest head alive, that fearful forms,
> Holy or reprobate, do page men's heels;
> That shapes, too horrid for our gaze, stand o'er
> The murderer's dust, and for revenge glare up,
> Even till the stars weep fire for very pity.

ALONG the sea of Solway, romantic on the Scottish side, with its woodland, its bays, its cliffs, and headlands; and interesting on the English side, with its many beautiful towns with their shadows on the water, rich pastures, safe harbours, and numerous ships; there still linger many traditional stories of a maritime nature, most of them connected with superstitions singularly wild and unusual. To the curious these tales afford a rich fund of entertainment, from the many diversities of the same story; some dry and barren, and stripped of all the embellishments of poetry; others dressed out in all the riches of a superstitious belief and haunted imagination. In this they resemble the inland traditions of the peasants; but many of the oral treasures of the Galwegian or the Cumbrian coast have the stamp of the Dane and the Norseman upon them, and claim but a remote or faint affinity with the legitimate legends of Caledonia. Something like a rude prosaic outline of several of the most noted of the northern ballads, the adventures and depredations of the old ocean kings, still lends life to the evening tale; and, among others, the story of the Haunted Ships is still popular among the maritime peasantry.

One fine harvest evening, I went on board the shallop of Richard Faulder, of Allanbay; and, committing ourselves to the waters, we allowed a gentle wind from the east to waft us at its pleasure towards the Scottish coast. We passed the sharp promontory of Siddick; and skirting the land within a stonecast, glided along the shore till we came within sight of the ruined Abbey of Sweetheart. The green mountain of Criffel ascended beside us; and the bleat of the flocks from its summit, together with the winding of the evening horn of the reapers, came softened into something like music over land and sea. We pushed our shallop into a deep and wooded bay, and sat silently looking on the serene beauty of the place. The moon glimmered in her rising through the tall shafts of the pines of Caerlaverock; and the sky, with scarce a cloud, showered down on wood and headland and bay, the twinkling beams of a thousand stars rendering every object visible. The tide, too, was coming with that swift and silent swell observable when the wind is gentle; the woody curves along the land were filling with the flood, till it touched the green branches of the drooping trees; while in the centre current the roll and the plunge of a thousand pellocks told to the experienced fisherman that salmon were abundant.

As we looked, we saw an old man emerging from a path that winded to the shore through a grove of doddered hazel; he carried a halve-net on his back, while behind him came a girl, bearing a small harpoon with which the fishers are remarkably dexterous in striking their prey. The senior seated himself on a large grey stone, which overlooked the bay, laid aside his bonnet, and submitted his bosom and neck to the refreshing sea breeze; and taking his harpoon from his attendant, sat with the gravity and composure of a spirit of the flood, with his ministering nymph behind him. We pushed our shallop to the shore, and soon stood at their side.

"This is old Mark Macmoran the mariner, with his granddaughter Barbara," said Richard Faulder, in a whisper that had something of fear in it; "he knows every creek and cavern and quicksand in Solway—has seen the Spectre Hound that haunts the Isle of Man; has heard him bark, and at every bark has seen a ship sink; and he has seen, too, the Haunted Ships in full sail; and, if all tales be true, he has sailed in them himself;—he's an awful person."

Though I perceived in the communication of my friend something of the superstition of the sailor, I could not help thinking that common rumour had made a happy choice in singling out old Mark to maintain her intercourse with the invisible world. His hair, which seemed to have refused all intercourse with the comb, hung matted upon his shoulders; a kind of mantle, or rather blanket, pinned with a wooden skewer round his neck, fell mid-leg down, concealing all his nether garments as far as a pair of hose, darned with yarn of all conceivable colours, and a pair of shoes, patched and repaired till nothing of the original structure remained, and clasped on his feet with two massy silver buckles. If the dress of the old man was rude and sordid, that of his granddaughter was gay, and even rich. She wore a bodice of fine wool, wrought round the bosom with alternate leaf and lily, and a kirtle of the same fabric, which, almost touching her white and delicate ankle, showed her snowy feet, so fairy-light and round that they scarcely seemed to touch the grass where she stood. Her hair, a natural ornament which woman seeks much to improve, was of bright glossy brown, and encumbered rather than adorned with a snood, set thick with marine productions, among which the small clear pearl found in the Solway was conspicuous. Nature had not trusted to a handsome shape and a sylph-like air, for young Barbara's influence over the heart of man; but had bestowed a pair of large bright blue eyes, swimming in liquid light, so full of love and gentleness and joy, that all the sailors from Annanwater to far Saint Bees acknowledged their power, and sung songs about the bonnie lass of Mark Macmoran. She stood holding a small gaff-hook of polished steel in her hand, and seemed not dissatisfied with the glances I bestowed on her from time to time, and which I held more than requited by a single glance of those eyes which retained so many capricious hearts in subjection.

The tide, though rapidly augmenting, had not yet filled the bay at our feet. The moon now streamed fairly over the tops of Caerlaverock pines, and showed the expanse of ocean dimpling and swelling, on which sloops and shallops came dancing, and displaying at every turn their extent of white sail against the beam of the moon. I looked on old Mark the mariner, who, seated motionless on his grey stone, kept his eye fixed on the increasing waters with a look of seriousness and sorrow in which I saw little of the calculating spirit of a mere fisherman. Though he looked on the coming tide, his eyes seemed to dwell particularly on the black and decayed hulls of two vessels, which, half immersed in the quicksand, still addressed to every heart a tale of shipwreck and desolation. The tide wheeled and foamed around them; and, creeping inch by inch up the side, at last fairly threw its waters over the top, and a long and hollow eddy showed the resistance which the liquid element received.

The moment they were fairly buried in the water, the old man clasped his hands together, and said: "Blessed be the tide that will break over and bury ye for ever! Sad to mariners, and sorrowful to maids and mothers, has the time been you have choked up this deep and bonnie bay. For evil were you sent, and for evil have you continued. Every season finds from you its song of sorrow and wail, its funeral processions, and its shrouded corses. Woe to the land where the wood grew that made ye! Cursed be the axe that hewed ye on the mountains, the hands that joined ye together, the bay that ye first swam in, and the wind that wafted ye here! Seven times have ye put my life in peril, three fair sons have ye swept from my side, and two bonnie grand-bairns; and now, even now, your waters foam and flash for my destruction, did I venture my infirm limbs in quest of food in your deadly bay. I see by that ripple and that foam, and hear by the sound and singing of your surge, that ye yearn for another victim; but it shall not be me nor mine."

Even as the old mariner addressed himself to the wrecked ships, a young man appeared at the southern extremity of the bay, holding his halve-net in his hand, and hastening into the current. Mark rose and shouted, and waved him back from a place which, to a person unacquainted with the dangers of the bay, real and superstitious, seemed sufficiently perilous: his granddaughter, too, added her voice to his, and waved her white hands; but the more they strove, the faster advanced the peasant, till he stood to his middle in the water, while the tide increased every moment in depth and strength. "Andrew, Andrew," cried the young woman, in a voice quavering with emotion, "turn, turn, I tell you! O the Ships, the Haunted Ships!" But the appearance of a fine run of fish had more influence with the peasant than the voice of bonnie Barbara, and forward he dashed, net in hand. In a moment he was borne off his feet, and mingled like foam with the water, and hurried towards the fatal eddies which whirled and roared round the sunken ships. But he was a powerful young man, and an expert swimmer: he seized on one of the projecting ribs of the nearest hulk, and clinging to it with the grasp of despair, uttered yell after yell, sustaining himself against the prodigious rush of the current.

From a shealing of turf and straw, within the pitch of a bar from the spot where we stood, came out an old woman bent with age, and leaning on a crutch. "I heard the voice of that lad Andrew Lammie; can the chield be drowning, that he skirls sae uncannilie?" said the old woman, seating herself on the ground, and looking earnestly at the water. "Ou ay," she continued, "he's doomed, he's doomed; heart and hand can never save him; boats, ropes, and man's strength and wit, all vain! vain!—he's doomed, he's doomed!"

By this time I had thrown myself into the shallop, followed reluctantly by Richard Faulder, over whose courage and kindness of heart superstition had great power; and with one push from the shore, and some exertion in sculling, we came within a quoitcast of the unfortunate fisherman. He stayed not to profit by our aid; for, when he perceived us near, he uttered a piercing shriek of joy, and bounded towards us through the agitated element the full length of an oar. I saw him for a second on the surface of the water; but the eddying current sucked him down; and all I ever beheld of him again was his hand held above the flood, and clutching in agony at some imaginary aid. I sat gazing in horror on the vacant sea before us; but a breathing-time before, a human being, full of youth and strength and hope, was there: his cries were still ringing in my ears, and echoing in the woods; and now nothing was seen or heard save the turbulent expanse of water, and the sound of its chafing on the shores. We pushed back our shallop, and resumed our station on the cliff beside the old mariner and his descendant.

"Wherefore sought ye to peril your own lives fruitlessly," said Mark, "in attempting to save the doomed? Whoso touches those infernal ships, never survives to tell the tale. Woe to the man who is found nigh them at midnight when the tide has subsided, and they arise in their former beauty, with forecastle, and deck, and sail, and pennon, and shroud! Then is seen the streaming of lights along the water from their cabin windows, and then is heard the sound of mirth and the clamour of tongues, and the infernal whoop and halloo, and song, ringing far and wide. Woe to the man who comes nigh them!"

To all this my Allanbay companion listened with a breathless attention. I felt something touched with a superstition to which I partly believed I had seen one victim offered up; and I inquired of the old mariner, "How and when came these Haunted Ships there? To me they seem but the melancholy relics of some unhappy voyagers, and much more likely to warn people to shun destruction than entice and delude them to it."

"And so," said the old man with a smile, which had more of sorrow in it than of mirth; "and so, young man, these black and shattered hulks seem to the eye of the multitude. But things are not what they seem: that water, a kind and convenient servant to the wants of man, which seems so smooth and so dimpling and so gentle, has swallowed up a human soul even now; and the place which it covers, so fair and so level, is a faithless quicksand, out of which none escape. Things are otherwise than they seem. Had you lived as long as I have had the sorrow to live; had you seen the storms, and braved the perils, and endured the distresses which have befallen me; had you sat gazing out on the dreary ocean at midnight on a haunted coast; had you seen comrade after comrade, brother after brother, and son after son, swept away by the merciless ocean from your very side; had you seen the shapes of friends, doomed to the wave and the quicksand, appearing to you in the dreams and visions of the night; then would your mind have been prepared for crediting the maritime legends of mariners; and the two haunted Danish ships would have had their terrors for you, as they have for all who sojourn on this coast.

"Of the time and the cause of their destruction," continued the old man, "I know nothing certain: they have stood as you have seen them for uncounted time; and while all other ships wrecked on this unhappy coast have gone to pieces, and rotted and sunk away in a few years, these two haunted hulks have neither sunk in the quicksand, nor has a single spar or board been displaced. Maritime legend says, that two ships of Denmark having had permission, for a time, to work deeds of darkness and dolour on the deep, were at last condemned to the whirlpool and the sunken rock, and were wrecked in this bonnie bay, as a sign to seamen to be gentle and devout. The night when they were lost was a harvest evening of uncommon mildness and beauty: the sun had newly set; the moon came brighter and brighter out; and the reapers, laying their sickles at the root of the standing corn, stood on rock and bank, looking at the increasing magnitude of the waters, for sea and land were visible from Saint Bees to Barnhourie. The sails of two vessels were soon seen bent for the Scottish coast; and, with a speed outrunning the swiftest ship, they approached the dangerous quicksands and headland of Borranpoint. On the deck of the foremost ship not a living soul was seen, or shape, unless something in darkness and form resembling a human shadow could be called a shape, which flitted from extremity to extremity of the ship, with the appearance of trimming the sails, and directing the vessel's course. But the decks of its companion were crowded with human shapes; the captain and mate, and sailor and cabin-boy, all seemed there; and from them the sound of mirth and minstrelsy echoed over land and water. The coast which they skirted along was one of extreme danger, and the reapers shouted to warn them to beware of sandbank and rock; but of this friendly counsel no notice was taken, except that a large and famished dog, which sat on the prow, answered every shout with a long, loud, and melancholy howl. The deep sandbank of Carsethorn was expected to arrest the career of these desperate navigators; but they passed, with the celerity of waterfowl, over an obstruction which had wrecked many pretty ships.

"Old men shook their heads and departed, saying, 'We have seen the fiend sailing in a bottomless ship; let us go home and pray;' but one young and wilful man said, 'Fiend! I'll warrant it's nae fiend, but douce Janet Withershins the witch, holding a carouse with some of her Cumberland cummers, and mickle red wine will be spilt atween them. Dod I would gladly have a toothfu'! I'll warrant it's nane o' your cauld sour slae-water like a bottle of Bailie Skrinkie's port, but right drap-o'-my-heart's-blood stuff, that would waken a body out of their last linen. I wonder where the cummers will anchor their craft?' 'And I'll vow,' said another rustic, 'the wine they quaff is none of your visionary drink, such as a drouthie body has dished out to his lips in a dream; nor is it shadowy and unsubstantial, like the vessels they sail in, which are made out of a cockel-shell or a cast-off slipper, or the paring of a seaman's right thumbnail. I once got a hansel out of a witch's quaigh myself—auld Marion Mathers, of Dustiefoot, whom they tried to bury in the old kirkyard of Dunscore; but the cummer raise as fast as they laid her down, and naewhere else would she lie but in the bonnie green kirkyard of Kier, among douce and sponsible fowk. So I'll vow that the wine of a witch's cup is as fell liquor as ever did a kindly turn to a poor man's heart; and be they fiends, or be they witches, if they have red wine asteer, I'll risk a drouket sark for ae glorious tout on't.' 'Silence, ye sinners,' said the minister's son of a neighbouring parish, who united in his own person his father's lack of devotion with his mother's love of liquor. 'Whist!—speak as if ye had the fear of something holy before ye. Let the vessels run their own way to destruction: who can stay the eastern wind, and the current of the Solway sea? I can find ye Scripture warrant for that; so let them try their strength on Blawhooly rocks, and their might on the broad quicksand. There's a surf running there would knock the ribs together of a galley built by the imps of the pit, and commanded by the Prince of Darkness. Bonnilie and bravely they sail away there, but before the blast blows by they'll be wrecked; and red wine and strong brandy will be as rife as dyke water, and we'll drink the health of bonnie Bell Blackness out of her left-foot slipper.'

"The speech of the young profligate was applauded by several of his companions, and away they flew to the bay of Blawhooly, from whence they never returned. The two vessels were observed all at once to stop in the bosom of the bay, on the spot where their hulls now appear; the mirth and the minstrelsy waxed louder than ever, and the forms of maidens, with instruments of music and wine-cups in their hands, thronged the decks. A boat was lowered; and the same shadowy pilot who conducted the ships made it start towards the shore with the rapidity of lightning, and its head knocked against the bank where the four young men stood who longed for the unblest drink. They leaped in with a laugh, and with a laugh were they welcomed on deck; wine-cups were given to each, and as they raised them to their lips the vessels melted away beneath their feet; and one loud shriek, mingled with laughter still louder, was heard over land and water for many miles. Nothing more was heard or seen till the morning, when the crowd who came to the beach saw with fear and wonder the two Haunted Ships,' such as they now seem, masts and tackle gone; nor mark, nor sign, by which their name, country, or destination could be known, was left remaining. Such is the tradition of the mariners; and its truth has been attested by many families whose sons and whose fathers have been drowned in the haunted bay of Blawhooly."

"And trow ye," said the old woman, who, attracted from her hut by the drowning cries of the young fisherman, had remained an auditor of the mariner's legend; "and trow ye, Mark Macmoran, that the tale of the Haunted Ships is done? I can say no to that. Mickle have mine ears heard; but more mine eyes have witnessed since I came to dwell in this humble home by the side of the deep sea. I mind the night weel: it was on Hallowmass Eve: the nuts were cracked, and the apples were eaten, and spell and charm were tried at my fireside; till, wearied with diving into the dark waves of futurity, the lads and lasses fairly took to the more visible blessings of kind words, tender clasps, and gentle courtship. Soft words in a maiden's ear, and a kindlie kiss o' her lip, were old world matters to me, Mark Macmoran; though I mean not to say that I have been free of the folly of daunering and daffin with a youth in my day, and keeping tryste with him in dark and lonely places. However, as I say, these times of enjoyment were passed and gone with me—the mair's the pity that pleasure should fly sae fast away—and as I could nae make sport I thought I should not mar any; so out I sauntered into the fresh cold air, and sat down behind that old oak, and looked abroad on the wide sea. I had my ain sad thoughts, ye may think, at the time: it was in that very bay my blythe good man perished, with seven more in his company; and on that very bank where ye see the waves leaping and foaming, I saw seven stately corses streeked, but the dearest was the eighth. It was a woeful sight to me, a widow, with four bonnie boys, with nought to support them but these twa hands, and God's blessing, and a cow's grass. I have never liked to live out of sight of this bay since that time; and mony's the moonlight night I sit looking on these watery mountains, and these waste shores; it does my heart good, whatever it may do to my head. So ye see it was

Hallowmass Night, and looking on sea and land sat I; and my heart wandering to other thoughts soon made me forget my youthful company at hame. It might be near the howe hour of the night. The tide was making, and its singing brought strange old world stories with it, and I thought on the dangers that sailors endure, the fates they meet with, and the fearful forms they see. My own blythe good man had seen sights that made him grave enough at times, though he aye tried to laugh them away.

"Aweel, atween that very rock aneath us and the coming tide, I saw, or thought I saw—for the tale is so dreamlike, that the whole might pass for a vision of the night—I saw the form of a man: his plaid was grey, his face was grey; and his hair, which hung low down till it nearly came to the middle of his back, was as white as the white sea-foam. He began to howk and dig under the bank; an' God be near me, thought I, this maun be the unblessed spirit of auld Adam Gowdgowpin the miser, who is doomed to dig for shipwrecked treasure, and count how many millions are hidden for ever from man's enjoyment. The form found something which in shape and hue seemed a left-foot slipper of brass; so down to the tide he marched, and placing it on the water, whirled it thrice round, and the infernal slipper dilated at every turn, till it became a bonnie barge with its sails bent, and on board leaped the form, and scudded swiftly away. He came to one of the Haunted Ships, and striking it with his oar, a fair ship, with mast and canvas and mariners, started up; he touched the other Haunted Ship, and produced the like transformation; and away the three spectre ships bounded, leaving a track of fire behind them on the billows which was long unextinguished. Now was nae that a bonnie and a fearful sight to see beneath the light of the Hallowmass moon? But the tale is far frae finished, for mariners say that once a year, on a certain night, if ye stand on the Borran Point, ye will see the infernal shallops coming snoring through the Solway, ye will hear the same laugh and song and mirth and minstrelsy which our ancestors heard; see them bound over the sandbanks and sunken rocks like sea-gulls, cast their anchor in Blawhooly Bay, while the shadowy figure lowers down the boat, and augments their numbers with the four unhappy mortals to whose memory a stone stands in the kirkyard, with a sinking ship and a shoreless sea cut upon it. Then the spectre ships vanish, and the drowning shriek of mortals and the rejoicing laugh of fiends are heard, and the old hulls are left as a memorial that the old spiritual kingdom has not departed from the earth. But I maun away, and trim my little cottage fire, and make it burn and blaze up bonnie, to warm the crickets and my cold and crazy bones, that maun soon be laid aneath the green sod in the eerie kirkyard." And away the old dame tottered to her cottage, secured the door on the inside, and soon the hearth-flame was seen to glimmer and gleam through the keyhole and window.

"I'll tell ye what," said the old mariner, in a subdued tone, and with a shrewd and suspicious glance of his eye after the old sibyl, "it's a word that may not very well be uttered, but there are many mistakes made in evening stories if old Moll Moray there, where she lives, knows not mickle more than she is willing to tell of the Haunted Ships, and their unhallowed mariners. She lives cannilie and quietly; no one knows how she is fed or supported; but her dress is aye whole, her cottage ever smokes, and her table lacks neither of wine, white and red, nor of fowl and fish, and white bread and brown. It was a dear scoff to Jock Matheson, when he called old Moll the uncannie carline of Blawhooly: his boat ran round and round in the centre of the Solway—everybody said it was enchanted—and down it went head foremost: and had nae Jock been a swimmer equal to a sheldrake, he would have fed the fish. But I'll warrant it sobered the lad's speech; and he never reckoned himself safe till he made auld Moll the present of a new kirtle and a stone of cheese."

"O father," said his granddaughter Barbara, "ye surely wrong poor old Mary Moray: what use could it be to an old woman like her, who has no wrongs to redress, no malice to work out against mankind, and nothing to seek of enjoyment save a cannie hour and a quiet grave—what use could the fellowship of fiends and the communion of evil spirits be to her? I know Jenny Primrose puts rowan-tree above the door-head when she sees old Mary coming; I know the good wife of Kittlenaket wears rowan-berry leaves in the headband of her blue kirtle, and all for the sake of averting the unsonsie glance of Mary's right ee; and I know that the auld Laird of Burntroutwater drives his seven cows to their pasture with a wand of witch-tree, to keep Mary from milking them. But what has all that to do with haunted shallops, visionary mariners, and bottomless boats? I have heard myself as pleasant a tale about the Haunted Ships and their unworldly crews, as any one would wish to hear in a winter evening. It was told me by young Benjie Macharg, one summer night, sitting on Arbiglandbank: the lad intended a sort of love meeting; but all that he could talk of was about smearing sheep and shearing sheep, and of the wife which the Norway elves of the Haunted Ships made for his uncle Sandie Macharg. And I shall tell ye the tale as the honest lad told it to me.

"Alexander Macharg, besides being the laird of three acres of peatmoss, two kale gardens, and the owner of seven good milch cows, a pair of horses, and six pet sheep, was the husband of one of the handsomest women in seven parishes. Many a lad sighed the day he was brided; and a Nithsdale laird and two Annandale moorland farmers drank themselves to their last linen, as well as their last shilling, through sorrow for her loss. But married was the dame; and home she was carried, to bear rule over her home and her husband, as an honest woman should. Now ye maun ken that though the flesh and blood lovers of Alexander's bonnie wife all ceased to love and to sue her after she became another's, there were certain admirers who did not consider their claim at all abated, or their hopes lessened by the kirk's famous obstacle of matrimony. Ye have heard how the devout minister of Tinwald had a fair son carried away, and bedded against his liking to an unchristened bride, whom the elves and the fairies provided: ye have heard how the bonnie bride of the drunken Laird of Soukitup was stolen by the fairies out at the back-window of the bridal chamber, the time the bridegroom was groping his way to the chamber-door; and ye have heard—but why need I multiply cases? Such things in the ancient days were as common as candle-light. So ye'll no hinder certain water elves and sea fairies, who sometimes keep festival and summer mirth in these old haunted hulks, from falling in love with the weel-faured wife of Laird Macharg; and to their plots and contrivances they went how they might accomplish to sunder man and wife; and sundering such a man and such a wife was like sundering the green leaf from the summer, or the fragrance from the flower.

"So it fell on a time that Laird Macharg took his halvenet on his back, and his steel spear in his hand, and down to Blawhooly Bay gade he, and into the water he went right between the two haunted hulks, and placing his net awaited the coming of the tide. The night, ye maun ken, was mirk, and the wind lowne, and the singing of the increasing waters among the shells and the peebles was heard for sundry miles. All at once light began to glance and twinkle on board the two Haunted Ships from every hole and seam, and presently the sound as of a hatchet employed in squaring timber echoed far and wide. But if the toil of these unearthly workmen amazed the laird, how much more was his amazement increased when a sharp shrill voice called out, 'Ho! brother, what are you doing now?' A voice still shriller responded from the other haunted ship, 'I'm making a wife to Sandie Macharg!' And a loud quavering laugh running from ship to ship, and from bank to bank, told the joy they expected from their labour.

"Now the laird, besides being a devout and a God-fearing man, was shrewd and bold; and in plot and contrivance, and skill in conducting his designs, was fairly an overmatch for any dozen land elves: but the water elves are far more subtle; besides, their haunts and their dwellings being in the great deep, pursuit and detection is hopeless if they succeed in carrying their prey to the waves. But ye shall hear. Home flew the laird, collected his family around the hearth, spoke of the signs and the sins of the times, and talked of mortification and prayer for averting calamity; and finally, taking his father's Bible, brass clasps, black print, and covered with calf-skin, from the shelf, he proceeded without let or stint to perform domestic worship. I should have told ye that he bolted and locked the door, shut up all inlet to the house, threw salt into the fire, and proceeded in every way like a man skilful in guarding against the plots of fairies and fiends. His wife looked on all this with wonder; but she saw something in her husband's looks that hindered her from intruding either question or advice, and a wise woman was she.

"Near the mid-hour of the night the rush of a horse's feet was heard, and the sound of a rider leaping from its back, and a heavy knock came to the door, accompanied by a voice, saying, 'The cummer drink's hot, and the knave bairn is expected at Laird Laurie's to-night; sae mount, good-wife, and come.'

"'Preserve me!' said the wife of Sandie Macharg; 'that's news indeed! who could have thought it? The laird has been heirless for seventeen years! Now Sandie, my man, fetch me my skirt and hood.'

"But he laid his arm round his wife's neck, and said, 'If all the lairds in Galloway go heirless, over this door threshold shall you not stir to-night; and I have said, and I have sworn it: seek not to know why or wherefore—but, Lord, send us thy blessed mornlight.' The wife looked for a moment in her husband's eyes, and desisted from further entreaty.

"'But let us send a civil message to the gossips, Sandy; and hadnae ye better say I am sair laid with a sudden sickness?—though it's sinful-like to send the poor messenger a mile agate with a lie in his mouth without a glass of brandy.'

"'To such a messenger, and to those who sent him, no apology is needed,' said the austere laird; 'so let him depart.' And the clatter of a horse's hoofs was heard, and the muttered imprecations of its rider on the churlish treatment he had experienced.

"'Now, Sandie, my lad,' said his wife, laying an arm particularly white and round about his neck as she spoke, 'are you not a queer man and a stern? I have been your wedded wife now these three years; and, beside my dower, have brought you three as bonnie bairns as ever smiled aneath a summer sun. O man, you a douce man, and fitter to be an elder than even Willie Greer himself, I have the minister's ain word for't, to put on these hard-hearted looks, and gang waving your arms that way, as if ye said, "I winna take the counsel of sic a hempie as you;" I'm your ain leal wife, and will and maun have an explanation.'

"To all this Sandie Macharg replied, 'It is written— "Wives, obey your husbands;" but we have been stayed in our devotion, so let us pray;' and down he knelt: his wife knelt also, for she was as devont as bonnie; and beside them knelt their household, and all lights were extinguished.

"'Now this beats a',' muttered his wife to herself; 'however, I shall be obedient for a time; but if I dinna ken what all this is for before the morn by sunket-time, my tongue is nae langer a tongue, nor my hands worth wearing.'

"The voice of her husband in prayer interrupted this mental soliloquy; and ardently did he beseech to be preserved from the wiles of the fiends and the snares of Satan; 'from witches, ghosts, goblins, elves, fairies, spunkies, and water-kelpies; from the spectre shallop of Solway; from spirits visible and invisible; from the Haunted Ships and their unearthly tenants; from maritime spirits that plotted against godly men, and fell in love with their wives——'

"'Nay, but his presence be near us!' said his wife in a low tone of dismay. 'God guide my gudeman's wits: I never heard such a prayer from human lips before. But Sandie, my man, Lord's sake, rise. What fearful light is this? Barn and byre and stable maun be in a blaze; and Hawkie, and Hurley, Doddie, and Cherrie, and Damson-plum will be smoored with reek, and scorched with flame.'

"And a flood of light, but not so gross as a common fire, which ascended to heaven and filled all the court before the house, amply justified the good wife's suspicions. But to the terrors of fire Sandie was as immovable as he was to the imaginary groans of the barren wife of Laird Laurie; and he held his wife, and threatened the weight of his right hand— and it was a heavy one—to all who ventured abroad, or even unbolted the door. The neighing and prancing of horses, and the bellowing of cows, augmented the horrors of the night; and to any one who only heard the din, it seemed that the whole onstead was in a blaze, and horses and cattle perishing in the flame. All wiles, common or extraordinary, were put in practice to entice or force the honest farmer and his wife to open the door; and when the like success attended every new stratagem, silence for a little while ensued, and a long, loud, and shrilling laugh wound up the dramatic efforts of the night. In the morning, when Laird Macharg went to the door, he found standing against one of the pilasters a piece of black ship oak, rudely fashioned into something like human form, and which skilful people declared would have been clothed with seeming flesh and blood, and palmed upon him by elfin adroitness for his wife, had he admitted his visitants. A synod of wise men and women sat upon the woman of timber, and she was finally ordered to be devoured by fire, and that in the open air A fire was soon made, and into it the elfin sculpture was tossed from the prongs of two pairs of pitchforks. The blaze that arose was awful to behold; and hissings and burstings and loud cracklings and strange noises were heard in the midst of the flame; and when the whole sank into ashes, a drinking-cup of some precious metal was found; and this cup, fashioned no doubt by elfin skill, but rendered harmless by the purification with fire, the sons and daughters of Sandie Macharg and his wife drink out of to this very day. Bless all bold men, say I, and obedient wives!"

DEATH OF THE LAIRD OF WARLSWORM.

IT happened on a fine harvest afternoon, that I found myself at the entrance of one of the wild and romantic glens or vales of Galloway; and as a Galwegian vale has a character of its own, it would mutilate my story to leave it undescribed. Imagine an expanse of brown moorland extending as far as sight can reach, threaded by innumerable burns or brooks, and only tenanted in appearance by flocks of sheep, or by coveys of red and black game. Here and there a shepherd was seen with his dogs, or a bare-headed maiden with her pails of milk, going homewards from the fold, and cheering her way with one of those old tender traditional ballads which some neglected spirit, like that of John Lowe, has scattered so largely among the pastoral glens of Galloway. A shepherd's house, or his summer sheal, rising like the "bonnie bower," of the two heroines of Scottish song, on a burn brae, and covered thick with rushes, while it threw its long wavering line of blue smoke into the clear sharp air, spoke of the presence of the sons and daughters of man, or said, in the quaint and homely language of the Galwegian proverb, "where four cloots go, man's twa feet maun follow."

But this heath, barren and wild as it seemed, had other attractions. At the distance of almost every little mile, numerous streams of smoke ascended from the brown moor; the sound and the hum of man, busied with the flail, the hatchet, or the hammer, was heard; the cry and the merriment of children abounded; and here and there a green tree-top or a chimney-head, a kirk-spire or a ruined tower, projecting above the horizon of blossomed heather, proclaimed to the traveller that Caledonia, amid her deserts, has her well-peopled glens and her fruitful places.

On a summer Sabbath morning the people of Galloway are to be beheld in their glory; then every little deep-green and populous vale pours forth its own sedate and pious and well-dressed multitude. From the dame in the douce grey mantle to the maiden in glittering silks and scarlets; from him in the broad blue bonnet to her in the gallant cap and feather; from the trembling and careful step of age to the firm and heedless stride of youth; from her who dreams of bridal favours and bridegroom's vows, to him bent to the earth with age, musing on the burial procession and the gaping grave—all are there, moving on staid and soberly to the house of God. Often have I stood and seen the scanty current of people issue out like the little brook of their native glen, join themselves to a fuller stream, and, increasing as they flowed on, become as a river ere they reached the entrance to the burial-ground, which, hallowed with their fathers' dust, encompassed their native kirk. I have heard the bell toll, and the melody of their psalms of praise and hymns of thanksgiving flow far and wide. I have thought, while these holy sounds arose, that the bleat of the flocks became softer, the cry of the plover less shrill, and that the divine melody subdued into music the rough brawling of the brook along which it was heard.

At the heathy entrance into one of these beautiful vales I accordingly stood and pursued the winding of a little stream, which, after leaping over two or three small crags, and forming several little bleaching grounds of greensward for the villagers' webs, gathered all its waters together, and concentrated all its might, to pour itself on a solitary millwheel at the farther end of the valley. On either side of the glen the shepherds and husbandmen had each constructed his homely abode, according to his own fancy; the houses were dropped here and there at random, facing east, and west, and south, each attached to its own little garden, the green flourishing of which was pleasant to the eye, while the fragrance of some sweet herbs, or a few simple flowers, escaped from the enclosure, and was wafted about me by the low and fitful wind. The whole glen was full of life, the sickles were moving beneath the ripe grain, the bandsmen were binding and stooking it, several low-wheeled cars were busied in depositing this rustic treasure in the farmer's stack-yard; while the farmer himself moved about, surveyed the fulfilment of his wishes, and rubbed the full ears between his palms, and examined with a pleased and a curious eye the quality of his crop. At the doors of the cottages the old dames sat in groups in the sun, twirling their distaffs, and driving the story round of wonder or of scandal; while an unsummable progeny of barefooted bairns ran, and rolled, and leaped, and tumbled, and laughed, and screamed, till the whole glen remurmured with the din.

I sat down by the side of a flat gravestone, bedded level with the grass; the ancient inscription, often renewed by the pious villagers, told that beneath it lay one of those enthusiastic, undaunted, and persecuted peasants, who combated for freedom of faith and body when the nobles of the land forgot the cause of God and their country. Presently the children desisted from their merriment, and gathered about and gazed on me, a man of an unknown glen, with a quiet and a curious eye. I ever loved the innocent scrutiny of youthful eyes; so I allowed them to descant at freedom on my southland garb, and wonder what could make me choose my seat by the martyr's tombstone, a place seldom visited, save by men in a devotional frame of mind. A venerable old dame, with a straggling tress or two of grey hair flowing from beneath her mutch or coif, laid aside her distaff, and advanced to free me from the intrusion of a dozen or more of her curly-headed descendants. The admonishing tone in which she said, "Bairns, bairns!" with the rebuke of her eye, accomplished her wishes; the children vanished from my side, and retired to a little round green knowe or knoll, which rose on the rivulet bank in the middle of the village, and seemed appropriated for rustic games, pitching the bar, casting the stone, for leaping and for wrestling. "A bonnie harvest afternoon, sir," said the Galwegian matron, "but ye would be wiser to come and rest ye in a comfortable house than sit on the cauld stane, though it lies aboon the dust of ane of the godly auld folk of the saintly days of Galloway, or maybe ye might like the change-house better to birl yere sixpence, and be behadden to none, and I cannot say that I can advise ye."

I was prevented from replying by another of the village dames, who thus broke in on our parley: "Birl his silver in the change-house!—wherefore should he? What can hinder him from slipping cannilie away up the brae to the gudeman of Warlsworm? he's either dead, or as good as dead; and if he's no departed, so much the better; he will leave the world with a perturbed spirit, for sore, sore, has he stuck to the earth, and loth will he be to leave his gowd and his gains, and his bonnie broad lairdships; and who kens but the sight of a stranger breaking his bread and drinking his milk may make him die through downright vexation for the unwonted waste? Andrew, my bonnie lad, take this strange man up to auld Warlsworm's hall-door; I would gang myself, but I vowed never to cross his threshold or enter his land, since he cheated my ain cousin out of the green holms of Dee: black be his cast, and bitter his doom!"

A little boy came to my side, and put his hand in mine; and, willing to know more of a man of whom I had heard so much, away I walked with my barefooted guide, and soon came within sight of the mansion of Warlsworm.

It was a rough old house, built of undressed granite, and covered with a slating of coarse sandstone. The smoke, despairing to find its way through the windings of a chimney almost choked with sides of bacon and soot, sought its passage in many a curl and turn along the roof, and, finally descending, streamed out into the pure air through window and door. Groups of black cattle, after browsing on every green thing which the garden contained, and trying to digest the withered thatch which depended from the sides of the barn and stable, stood lowing knee-deep in a pool of muddy water before the mansion, and looking wistfully on the green hills and the golden harvest around them. The fowls, undismayed by foumart or fox, plundered the corn which hung drop-ripe and unreaped in the field; while a multitude of swine, breaking, in the desperation of hunger, from their pens, ran grunting through the standing grain, crushed the growing potatoes in unwieldy joy, and finally cooled their sides, and fulfilled the Scripture proverb, by wallowing in the mire which encompassed as with a fosse this miserable mansion.

The door stood open. In summer, in the pastoral districts, few doors are closed; and, with the privilege which a stranger claims in a hospitable land, I entered the house. Wheeled towards the fire, and bedded thick with sheepskins and soft cushions, stood the lang settle, or rustic sofa; and on it lay a man bald and feeble with age, and kneeling by his side I saw a fair-haired girl, her hands clasped, and her large blue eyes fixed with a moist and motionless gaze on his face. This was the owner of the mansion, the far-famed Laird of Warlsworm; and the maid was his niece, as remarkable for her gentleness and beauty as her relative for his grasping and incessant greed. As my shadow darkened the floor, she looked up, and motioned me to silence and a seat. I accordingly sat down, and looked with an eye of deep interest on the touching scene before me. There lay Age, his face gross and covetous, his mind seeking communion with the riches of the earth, while his body was fast hasting to dust, and his soul to its final account; and there knelt Youth, glowing in health and ripe in beauty, her tresses bright, and flowing over her neck, like sunshine visiting a bank of lilies; her hands, white and shapely and small, clasped over a white and a perturbed bosom; while from her long dark eyelashes the tears of sorrow descended drop by drop. On both, a young man in a homely garb, but with a face comely and interesting, sat and looked, and looked too with a brow on which might be read more of love for the maid than of sorrow for the man.

The old man uttered a groan, turned on his couch, half opened his eyes, and said, "Bessie, my bairn, let me have hold of thy hand; my sight is not so good as it ought to be; and I think I see queer things, that should not be seen by a man when he lies down to die. But I have wronged no man; I took but what the law gave me; and if the law grips with an iron hand, it's the worse for them that made it. I thought I heard the footstep of the young portioner of Glaiketha; he'll be come to borrow gold and to wadset land. But, Bessie my lass, gold's scarce, and land abundant; no that I refuse the minted money when the interest will do thee good, and when the security's sicker; sae gang thy ways, my wean, to the old pose ahint the cathud, or hear ye me; there's a saddle bag of good red gold riding on the rannel-tree that has nae seen sun or wind these seven-and-twenty summers."

"Oh! forget the cares of the world," said the maiden, with a voice smothering with sorrow, "and think of your health. This is not the young portioner of Glaiketha seeking for gold to cast away in eating and drinking and dancing, or in more evil pursuits; but a stranger youth come to repose him all night as strangers do, and recommence his journey in the morning."

"Repose him!" re-echoed the old man, his voice deepening and his faded eyes brightening as he spoke. "Have I wranged any of his kin, that he comes hither to riot on my substance? Have I ever darkened his father's door, that he should presume to darken mine? Alas! alas! the bonnie haughs of Orr, and the fair holms of Dee, will be wasted on loons and limmers, and I shall no find repose where all men find rest. Ay! ay! my hall will soon be a changed place; there will be fizzenless tea instead of weel-buttered breakfast brose; a pudding with spices and raisins for a gallant haggis dropping with fatness, and full of marrowy strength; and for the pleasant din of the spinning-wheel there will be the sounding of fiddle-strings, and the leaping of wanton feet. Strangers will feast at my supper-board, where strangers never feasted before; and auld men will shake their heads and say, 'Away fly the riches of honest Warlsworm.'"

And putting his hands over his eyes, as if to hide the hideous picture of extravagance which his imagination had painted, and uttering groan succeeding groan, he stretched himself at full length on the lang settle.

His niece turned pale as she beheld him writhing under the infliction of the spirit which she mistook for a deadlier pang, and thus she addressed the young man, who seemed to remain there that he might gaze without intermission on her beauty. "Oh, Willie, lad, if ye wish for wealth in this world, and weal in the ane to come—rise up, and run."

The youth leaped to his feet, stood with his lips apart, his left foot forward, and his whole face beaming with joy at being commanded by so sweet a tongue. "Oh run, William, run! fly over moor and moss, and seek and bring auld Haudthegrup, a man gifted in prayer and conversant with godly things; he will cheer my uncle's spirit. For oh, they're gladsome when they get thegither. I have seen them sit in the howe heart of winter, laying schemes for gripping and guiding wealth, when the snow was on the hill, and the icicle on the house-side, with less fire to thowe them than would warm a bairn's breakfast. Oh run, William, run! tell him to hasten; for the sands of life are nearly out; and that my uncle talks of the gathered gold of faith, and the set siller of redemption; and that's nae symptom of health with him."

The youth looked at her for a moment, then away he darted from the door, climbed the hill with the swiftness of a fowl in its flight, tarried for a second on its summit, to look back on the dwelling; nor were his glances unrewarded; he then vanished along the moor, to seek the home of auld Haudthegrup.

This devotional auxiliary soon made his appearance; he seemed a personification of penance and famine. He was tall and lean, with a frame of iron, a forehead villanous low, and eyes small, restless and glimmering about in quest of gain, like those of a cat seeking prey in the twilight. His nose was sharp and thin, like the style of a sun-dial; while his lips, though very broad, were too scanty to cover a seam of teeth as rusty as the jaws of an unused fox-trap, and wholly unacquainted with the luxury of the pastoral district, the flesh of lambs or ewes, unless when a friend's house had the scourge of his company. He carried under his arm a mighty Bible, garnished with massy clasps of iron; and entered the abode of his dying friend with the satisfied look of a man proud of his gifts, and conscious of the extensive influence of his intercessions. "Peace be among you," said the goodman of Haudthegrup, "and may God claim his ain in his blessed time and way; when the grain's ready let it go to the threshing-floor, and when the grapes are ripe, take them to the wine-press." So saying, he made a stride or two, and, looking in the face of his ancient friend, thus proceeded to comfort him.

"Bless me, Laird of Warlsworm! ye're no going to leave us; leaving us, too, when golden days are at hand? Never was there such an appearance of a harvest of gold, and the precious things of the earth, all ripening and getting ready for thy sickle and mine. Cheer up, man, ye'll hear the chink of gold in yere left lug for mony a bonnie year yet. Wou'd ye lie there, and let the breath sough away frae atween your lips, like a cow strangled with her tether in a field knee-deep of clover? Look me in the face, I say; bankers are breaking, and the credit of cattle-dealers is cracked—gold will be gold soon, and the rate of interest will rise in Galloway. The crouse and ringing frosts of winter will soon come to purify the air, and make yere auld blood course boldly in yere veins. Then the grass will grow green, the bushes will bud, and the primroses will blow on the bonnie burn bank, and ye'll get yere feet among the braw blooming gowans, that lie scattered o'er the face of the earth, like as mony pieces of a spendthrift's gold. Sae cheer up, man, ye would do wrong to die, and so many blessings awaiting ye."

The Laird of Warlsworm sat erect for a moment; the prospect of life, and the hopes of future gain, passed by him like a bright pageant; his eyes sparkled with that unholy light by which Mammon sums his treasure, and he stretched forth his hand to clutch the visionary gold, which deceitful fancy heaped up before him. But nature could not sustain the effort, the light faded in his eyes, his hand sank and his head declined, and sinking on the cushions, he muttered, "Na, na, it winna do, it winna do, I maun away to the worms, and my bits of bonnie gold will get a fearful scattering;" and fixing his looks on the old bag of coin, which was suspended in the chimney, he lay for a while in woeful rumination, and thus proceeded: "Ay, ay, ye'll no hang lang in that cozie place now; the hand of the spoiler will come, and thy braw broad pieces which I gathered with care and with sorrow, and regarded as gods, will gang to the silk shop and the maker of golden gimcracks, glancing with polished stones for woman's neck and bosom." And shutting his eyes in despair, and clutching his hands in agony of spirit, he resigned himself to his fate.

Meanwhile the devout twin-brother of Mammon seated himself in an old chair, laid his Bible on his knees, uncovered his head, placed his long iron fingers on the clasps, and with a prolonged preliminary cough, which hypocrisy had taught to imitate the listless and weary end of a dull sectarian sermon, he opened the volume. He glanced his eye around, to see if his auditors were composed, and commenced his search for a chapter befitting the perilous state of his friend. I was seated beside him, and thus I heard him converse with himself, as he turned over the leaves: "A chapter fit for a sinner's state! I mauna read about repentance, nor speak of the benefits of redemption. He'll never forgive me for directing his thoughts to such strange objects."

The laird uttered a low groan, and the devout man proceeded with his mutterings. "He's going gear, he's going gear; he winna shoot over the coming midnight: he'll be a stretched-out corse, and Bessie Lamond, his niece there, a braw rich heiress before the morning light. She'll be a weel tochered lass, when auld Gripagain travels. Let me see, there's Hurleyhawkie, a rich land and well watered; there's Auchenling, a dreary domain it's true, but there's gallant shooting on't, though it bears little but cranberries; then there's Wyliehole, and the sixteen acre parks of Warlsworm, forbye bails and bonds and gathered gold; my sooth, Bessie my lass, many a gallant will cast his cap at thee." And he glanced his sharp considerate eyes on the young maiden, to whose mind her uncle's danger seemed alone present. "Ay, ay," he resumed, "she's a well-favoured lass, and I'll warrant has a gift of knowing on't; deil a doubt of that, but I am not so very auld, and have been single for seven year, and bating a sad cough, which I can mend when I like for sixpence, and sundry grey hairs, the lass may have sillier woosters than me. When I cock my bonnet, and put on my crousest coat, and give my horse a tasting of corn, and then a tasting of the spur, I think the quean will no be a draps-blood to her uncle if she say me nay. And the lassie, too, is modest of demeanour, she wears nae silver in her shoon, nor frights the fowls with the feathers of her cap; and weel I mind it was her thrifty mother's boast that she should never sit on a sark till she could spin ane. I'll warrant her a gallant lassie, and a gude guider of gear. I should like to lead her to a brankan bridal." And, resuming his search of a suitable chapter, he withdrew his looks from the maid, who with brimful eyes, a troubled brow, and quivering hands, ministered to the sick man.

Her pure sincerity of heart won its way to auld Warlsworm's bosom, frozen as it seemed, and shut up resolutely against the charities of nature. "Ah, Bessie, lass," he murmured, "thy uncle maun leave the bonnie links of Orr, and the gowany braeside of Dee. Many a tug, and many a toiled brow, has it cost him to get them; but the strength of man cannot endure like the hills, nor his spirit flow for ever, like a running stream. And talking of running streams, that reminds me that Miller Macmillan owes me a year's rent, past on Tuesday; gar Jack Candlish gang and fetch it: the miller's a sicker ane; he thinks my dam is nearly run, and that my wheel of existence lacks the water of life, and sae he'll keep up the rent till my head's happit, and then wheedle or swear thee out on't. So that's settled, and my spirit's all the calmer for it. And now for thee, lass, ye'll be a rich quean, Bessie, and the lads will like ye nae the waur because he who lived before ye had a gathering eye and a sicker grip. But ye maun never wear a towering bonnet with a long feather; for that is an abomination in devout eyes, and a sad drain for the pocket; and sair I slighted bonnie Jenny Duff for the pride of her apparel: wear the snood of maiden singleness as lang as ye can, lassie; and, if ye maun be a wife, wear a douce hood, or a devout mutch;

ye'll find ane of yere grandmother's treasured by among my bonds; for I loved my ain mother better than ever I loved gold; ye'll hardly credit that, Bessie; and I love thee, too, my ain sweet sister's wean."

He laid his arms around her neck, looked full in her face, with a kind and a glistening eye, and the demon of lucre spread his wings, to forsake the mansion where he had lived so long. But it was otherwise ordered. The poor weeping girl knelt over him, and wiped away from his face the tears which flowed from her own eyes, for tears never flowed from his, and hid her face in his bosom with many a bitter sob.

"Ah, ye waster hussey!" exclaimed the laird, in a tone above his strength, "wherefore wipe ye my face with a damask napkin, when a cloth three threads to the pound is too good for a wadset about to be redeemed like me? And see, as I hope to be saved, if ye are not consuming the good dry wood which I kept for the cozie winter night; ground-elding (dried turf) is good enough to warm such an old sapless bough as me, which the feller's axe is fast lopping away from the green tree of existence."

This appearance of unwonted profusion smote sore on the heart of the parsimonious old man, and in a tone of rebuke and bitterness he continued his discourse. "I may waste my breath—and I ought to leave some for a scrap of prayer, it may help me where I am going; I may waste my breath, Bess, I say, in counselling ye how to choose a husband. When a woman's eye is bright, her ear is deaf. Take not a man, Bess, who counts kindred four generations back; he'll call his ancestor a gentleman, and spill the brimming cup of thy fortune in justifying his descent. Nor yet marry a man who scorns his ancestors; the man who mocks his forefathers, tramples on their dust. I hold a father's fair name equal with hoarded siller. Above all things wed not a lawyer, lass; ye should aye strive to mend your fortune and better your fame. Think not of a sailor, for he thinks there is no Sunday in five fathoms of water, and finds a love in every land. Shun too the soldier, for shining scarlet, golden shoulder-knots, and a hat filled with fowls' feathers, will consume thy gold, and fly away with thy happiness; and, oh, what a gowk he maun be, who stands up to be shot at for saxpence a day, Sunday included! But marry, lass, for all women love to be married, were it only for the sake of having somebody to scold at, and to bear the fault for their folly,—weu, I say, a strong-handed chield, who can keep the crown of the causeway, and make himself be obeyed at his own fireside. A cannie homely lad, who can clip seven score of sheep while another clips six; kens the buttered frae the bare side of the bread; loves nought so well as his own wife but the knotting of his own purse-strings; and who fears the Lord, and can back five bushels of barley."

This grave and worldly counsellor fairly exhausted himself, and, laying his head on the cushion, and fixing his eye on his bag of gold, which common fame calculated at a thousand pieces, remained silent while that devout person, Haudthegrup, commenced family devotion. He had examined the New Testament for a fitting and seemly text; but the divine meekness and charity and self-denial, and scorn of all terrestrial grandeur, which inspire its pages, rejected all community of feeling, and obliged him to seek consolation under the splendid and ostentatious dispensations of the Mosaic law.

"Spoiling the Egyptians," I heard him mutter, as he hastened along, " the heathen Egyptians of their jewels of silver, and jewels of gold, a meritorious deed; making the molten calf, a piece of dark idolatry, and a waste of precious metal; spoiling the Amalekite, a rich and a pagan people, a pleasant act and an acceptable. The Temple, ay, ay, the Temple of Solomon, the roof thereof was of fine cedar, the pillars of ivory, the floor of pure silver, and the walls of beaten gold—this has often consoled me, and doubtless will console him. It would be pleasant to die with a vision of this golden palace before him." Here he raised his head and said audibly: "Let us begin the worship of Him on high, by readfng in his praise first Kings, chapter the sixth." And, elevating his voice, he chanted forth the history of the building of Solomon's Temple, adorning it with the prolonged tone and quavering grace-notes of an ancient Cameronian professor. Nor did he fail to express his own admiration at the profusion of precious metal, by dwelling, with a delight that seemed unwilling to depart, on the passages recording the overlayings of the wall with gold, and the altar, and the floor. As he proceeded, the eye of old Warlsworm looked on his own sooty rafters, and on his coarse unhewn floor, and on the ark which contained his meal; yet what were they, covered, as his imagination made them, with beaten gold, compared to the immeasurable riches of the Jewish temple! Devotion fell prostrate before the divinity of wealth, and the man who had not five hours to live, leaped to his feet, smote his hands together, and exclaimed, "Oh Lord, what, o' gowd! what, o' gowd!"

"Ay, lad, and pure gowd too," responded Haudthegrup, casting the Bible from him as he spoke, and pacing round the room with a proud look and an augmented stride.

At this lamentable conclusion to family worship and intercession for the soul of a departing sinner, the beauteous relation of Warlsworm seemed deeply affected and incensed. She caught the laird in her arms, replaced him on his cushions, soothed down his worldly spirit, and wiped from his face the moisture which disease and excitement had brought to his brow, and that, too, with a cloth of a texture very unlike the fine twined linen and needlework of Egypt which had contributed to this unseemly rapture. While this passed, I observed the shadow of a man, lengthened by the departing sun, moving on the hall-floor, and seeming to whirl round and round with the agility of a dancer. I looked about, and beheld a singular being, a man about the age of fifty, clad in coarse cloth, called by the shepherds hiplock plaiden, bare-foot, bare-legged, bare-necked, and bare-headed. About his shoulders hung a mass of withered and matted hair; and he carried in his hand a long straw, which he held up before his face, moving all the while round and round, and accompanying his gestures with wild and disjointed words.

"Alas, alas!" said the young maiden, "what can have brought that poor demented simpleton here? He knows our doors were ever closed against him, and that our meal never augmented the little store which he obtained, more by the intercession of his own innocent face than by the entreaty of his tongue, from the scrupulous charity of our neighbours. Ah, poor houseless, homeless, hapless creature! he is come to express the sorrow of his own harmless heart for the illness of the head of this house; and hame shall he not go without partaking of the mercies with which we have been so long blessed." And with meat and drink in her hands forth she walked, and approached, not without hesitation, to the little green knoll on which the poor maniac had stationed himself, in order perhaps to give greater effect to the singular ceremony he was performing.

"East and west, and north and south," he chanted in a tone

of dissonance equal to the croak of the raven—" east, west, north, and south; not a cloud—not a breath of wind—a burning heat, and a scorching drouth—the grasshopper cannot sing for want of her evening dew." He paused, and reversed the straw, and, holding it up before him, renewed his dancing and his chant. "North, south, west, and east, the morning sun cannot ascend for the concourse of clouds—the little streams sing among their pebbles, for their banks will soon be overflowed; and the little flowers, bless their bonnie faces, hold up their parched heads, rejoicing in the descending shower. The rains fall, the winds blow, the rivulets swell and the thunders roll, and rock the green hills. The wide and winding water—even the links of my bright and stately Orr—flows like a wild and a raging sea. I see it, I see it, I see it; man may not ride it; and the saddled steed neighs across the flood, which it trembles to take. Ah! I would not go to be buried in the old kirkyard, beyond that roaring river, though ye were to make me a bed three ell deep, and lay the greenest turf in Galloway aboon me."

"Gawain, Gawain," said Bessie Lamond, in her sweetest tone, and with a smile of sympathy and kindness on her lips; "Gawain—hinnie, have ye forgotten how many bowls of curds and cream, and pieces of bread and cheese, I have stolen from our penurious board to feed ye in the glen? Turn and speak to me, my bonnie man, and spae nae mair about uncannie things, and see nae mair unsonsie sights."

But Gawain was possessed beyond the influence of the tongue and charms of the fair niece of the penurious laird, and continued to elevate and dandle the straw with an increasing wildness of look and gesture. "But who are those who ride mourning on their coal-black steeds, two and two, and bear a coffined corse before them? I see some whom I shall not see long, and the owner of this house is among them; stretched full gay in his burial linen, and a velvet pall aboon him—the siller it costs would be a sore sight; it is well for him that his senses are shut, else the expense of the burial wine would break his heart. There is a deep grave dug, and the bedral leans on his spade, and looks to the burial train about to pass the river. Aha! Johnnie Feastheworm, ye're cheated, lad, ye're cheated," shouted Gawain, changing the wild seriousness of his tone to that of laughter and merriment. "Fill your kirkyard hole again with the black mools, for auld Warlsworm's floating down the links of Orr, and his bonnie black coffin will frighten the seamen on Solway; and wha should float aside him but auld Haudthegrup? But he'll no float far, for twa pouchfuls of stolen gowd will tug the sinner down, and sink him to perdition: ye're cheated, Johnnie Feastheworm, ye're cheated, sae fill yere kirkyard hole with the fat mools again, my cannie man."

These concluding words were too loud to escape notice, and out upon him sallied Haudthegrup, his face inflamed, his hand clenched, and burning anger on his tongue. "What fiend hath possessed himself of this man, and utters this falseness through his foolish lips? Verily, I will cast him out; a sore buffeting shall the foul thief abide, that presumes to enter into the living image of the High One, and prophesy against righteous men. Lo! I will rebuke him with my right hand, and chasten him sorely with this rod of rowan-tree, with which I once combated and overcame three witch women in the wicked parish of Penpont." And, advancing upon Gawain as he spoke, he aimed a blow, which the maniac turned aside, exclaiming: "Aha! auld greedy Haudthegrup, I have ye now, I have ye now; take that, man, for throwing a bone at me, at Joe Tamson's bridal, seven-and-thirty years syne come beltan." As he uttered these words, he dashed his opponent from him with such force that he reeled several paces, and plunged into a miry hole, fairly under the verdant mantle with which the summer warmth had decked it. Gawain, having performed this feat, stalked perpendicularly into the hall—seated himself by the warm ashes on the hearth, and, looking on the sick man, said, "Ye lie soft and braw on your bonnie white cushions there; and deed and trouth, an I was you, I wad nae die till the cauld frost and winter should come, when I care na to accompany ye to the kirkyard hole mysel, and take my word for't, ye'll lie saftest and fealest on the Buittle side of the kirk; I aye think the gowans are bonnier, and the grass the fairer, and the blinks of the simmer sun sweeter on that side than the other: 'od, but lad, if ye hope to lie wi' me, ye maun lie quiet, and nae trouble ane with your weeping, and wailing, and gnashing of teeth—the cauld grave's a bad place to repent in."

We were now rejoined by old Haudthegrup, purified by the fair hands of the maiden from the soil of the pond, and anxious to drown shame and mortification by a long and lamentable prayer. The sun was set, and a soft and balmy twilight·had succeeded. The sound of the reaper's returning song, and the repeated call of the harvest-horn, were audible on all sides; and in the hall of Warlsworm we had that silence which ushers in prayer, and that fitful and glimmering light afforded by the decaying beams of day, and the twinkling gleam of fading embers. As we knelt, I could not refrain from looking on the singular group thus strangely assembled.

Gawain, abasing himself in the ashes, and stooping his forehead quietly into the dust, accompanied with a chorusing groan the melancholy cough of the sick man; the maiden knelt by the couch, watching with a steady and uninterrupted gaze the changing looks of her uncle; while Haudthegrup himself clasped his hands, drew down his cheeks to a most hypocritical length, and, fixing his eyes on things above, namely, on the golden hoard which hung beyond reach in the chimney, proceeded with his prayer. The prayers of the righteous avail much, says the Fountain of Belief, but what avail the prayers of the hypocrite? Unwise would that man be who would give them a record and a sanctuary. A strong and a burning faith, a day of firm belief, and an hour of deathbed repentance, were pressed with many a mighty word and many a weary groan. He recommended the health of his friend to Him who sweetened the waters of Marah, and his spirit to that Being who presided over angels and thrones, and the souls of just men made perfect. "To thee," said he, making a concluding address to the Fountain of all glory, "to thee, who can make silver into gold, and the dust upon which we tread into precious gems, it can be little to mend a broken body and revive a contrite spirit. To thee, who made my lambs worth five half-crowns at the St. James's fair of Lanark, though when I supplicated thee they were worth but five and sixpence, the renovation of this frail and fainting man is but a breath from thy nostrils. But if it is thy will to glean this ripened ear, to snatch this brand from the fires of this sinful world, let him honour thee and serve thee, and leave a moiety of that worldly dross, which men call gold, even unto him who thus wrestled with thee for his welfare and salvation." Here the sick man moaned, and the glances of his gifted friend and him flashed towards the hidden gold like the hostile lights of two adverse planets.

DEATH OF THE LAIRD OF WARLSWORM.

Haudthegrup concluded, "And, leaving his red gold in thy servant's hand, let him dwell in that house not built with hands, eternal in the heavens."

"A house not built with hands," re-echoed Gawain in the tone of the prayer, and leaping to his feet, "I never saw a house not built with hands except a magpie-nest in the foot of my mother's garden." With him, too, rose the Laird of Warlsworm, the deadly paleness of rage and receding life in his face; he fixed his eyes, shining with a light that seemed of the world below, on Haudthegrup, and stretching his hands towards him to pour forth his departing malediction, seemed inspired by the fiend who presides over the last hours of evil men. He opened his lips, the curse trembled on his tongue; but words never came, for he was stricken speechless, and fell back on the settle, his lips apart, his eyes fixed, and his hands clenched. "He'll never hound me frae his door mair," said Gawain, "nor tell me that wet straw is owre good a bed for a beggar bodie."

"Let us carry him into the spence," said Haudthegrup, "his spirit winna part in peace while his eye is fixed on that dross called gold, and his worldly good." The dying man seized his niece's hand, and pointed to several bags which hung among hams and tongues in the chimney. "Ah, he's making an edifying hinder end," said his parsimonious friend, "his hopes are with things aboon, with the blessed, doubtless." And away he bore him amid some faint resistance to a little secluded chamber, his hands still stretched towards the chimney, and his lips moving with the rapidity of one who speaks in haste. His dumb warnings were all in vain.

"Now, my bonnie young lady of Warlsworm," said this sanctified person in a whisper, "watch over the last moments of the righteous, and let these two youths and this simple innocent attend you; verily, they may profit by such an edifying sight; I, even I, a man dead to the things of this earth, will go and kneel down even where I lately knelt, and my intercession shall arise and go upward for the welfare of the body, and the glorification of the spirit."

The maiden wept, and, half insensible with sorrow, bathed her cheeks in tears, while away strode the comforter to the hall, and presently his voice arose in vehement intercession —the sick man groaned. In a little while, the sound of the prayer seemed to ascend from the floor, the laird made a convulsive effort to rise, the voice of Haudthegrup quavered and hesitated, as the voice of a man will do when his hands are busied, and then the sound as of gold falling was heard. At this mishap the tongue of the inteceder uttered a curse, and the power of speech returning to the dying man, he smote his hands together and exclaimed, "He's herrying me, he's herrying me, and I maun gang to the brimstone pit with no a penny in my pocket." And with these words he expired.

The singular prophecy of Gawain met with a remarkable fulfilment. The day of the burial of the laird was wild and stormy, the place of interment was in an old churchyard on the south side of the river Orr. The mourners were mounted, and the coffin was borne on horses' necks, covered with a pall of black velvet, the parochial mortcloth, which reached nigh to the ground. Haudthegrup was chief mourner, and, to elude the expense of a toll-bar, he proposed to ford the river, red and swollen with rain. When he reached the middle of the stream, his horse, unaccustomed to such processions, startled and plunged, and fairly flung his rider over his ears. In his fall, he seized the coffin of Warlsworm, and the quick and the dead alike found a grave in the links of the Orr.

"Alas, for Haudthegrup!" said one of the mourners; "watch when he swims, and let us try to save him."

"Swims!" rejoined another mourner, "how think ye will he swim, and seven hundred stolen pieces of Warlsworm's gold in his pocket? I'll prophesy, when his body's found he'll be holding his hands on his breeches-pockets to preserve his treasure."

THE SEVEN FORESTERS OF CHATSWORTH.

AN ANCIENT DERBYSHIRE BALLAD.

In presenting this somewhat rude but curious ballad to the reader, it may be proper to observe that those who profess to be charmed with truth only, and would wish one to swear to the certainty of a song, will learn with pleasure, perhaps, that tradition has recited, or sung, I know not which, this singular legend, for centuries, in the beautiful vale of Derwent, in Derbyshire. It is a tale current in the county. The projecting rock in Chatsworth wood, still bearing the name of the Shouter's Stone, is pointed out by the peasantry as the place on which this famous and successful outlaw stood and shouted. It overhangs a wild and winding footpath in the preserve, and in former times, before the wood became so luxuriant, commanded a fine view of the valley, in the midst of which stands Chatsworth House, the favourite mansion of the ancient and noble family of Cavendish. In the house itself, this tale has sought sanctuary. There is a painting from no less a hand than that of Prince Nicolas, in which a portion of the tradition is sought to be embodied; but the illustrious artist has, with poetical license, put a gilded horn in the outlaw's hand; and with a departure from the story, which all lovers of oral literature will deplore, has given to the cavern below a couple of outlaws, who rouse and bestir themselves to the sound of their leader's horn. The ancient oaks of Chatsworth are to be found everywhere in the valley; and, perhaps, no oaks in England, except those in Sherwood Forest, can claim to be their coevals—they are upwards of a thousand years old.

Chatsworth has many other attractions. The flower garden of the beautiful and unfortunate Queen of Scotland, a plat of earth elevated on a squat tower, and guarded with a fosse, stands on the banks of the Derwent, within a stone's-throw of the house. All around, the hills ascend and recede in woody or naked magnificence; and indeed the grandeur of Nature is such, that the beautiful mansion is diminished in the contemplation.

An attempt was made to abate the occasional provincialism of the ballad, but the experiment threatened to ravel the entire web, and it was not persisted in.

BALLAD.

The sun had risen above the mist,
   The boughs in dew were dreeping;
Seven foresters sat on Chatsworth bank,
   And sung while roes were leaping.

"Alas!" sung one, "for Chatsworth oaks,
   Their heads are bald and hoary,
They droop in fulness of honour and fame,
   They have had their time of glory.

"No stately tree in old merry England
   Can match their antique grandeur;
Tradition can tell of no time when they
   Towered not in pride and splendour.

"How fair they stand amid their green land,
   The sock or share ne'er pained them;
Not a bough or leaf have been shred from their strength,
   Nor the woodman's axe profaned them."

"Green," sung another, "were they that hour
   When Scotland's loveliest woman,
And saddest queen in the sweet twilight,
   Aneath their boughs was roamin'.

"And ever the Derwent lilies her tears
   In their silver tops were catching,
As she looked to the cold and faithless north,
   Till her eyes waxed dim with watching."

"Be mute now," the third forester said,
   "The dame who fledged mine arrow
With the cygnet's wing, has a whiter hand
   Than the fairest maid on Yarrow."

Loud laughed the forester fourth, and sung,
   "Say not thy maid's the fair one;
On the banks of Dove there dwells my love,
   A beauteous and a rare one."

"Now cease your singing," the fifth one said,
   "And choose of shafts the longest,
And seek the bucks on Chatsworth chase,
   Where the lady-bracken's strongest.

"Let every bow be strung, and smite
   The fattest and the fairest;
Lord Devonshire will taste our cheer,
   Of England's lords the rarest."

"String them with speed," the sixth man said,
  "For low down in the forest
There runs a deer I long to smite,
  With bitter shafts the sorest.

"The bucks bound blythe on Chatsworth lea,
  Where brackens grow the greenest;
The pheasant's safe 'neath Chatsworth oaks,
  When the tempest sweeps the keenest.

"The fawn is fain as it sucks its dam,
  The bird is blythe when hatching;
Saint George! such game was never seen,
  With seven such fellows watching.

"In the wild wood of fair Dove dwells
  An outlaw, young and handsome;
A sight of him on Chatsworth bank
  Were worth a prince's ransom.

"He slew the deer on Hardwick Hill,
  And left the keeper sleeping
The sleep of death; late—late yestreen
  I heard his widow weeping.

"Now bend your bows, and choose your shafts"—
  His string at his touch went sighing;
"The outlaw comes—now, now at his breast
  Let seven broad shafts be flying."

The outlaw came—with a song he came—
  Green was his gallant cleeding;*
A horn at his belt, in his hand the bow
  That set the roebucks bleeding.

The outlaw came—with a song he came—
  O'er a brow more brent and bonny
The pheasant plume ne'er danced and shone,
  In a summer morning sunny.

The outlaw came—at his belt a blade,
  Broad, short and sharp, was gleamin';
Free was his step, as one who had ruled
  Among knights and lovely women.

See, by his shadow in the stream
  He loves to look and linger,
And wave his mantle richly flowered
  By a white and witching finger.

"Now, shall I hit him where yon gay plume
  Of the Chatsworth pheasant's glancing;
Or shall I smite his shapely limbs
  That charm our maidens dancing?"

"Hold! hold!" a northern forester said,
  "'Twill be told from Trent to Yarrow,
How the true-love song of a gentle outlaw
  Was stayed by a churl's arrow."

---

* *Cleeding*, a word still used in the north of England; clothing, apparel. South of Germany, *kleidung*; Icelandic, *klaede*; Teutonic, *kleed*.

"It shall never be said," quoth the forester then,
  "That the song of a red deer reaver
Could charm the bow that my grandsire bent
  On the banks of Guadalquiver."

And a shaft he laid, as he spoke, to the string,
  When the outlaw's song came falling
As sweet on his ear, as the wind when it comes
  Through the fragrant woodlands calling.

There each man stood, with his good bow bent,
  And his shaft plucked from the quiver:
While thus then sung that gallant outlaw,
  Till rung both rock and river:

"Oh! bonny Chatsworth, and fair Chatsworth,
  Thy bucks go merrily bounding;
Aneath your green oaks, as the herds flew past,
  How oft have my shafts been sounding!

"It is sweet to meet with the one we love,
  When the night is nigh the hoarest;
It is sweet to bend the bow as she bids,
  On the proud prey of the forest.

"One fair dame loves the cittern's sound,
  When the words of love are winging;
But my fair one's music's the outlaw's horn,
  And his bow-string sharply singing.

"She waves her hand—her little white hand,
  'Tis a spell to each who sees her;
One glance of her eye—and I snatch my bow,
  And let fly my shafts to please her.

"I bring the lark from the morning cloud,
  When its song is at the sweetest;
I stay the deer upon Chatsworth lea,
  When its flight is at the fleetest.

"There's magic in the wave of her hand,
  And her dark eye rains those glances,
Which fill the best and the wisest hearts
  With love's sweet influences.

"Her locks are brown—bright berry brown,
  O'er her temples white descending;
And her neck is like the neck of the swan,
  As her way through heaven she's wending.

"How I have won my way to her heart
  Is past all men's discernin';
For she is lofty, and I am low,
  My lovely Julia Vernon."

He turned him right and round about,
  With a step both long and lordly;
When he was aware of those foresters bold,
  And he bore him wondrous proudly.

"Good morrow, good fellows!" all fearless he said,
  "Was your supper spread so sparely;
Or is to feast some sweet young dame,
  That you bend your bows so early?

"The world is wide, and the world is broad,
  There's fish in the smallest river;
Deer leap on the hill—fowls fly in the air—
  Was, is, and will be ever.

"And now I feast on the ptarmigan,
  And then I taste the pheasant;
And my supper is of the Chatsworth fawn,
  Which my love dresses pleasant.

"But to-morrow I feast on yon bonny roebuck;
  'Tis time I stayed his bounding."
He twanged his string—like the swallow it sung,
  All shrilly and sharply sounding.

"By my grandsire's bow," said a forester then,
  "By my shafts which fly so yarely,
And by all the skill of my strong right hand,
  Good outlaw, thou lords it rarely.

"Seest thou yon tree, yon lonely tree,
  Whose bough the Derwent's laving?
Upon its top, thou gallant outlaw,
  Thou'lt be hung to feed the raven.

"So short as the time this sharp shaft flies,
  And strikes yon golden pheasant—
There—thy time is meted, so bid farewell
  To these greenwoods wild and pleasant."

The outlaw laughed. "Good fellow," he said,
  "My sword's too sure a servant
To suffer that tree to bear such fruit,
  While it stands on the Derwent.

"She would scorn my might, my own true love,
  And the mother would weep that bore me
If I stayed my step for such strength as thine,
  Or seven such churls before me.

"I have made my way with this little brown sword
  Where the war-steeds rushed the throngest;
I have saved my breast with this little brown sword,
  When the strife was at the strongest.

"It guarded me well in bonny Scotland,
  When the Scotts and Graemes fought fervent
And the steel that saved me by gentle Nith,
  May do the same by Derwent."

"Fair fall thee, outlaw, for that word!
  Oh, Nith! thou gentle river,
When a bairn, I flew along thy banks
  As an arrow from the quiver.

"The roebucks run upon thy braes
  Without a watch or warden;
And the tongue that calls thee a gentle stream
  Is dear to Geordie Gordon."

The outlaw smiled. "'Tis a soldier's saye
  That the Gordons, blythe and ready,
Ne'er stooped the plumes of their basnets bright
  Save to a lovesome lady."

"Now by Saint Allan," the forester said,
  "And the saint who slew the dragon;
And by this hand that wields the brand,
  As wight as it tooms the flagon;

"It shall never be told of the Gordons' name,
  Of a name so high and lordly,
That I took a gallant outlaw in the toil,
  And hanged him base and cowardly.

"I'll give thee the law of Lord Nithisdale,
  A good lord of the border;
So take thy bow, thou gallant outlaw,
  And set thy shafts in order.

"And we will go each one to his stance,
  With bows and arrows ready;
And thou shalt climb up Chatsworth bank,
  Where the wood is wild and shady.

"And thou shalt stand on yon rough red rock,
  With woodbine hung and bracken;
And shout three times o'er Derwent Vale,
  Till all the echoes waken.

"Then loose thy shafts, and slay a buck
  Fit for a monarch's larders;
And carry him free from Chatsworth Park,
  In spite of seven warders.

"Do this and live, and I do vow
  By the white hand of my mother,
I'll smite him low who runs ere thou shout,
  Were he Saint Andrew's brother."

The outlaw smiled. "Good Gordon," he said,
  "I'll shout both high and gaily;
And smite a buck, and carry him off:
  'Tis the work I'm bowne to daily."

The outlaw stood upon Chatsworth rock,
  Like light his looks did gladden;
The sun was shining on Bakewell Edge,
  And on the heights of Haddon.

The outlaw stood upon Chatsworth rock,
  He looked to vale and mountain,
And gave a shout so shrill, the swans
  Sprung up from stream and fountain.

The outlaw stood upon Chatsworth rock,
  And shouted shrill and gaily;
Till the dun deer leaped from brake and bower,
  Two miles down Derwent Valley

The outlaw stood upon Chatsworth rock,
  Looking o'er the vale so narrow;
And his voice flew fleet as away from the string
  Starts off the thirsty arrow.

And loudly it rung in Haddon Wood,
  Where the deer in pairs were dernan:*
And loudly it rung in Haddon Hall,
  And up rose Julia Vernon.

"If ever I heard my true love's voice,
  'Tis now through my bowers ringing;
His voice is sweet as the wild bird's note,
  When the buds bloom to its singing.

"For well I know my true love's voice,
  It sounds so gay and clearly:
An angel's voice in a maiden's ear
  Would ne'er drop down so dearly."

She took her green robe in a hand
  White as the opening lily,
And the morning sun and the lovely maid
  Looked down on Chatsworth Valley.

Around the brow of the high green hill
  The sun's fair beams were twining,
And bend and fall of the Derwent stream
  In golden light were shining.

The silver smoke from Chatsworth tower,
  Like a pennon broad went streaming,
And gushed against the morning sky,
  And all the vale was gleaming.

She gave one look on the broad green land,
  And back her tresses sheddin',
With her snowy neck, and her bonnie blue eyes,
  Came down from the hill of Haddon.

She saw the wild dove start from its bower,
  And heard the green boughs crashing;
And saw the wild deer leap from its lair,
  And heard the deep stream dashing.

And then she saw her own true love
  Bound past by bush and hollow;
And after him seven armed men
  With many a shout and hollo.

---

* *Dernan*, concealing. "Abusing and harming his Majesty's good subjects by their darned (concealed) stouths."—*Acts of James I. of England.* Anglo-Saxon, *dearn-an*.

"Oh! had I but thy bow, my love,
  And seven good arrows by me,
I'd make the fiercest of thy foes
  Bleed ere they could come nigh thee.

"Oh! had I but thy sword, my love,
  Thy sword so brown and ready,
I'd meet thy foes on Chatsworth bank,
  Among the woodlands shady."

On high she held her white white hands
  In wild and deep devotion,
And locks and lips, and lith* and limb,
  Were shivering with emotion.

"Nay, stay the chase," said a forester then,
  "For when the lion's roaring
The hound may hide. May the raven catch
  The eagle in his soaring?

"Farewell, my bow, that could send a shaft,
  As the levin leaves the thunder!
A lady looks down from Haddon height
  Has snapt thy strength asunder.

"A lady looks down from Haddon height,
  O'er all men's hearts she's lordin';
Who harms a hair of her true love's head
  Makes a foe of Geordie Gordon."

The bank was steep—down the outlaw sprung,
  The greenwood wide resounded;
The wall was high—like a hunted hart
  O'er it he fleetly bounded.

And when he saw his love he sunk
  His dark glance in obeisance:
"Comes my love forth to charm the morn,
  And bless it with her presence?

"How sweet is Haddon Hill to me,
  Where silver streams are twining!
My love excels the morning star,
  And shines while the sun is shining.

"She and the sun, and all that's sweet,
  Smile when the grass is hoarest;
And here at her white feet I lay
  The proud buck of the forest.

"Now, farewell, Chatsworth's woodlands green,
  Where fallow-deer are deman;
For dearer than the world to me
  Is my love, Julia Vernon!"

* *Lith*, joint. Anglo-Saxon, *lith*.

www.ingramcontent.com/pod-product-compliance
Lightning Source LLC
Chambersburg PA
CBHW032105220426
43664CB00008B/1144